Letters
from a whoremonger's wife

DANITA CLARK ABLE

ISBN: 1477684050
ISBN 13: 9781477684054

Linds and Garrett,
Every mom should be so lucky.
I love you more than all the stars

Justin, Linds & Garrett,
You are the three strongest people I've ever known.
You deserve better than you got…
The three of you will always own my heart.

An Ode to a Former Man

Where you came from I do not know…
Your past is as mysterious as your present and your future…
I now find the exit of you from my life as much a blessing as you coming into it…
You held my heart, soul, and mind and gave me joy and wishes…
You left me with sadness and disappointment…
What lets me down more than anything is seeing someone I love and care for letting
themselves down even more…
I will hurt, but with <u>MY</u> family I will move on and be happy…
As for someone that I love, I can only hope that you can also move on beyond us,
and hopefully be happy…
I can forgive you, but I will never forget…

Justin Clark

Author's Note

Since its first publication, I've been asked why I chose to write this book, this raw memoir.

I've been accused of writing for revenge.

I've been accused of writing because I'm filled with hatred.

I've been accused of writing because I'm incapable of letting go of the past.

*None of these reasons are accurate. I wrote **Letters, From A Whoremonger's Wife,** because I want to help others. I don't want you, or someone you love, to blow twenty-four years of life in a bad relationship. I don't want you to hurt your children by staying in a bad marriage. I want you to know that there is true love in the world, but I want you to know true love doesn't hurt and deceive.*

I wrote because I want you to give a second chance, one time. I don't want you to destroy yourself or your children, by giving second chances over and over, to someone who hurts and manipulates you. Don't give up your chance at a good life. Concentrate on your children, love them, love yourself. Move on.

I wrote because I want you to know you might lose your mind and yourself, and find both again.

I wrote this book because I want you to understand that silence is deadly. There are people who love you, who will help you. But they must know what you're going through to do so.

I wrote because I want you to see that no matter how hard you try, if your partner is not interested in being a life partner…. Nothing you do will fix him/her.

I wrote because I want you to recognize Red Flags.

I wrote, because I don't want you to make the same mistakes I've made.

Danita

This book is based on a true story. More accurately, it's a true story with a few changes. I've changed the names of some people because it's just easier that way. So while some of the names are not real, the people are. The environment and locations are true too, i.e.: Cartersville, Georgia and Cheyenne, Wyoming. Professions, seasons of occurrence, ages, etc...all true.

When you read my story, you may say to yourself, "This girl is crazy. What was she thinking? If it were me, I would have left that sonofagun long before she did." Please don't judge my choices and my mistakes, but use them to help yourself or someone you love... Sometimes a person disappears so gradually no one notices.

In my early twenties I fell in love with and married a selfish and hollow man. Outwardly, he appeared to be an amazing man. Inwardly he was filled with rage, bitterness and resentment. His resentment and anger chipped away at the young woman I was until I no longer recognized myself. I'm only now remembering who I used to be and I'm just on the brink of discovering who I can be. A few years ago, three years before my divorce, a college friend and her family visited from another state to attend my daughter's graduation party. They stayed after the other guests left so we could chat, I had not seen them since my children were very small. A couple of hours into our visit, the husband of my friend said this to me: "Danita you used to be fearless! What happened to that brave girl? Where is she?" I didn't know how to answer him until now: *She's been buried under the garbage heap her husband heaped on her. He almost smothered her with the filthy trash he accumulated. The stench of life with him almost killed her spirit, too. But one rainy summer night she saw a small stream of light breaking through the dark debris piled on top of her. And she heard angelic voices, which sounded much like the voices of her children saying, "You don't have to do this any longer". So that's where she's been, Frank. But she's back and she's remembering how to be fearless…*

Special Thanks To

Numerous friends and family have helped Linds, Garrett and me over the years. I wish I could list all of your names, thank each of you individually. If your name isn't mentioned in these acknowledgements, please know you are not left out of my appreciation or my prayers of thanksgiving.

Linds & Garrett, I ask your forgiveness for the times I didn't know what I was doing. I thank you for allowing me to display pieces of your lives on paper. You have been towers of strength for me. Because of you, surrender has never been an option. It's an honor and a privilege to be your mom.

Justin, thank you….you also allowed me to share bits of your life on these pages; you gave me the 'go ahead' to share your poem, even while it breaks my heart. Both you and Rebecca were barely out of UGA and still newlyweds when you stood in the gap for Cissy and Garrett. I will never be able to thank you enough…The two of you are a wonderful team. I'm so happy we're in the same "flamly".

Nanny & Poppy, for providing an example of parental love and perseverance…and for believing in me when I didn't believe there was any good left. And for everything else you do. Without your help, who knows where I would be.

My brother Dwight, for the letters of encouragement you continue to send me. You've been my most vocal cheerleader.

The Lloyds, on that fateful evening, you provided Garrett a place out of the rain. When I was frightened, you gave me a safe place to hide.

The Kings, you provided encouragement, wonderful meals and a room with a view while I completed LFAWW. You stepped in with financial support when I didn't have a dime to my name. You selflessly provided funds when my daughter needed University book money and when my son needed help getting to his internship. ..I hope one day to be able to pass the love on to another.

The Alexandersens, *your encouragement is never ending, how do I begin to thank you?* You supplied lifesaving motorcycle lessons and a safe haven for my son in those excruciating first days of August 2009 and again in 2012... Your friendship is a powerful waterfall of love. You provided a warm environment and a welcoming place for me to hang out while this book was being published. Without you, I would not have had the opportunity to see it to completion. Thank you for your continuing love, friendship, prayers, great food, lots of laughs and good conversation.

Christina A., For the healing note, E♭.

Chrissy R., for many things, most of all your love and friendship... I will always be thankful.

Jayta, my "ride or die" girl. Though you may never be able to read this.... early on, you got me through some of the darkest days. May you rest peacefully in the Arms of God.

I love you.

Laughridge Family...I could write another book based solely on your love and generosity. Claudia, thank you for sharing motherly love with my children and sisterly love with me. Christmas 2009 would have been the first Christmas of my life without a tree, but you didn't allow that to happen....you even sent little elves to deliver and set up the beautiful nine foot Frazier Fir! And...Terry Reid Kia, when I was left without wheels, you made certain I had reliable transportation. Thank you.

Delilah, Donna & Sherry, my sister-cousins. I love you.

Jean & TC, for friendship spanning decades, solid practical advice and hours of late night phone calls....I love you, my friends.

My Aunt Mae, your love and naturally funny personality has always provided a soft cushion. You and William raised children who were willing to help others in need. Tyra & Adrian, you helped more than you know.

J. Middleton, for your beautiful example of Grace....

Tammy S., for a sofa to sleep on.

Williams Brothers (aka The Willies), for bringing in my firewood, planting trees, pulling weeds...and tons more.

Laura R., for suggesting I combine the two nicknames...Dick Crisco.

Your daddy's demons are callin' your name
Don't you listen to them 'cause they've got no claim.
Temptations may come, that ain't no sin,
You get stronger every time that you don't give in.

Walk Like A Man, Tim McGraw

"Stepping into a brand-new path is difficult, but not more difficult than remaining in a situation, which is not nurturing to the whole woman."

Maya Angelou

The Warning

I wore no veil as I stood in the open doors of the church, nervously clutching a bouquet of white roses. Tentatively, I stepped onto the center aisle and looked toward the altar, expecting to find Dick, my groom, smiling brightly, perhaps anxiously, waiting for me. I couldn't see him; candlelight and shimmering panes of multi-hued stained glass, backlit by sunlight, mingled and formed a bright haze, obstructing my vision. The guests to my left and right were a blur of subdued colors as I slowly made my way down the long aisle in a sleeveless, white bridal gown. A long train of chiffon trailed softly behind me. My dark hair was pulled away from my face and twisted into a French Knot. Another dark knot twisted in my gut, dread beat rapidly in my chest as I crept through the haze toward my destination.

In time the haze lifted and I saw him; my groom. He was standing erect in his black tuxedo and white shirt, hands clasped casually behind his back, waiting for me to come to him. I could not see his face. I tilted my head to the side so that I might have a better view of him. Still, his face was obscured. Apprehension clamped tightly in my throat as I moved closer to the altar, desperately attempting to see my groom's handsome face. Something was wrong. "Why can't I see him?" I wondered. I could see reflections of candlelight in his black shoes but I could not see his face. His groomsmen stood beside him and I could see them clearly. All but one groomsman was smiling sweetly, each making eye contact with me. My groom's uncle stared gloomily at me and slowly turned his head from one side to the other, as if he were disagreeing with me about something. The behavior of the uncle disturbed me and I averted my eyes from him, looking again toward my groom, trying in vain to see his face. As I neared the end of the aisle I knew I would finally see his smile, the grey of his eyes. But at the very moment I took the final step toward him, he turned and faced the minister, the fingers of his hands still casually intertwined behind his back. When I took my place beside my future husband the minister began speaking, his words were jumbled and fuzzy, *and I couldn't understand what he was saying. I felt confused and disoriented. Darkness swelled in my chest and nearly suffocated me.*

Almost as soon as it began, the ceremony was over. The minister placed a hand on each of our shoulders and gently turned us to greet our guests. Dick reached for my hand and in that moment I realized my beautiful bridal gown was made of paper, thin and fragile, the color of fresh snow. I could hear the sounds of crumpled paper as Dick and I hurriedly walked toward the front doors of the church and I wondered if the guests had noticed. I was shamed by the dress and wondered how I had made such an oversight, yet I smiled up at my faceless groom and tried to appear as if nothing was out of the ordinary. Arms linked, we approached the narthex as masculine hands opened a massive pair of walnut and stained glass doors. Beyond the doors, an azure sky hung over the front lawn of the church. Weeping Willows waltzed along the cobbled driveway. Dick, his face still blind to me, placed his arm around me as we stepped from the soft light of the sanctuary into the bright sunlight. And then the rainstorms came. Large, cold raindrops pelted me and stung the bare skin of my shoulders and arms. Lightning streaked fire across the now darkened sky and thunder roared like the wrath of God. Dick slid his arm from my waist and when he did, my rain soaked paper dress ripped across my hips. I forced a pale smile and desperately tried to hold the dress in place, just when I thought I was holding it together, the dress began to rip down the center, between my breasts. I held the torn pieces against my body with both *hands and asked Dick to cover me with his tuxedo jacket. He stepped away from me and began to laugh as he ran toward a waiting black truck. Without looking back I heard him yell, "That's the ugliest damn dress I've ever seen!" I never saw his face.*

Disconcerted, I woke from that nightmare with my heart beating loudly in my ears, barely able to catch my breath. A fine layer of perspiration moistened my skin. For a few eternal seconds I felt lost and frightened, panic stricken, uncertain I had been dreaming. I looked at the bedside clock and took in the time and date: Four o'clock in the morning, February 20, two days before my wedding. Reality rushed in and relief swept over me; it was a dream, a terrible dream, a nightmare. I lay back on my pillow and tried unsuccessfully to relax tensed muscles, even while the nightmare kept replaying in my mind.

Sleep eluded me as I attempted to dissect the dream. In the end I chalked it up to nothing more than pre-wedding jitters. I told myself the part of the dream where Dick's uncle moved his head in a negative way was simply because he didn't want Dick to marry and leave him alone in their bachelor pad. Not only were they uncle and nephew, they were friends and roommates. A few weeks earlier the uncle had said to me, "Little Dick should never marry because he will never be responsible enough for marriage and a family. He lies. He will never settle for one woman." I thought the uncle was rude and immature, soured on marriage because his own had failed. When I mentioned the uncle's comment to Dick, he shrugged it off, "He's crazy. Forget about him." When I mentioned the comment to Dick's mom she had advised me to pay no attention to the uncle. Just a few years older than Dick, BJ said he had "always been jealous of Dick". "Ignore him. He's jealous, he wanted to date you and he's never wanted Dick to be happy. They have a love hate relationship and he will cause Little Dick trouble when he can. Just ignore him, he's messed up from his first wife and the girl he's dating now is no better."

So I ignored the comments made by the uncle. After hearing what B.J had to say about him, I began to distrust him, assuming there were ulterior motives behind everything he said.

Today, I realize I should have listened to him. He knew Dick better than anyone else and he was risking a relationship with his nephew when he gave me the warning. But I couldn't or wouldn't see it that way at the time. The uncle's description of Dick was nothing like the man I knew, the man I loved, so I easily disregarded the warning and believed the excuse my future mother-in-law gave me.

The problem is this: *the man I loved only allowed me to know the man he wanted me to know.*

It would be twenty-four years before I understood the significance of the pre-wedding nightmare. It would be twenty-four years before I would stop making excuses for Little Dick. And almost twenty-four years before I would admit to myself and others that Little Dick was and is a self-absorbed chronic liar, adulterer and sociopath.

The Degradation

His degradation of my life began the day we married. At times his delivery of my humiliation was subtle and easy, at other times the insults were powerful and bold. They were always well-timed, out of sight and out of hearing of anyone else. They were designed to reduce me to nothing.

In short order, the verbal abuse became physical, less frequent than the verbal attacks and not as damaging. Those deliveries were also powerful, well-timed and out of sight. They were never subtle. The fissures lay unseen, just beneath my surface. I was every bit as shattered and cracked as the brittle red clay of a dried up Georgia lake bed, but the cracks were not readily apparent. The emotional fissures and cracks became crevices and the crevices became canyons. Every ounce of self-confidence and self-esteem I had ever possessed was crushed and trampled upon and quietly began to leave me. In time there wasn't an emotional part of me that had not been broken by the man who had vowed to love me till death, there would be few physical parts to miss the pain of his hands. His hands were strong, they stung when he slapped me and they bruised when he grabbed me, but his hands never equaled the damage caused by his words.

When I think back to the beginning of our marriage I'm amazed at how quickly and easily I became his enabler. I'm sickened with the realization that I had a hand in my deteriorating life. My faith in him and a belief that his anger and our bad times were temporary, my tendency to defend his behavior with forced excuses, all became handicaps that eventually crippled me emotionally. I smiled for family and friends and co-workers, my smile told unspoken lies and convinced friends, acquaintances, family and strangers that I had an amazing marriage, a life to be envied. Friends came to me for advice in their times of relationship trouble. *Smiles lie.* So do random hugs and a strong hand gently placed on the small of the back at just the right moment or a hand being held walking into a movie theater even after years of marriage. A kiss on the cheek lies too. A question, *"Hey girl, do you know you're beautiful?"*, asked in front of church friends and colleagues lies best of all. Dick's lies were spoken so gently they felt like a caress. I wanted his lies to be true.

It's easy to believe a liar when his victim keeps secrets.

Dick understood people would have a difficult time believing me, had I chosen to tell his secrets. He had made certain everyone saw the loving family man persona he so carefully crafted. I was hemmed in by the perfect family image we had created and my silence gave him permission to add more lies and deception. He knew my pride would never allow me to reveal his secrets. He realized I had begun to doubt everything I had ever known about myself. His degradation of me had been very successful.

I was nothing. He said so. Who would believe me?

In a few short years I became fragile and vulnerable, shattered and crushed and no one knew. Even I wasn't fully aware of how broken I was. The impossible dream of having a stable home life with Dick and our children, and a deep well of faith, is what held me together. Ernest Hemmingway is quoted as saying, "The world breaks everyone, and afterward, many are stronger at the broken places". I hang on to those words and I believe they're descriptive of me today. I believe they describe my children, now adults, as well. We were broken by the hatred and resentment that festered in the man who was supposed to love us. Hatred, anger, bitterness and resentment which manifested in rage had been generously poured over us, his family. But now, our broken places are healing and we're stronger than the little man that wounded us.

Summer 2009

I woke without prelude, feeling as if I had been suddenly snatched from a peaceful place and unexpectedly plopped down in the middle of turmoil. A heavy, foreboding feeling disturbed my spirit and formed a knot in my chest, my eyes adjusted slowly to the darkness. Moonlight came gently through the sheer white fabric of the curtains and puddled softly across the mahogany dresser, reflecting in the mirror above. Nothing looked out of the ordinary, but everything felt wrong. Dick was not in our bed with me, but there was nothing unusual about that, he had a tendency to stay up late, watching TV. I glanced at the digital clock on the chest beside the bed; half past midnight. The air in the house felt different, heavier than it had an hour earlier when I was awake, waiting for Garrett to come home. Our nineteen year old son had been out on his motorcycle when a late summer storm blew in. The winds were fierce and the rain had peppered down in torrents. Garrett was a new biker and I had been unable to sleep until he was safely home. But once he sauntered through the door and down the hall, calling out, "Goodnight Mom," as he walked past the bedroom door, I was able to drift off to sleep. He had just returned home from spending several weeks in Australia and tomorrow he and my husband and I were driving to Athens, Georgia to help our daughter Cissy move into her new apartment. My last waking thought had been a prayer of thanks, for having both my children in safe places. *So why had I wakened with this foreboding feeling?* I lay still for a few seconds, listening to the sounds of the house: the mumbled, tinny sound of television voices echoing in low tones down the long center hallway of our home, the purring of central air was almost undetectable, whirring blades of a ceiling fan whispered softly above me, the faint but unmistakable sound of Daisy's tail thumping against wooden floors. Nothing was out of place, but something felt wrong. I lifted my sleepy body from the bed and walked down the long hallway, my bare feet chilled on the hardwoods. Garrett's door was closed, probably already sleeping, I thought. Bright lights from the den spilled sideways into the hall, too many lights for this time of night or early morning. *Dick usually watches television with all the lights shut off.* I walked into the den expecting to find him in his usual place, stretched out on the sofa in front of a late night re-run of America's Funniest Home Videos or a John Wayne movie. He wasn't there and his absence sparked more concern. Painful memories of his prior nocturnal wanderings rose swiftly to my conscience. I pushed the thoughts aside. Maybe he was in Garrett's room, behind the closed door. In the past they had occasionally played video games late into the night. Garrett had been away at school in New York City the past year and then spent the summer out of the country, so perhaps they were catching up. I turned on my bare heels and walked back down the hall to Garrett's bedroom, but even before I got to the door I knew I would not find them there. There were no sounds of laughter, none of the victory shouts or the cries of defeat that usually accompanied the video games. Still, I hoped. I pushed the bedroom door open and was greeted with stillness, silence. Garrett's bed had not been touched. A wet pair of black Converse, laces untied, had been dropped next to his desk chair. Garrett's iPhone lay on the floor, the screen foggy with moisture. Obviously he had been thoroughly drenched by the rain. It occurred to me that Garrett and Dick must be out in the garage, drying off the new Suzuki Boulevard C50, a source of pride for my son since he had purchased it solely on own. I didn't leave immediately to check the garage. A foreign feeling compelled me to linger in my son's room. His room, with the Hunter Green walls and wide, crisp white crown molding; outfitted with a tall oak bed covered in the dark greens, blues and burgundy plaid of a boy, had always been a pleasant and inviting messy jumble of books, swords, world maps, journals, knives, paintball guns, rocks and other things of interest to him. Tonight, the atmosphere in his room was heavy, unlike anything I had ever felt in here before. Sadness and desolation filled the spaces usually occupied by vibrant hope. Internally, I felt something slipping away. Innately, I knew life had changed. I said a prayer for Garrett and backed out of his room, flipping the lights off and closing the door as I left.

Walking toward the garage I began to feel nauseous and cold, drained of energy. My legs were heavy and weak as I moved from the hallway into the laundry room and out the side door, into the bright fluorescent light of the garage. The angriness of the storm had subsided, and when

I stepped into the early morning air I was hit with the overwhelming thickness of Georgia's 'after a summer rain' humidity and the unsettling realization that Garrett, his bike and Dick were nowhere to be seen. I walked to the open garage door and stepped into the damp darkness, instinctively looking toward the end of our long, tree lined driveway for any sight of the bike or the guys. I walked toward the front yard and found only Dick, illuminated by an outside security lamp, standing in the wet grass with his arms hanging loosely by his side, looking toward the quiet country road that runs in front of our property.

"Where's Garrett?" I asked.

"I don't know. He just took outta here like a bat out of hell for no reason. I don't know what his problem is." Dick kept his back to me.

"What? That isn't like him at all. What did he say? Something must have happened for him to leave like that. Did he say anything?" I asked.

Dick turned toward me and rubbed his chest, "I don't know. He said nothing. He just threw my phone at me and hit me right here and ran out! I don't know what's up with him. You know how he is." Dick's face had an expression I had come to recognize as his 'lying mask'.

"Yes, I do know how he is and I know he wouldn't angrily take off in the pouring rain, without a phone, unless there was an emergency, or something was wrong. He just got home a short time ago and he was happy to be here, he told me how nice it was to be back in his own room. And he was in a good mood when he came in tonight. He said goodnight to me when he walked down the hall, he was singing in the bathroom while he washed his face. So what happened between then and now, Dick?" I wasn't going to pretend I believed Dick's pathetic explanation. Not this time, and never again. Something was welling up in me that I couldn't explain; strength I had not felt in years had found its way home. Dick's lies, hanging in the space between us, were nauseating.

The fight building in me, however, didn't clear the bewildering fog surrounding me. I was still in that confused frame of mind one finds herself in when life begins to rapidly unravel. But somehow, something Dick said inched its way through the murkiness of my early morning confusion and found clarity.

"Why did he throw your phone at you?" I asked.

"Hell if I know! He was mad at something. Probably mad at some girl. His phone got wet in the rain and he used mine to call somebody. Next thing I know, he walks into the den and he's throwing the damn thing at me. He hit me in the chest with it!" For good measure, Dick rubbed the center of his chest one more time with his right hand, emphasizing inflicted pain.

Understanding trickled slowly into my bleary consciousness. During the last few weeks Dick had received several phone calls in the late evening hours, the text message indicator on his Blackberry pinged throughout the night. When I questioned him about it, he had an excuse for the calls and messages. Work. His "damn employees" wouldn't leave him alone, he said. There was "always a problem with those rednecks", he insisted.

A few weeks earlier we had had an argument when I had been unable to access and pay our cell phone bill online, that's how I learned Dick had changed the password and taken me off the account as a primary user. He claimed it was an accident; that he hadn't intended to remove me from the account. I knew better, I wasn't fooled by his easy lie. The suspicious business of the phone and several other incidents had begun to resemble a familiar road map and tonight we had arrived at our destination. Marriage to Dick Crisco had been a long, rough road to travel. Rough, in part, because I chose to walk it with one hundred ounces of hope in my soul and the blindfold of denial covering my eyes. On this night, I felt all hope drain out, and I allowed the blindfold to slip away. I was done.

I was too concerned about my son to waste time arguing with this lying, immature man. From previous arguments, I knew Dick would never tell the truth, not if he was trying to cover his trail about something. He would argue with Jesus, blame it on Jesus and claim Jesus lied before he would admit the truth or accept responsibility for his behavior. Even though I knew of his propensity for deception, full awareness of the depths of Dick Crisco's despicable nature came to me slowly. When I finally realized he would even lie about his only son, I found myself loathing him. His name was bile on my tongue.

I didn't sleep the rest of the night.

For a while that night, I drove around town in my bare feet, clad in summer pajamas, searching for my son, marveling at how quickly a wonderful day had deteriorated into a horrific evening. Earlier in the day, Garrett had entertained me with stories of Australia, now I was distraught with fear for his safety. The night was hot and sticky, but I was covered in a cold sweat, freezing with worry over my son. I looked in ditches and behind guardrails for evidence of an accident, a motorcycle leaving the road. I called the emergency room and inquired about recent patients with motorcycle injuries. I drove by Daniel's house, Garrett's longtime friend. I drove along the country road leading to Aric's house, another of Garrett's childhood friends. I drove past the Cochran's house. Eventually I admitted the futility of my search and returned home, where

I made worried calls to my daughter and some of Garrett's friends. No one had heard from him. I sat in our home office with cell phone in hand, anxiety and fear dancing around me, and tried to decide what I should do. Dick had gone to bed and fallen to sleep immediately, as if there was nothing in the world to worry about, I could hear his snores all the way down the hall. For a moment, I thought of calling my mom. I knew she would be more than happy to talk to me and could probably shed new light or offer a different perspective on the circumstances of the evening. But I also knew she would be worried, and worry would only worsen the health problems she had suffered lately. Eventually, I decided to make another attempt at getting some answers from Dick. Intellectually, I knew interrogation would be a waste of time and energy. I knew Little Dick would stick to his lies like flies in glue, and I knew his lies would only create frustration and anger within me. I knew he would turn the current situation around to be about me, it would become my fault. It's what he always did. It was insane to think Dick would tell me anything other than what he wanted me to know. But I needed to try and put the pieces of this night together. I needed to understand what was going on with my son and I knew my husband held the answers. I always held onto hope that one day, Dick Crisco would speak the truth rather than the lies he had always spun so well. Perhaps tonight he would have the same concern for our son that I felt, and would be compelled to be honest with me. Perhaps it would be his first night of truth. *I knew better, but I had to try.*

"Dick, wake up", he didn't budge. I tried again, "Dick, I need to talk to you." My hands were cold and clammy from fear as I switched on the bedside lamp. I crawled onto the bed beside Dick and nudged him awake, "Tell me one more time what happened. I don't understand why Garrett would leave in a huff without saying anything."

"Shut the fuck up and stop your whining! I need some sleep! He's fine! Why are you worried about him? He's not worried about you! Do you think he gives a fuck that you're awake and keeping me awake? Get in the damn bed! Or go to the sofa. Leave me the hell alone! Are you forgetting we have to get up in a couple of hours and drive to fucking Athens? You're just a fucking bitch! You don't care a fuck about me! Either shut up or get the fuck out of here!" I could almost see venom mixed with the spit spewing from Dick's mouth.

Little Dick's degrading verbal assaults had become commonplace over the years. Had you been a silent observer, watching the red-faced, screaming monster lash out at me…and if you had observed me, silently absorbing the insults, you may have considered me to be weak. The truth is this: I was weak with fear. Fear preceded my weakness. I was afraid. Afraid to fight back; afraid to return the screaming insults. Once Dick had told me he could kill me with one blow to my face and I knew in this he told the truth. Fear of Dick's temper had shoved me into a pit of insecurity and intimidation. Fear of leaving my children alone with his anger had crippled me years earlier. Dick knew this, the fear he saw in my eyes empowered him. But tonight, I was no longer afraid of him. I saw him for what he is: a pathetic, little man of lies; weak in character and void of the ability to feel true love. In that instant, when I recognized and admitted his mental cowardice, Dick lost power and I took the first breath of my new life. At that moment, sitting on the bed beside him, I literally felt inner strength being restored to me. An image of hot, liquid steel being poured into a cast of me, burned in my mind. Dick Crisco could still hurt me physically. But he had just lost his control over me.

Keeping my voice steady, I responded, "He doesn't know I'm awake and worried, Dick. I was sleeping when he left. I don't understand why you aren't concerned about him. What's going on here? What do you know that I don't?"

"I don't know nothin'! Leave me alone. He'll be here in the morning. He needs to grow up, so let him! That's the problem with these damn kids! You worry too much about them and they don't give a shit about you. Leave me and them alone! You bother every one of us and we're all sick of you and your shit and bitching!" Dick rolled over on his side, his back facing me, and pulled a pillow over his head.

For the remainder of the night I sat on the sofa and prayed. I asked God to watch over and protect Garrett; to get him to a safe place; to let him know how much I love him; to guide me. God granted me peace and I knew Garrett was under His watchful eyes. I knew the core of this latest turmoil was about my husband and not about my son. More than likely, once again, Garrett was collateral damage in the hellacious life of women and drunks Little Dick was so drawn to. These were the greasy things Dick Crisco had always loved. He is incapable of staying away from them.

With daybreak, I showered and went through the motions of dressing. I moved silently about the house with the song, **A Change is Gonna Come,** stuck on replay in my head. I still didn't know what was going on with my son, but intuitively I knew his quick departure from our home had something to do with his dad and I knew there was going to be a change. After almost twenty-four years of marriage, I was finally willing to admit my husband would never be an honest, responsible, respectable man. I was fully aware of every lie sliding out of Dick's slimy mouth and I was tired of the lies, the pain, and the deception. If nothing else, *that* was going to be the change. I decided from that day forward, not only would

I no longer be afraid of him, but I would no longer pretend to believe him when he lied. Instead, I would call him out on every lie. No matter where we were or with whom, I would no longer cover for him. The days of sitting back and biting my tongue to avoid an argument were over. I was stepping out of the darkness I had lived in for more than two decades.

After showering, I found Dick engaged in one of his favorite activities: lying on the sofa in his boxers watching an early morning fishing show, eating a breakfast of oatmeal cream pies. Disgust swelled within me. He had insulted our son and lied about him and I hated the sight of Crisco because of it. I knew he was hiding the truth to protect himself. Crisco, who possessed what most men could only hope for: good kids, a faithful wife, numerous career opportunities, a beautiful home on five country acres, and more, had never been content or satisfied with family life. Numerous times he had been willing to leave us behind for another woman, and now I hated myself for believing life with him would turn out differently. I hated myself for believing his promises, for having wasted too much time and effort on a lost cause, for tolerating a manipulative bum. Guilt ripped at my soul, how could I ever make up the painful years of lost innocence to my children? Could they ever forgive me?

Even in the midst of uncertainty and chaos, life must go on, obligations and promises have to be kept. "Are you ready to go to Athens?" I asked Dick.

"I guess so. I just need to hook the trailer to the Kia."

Leaving Cartersville, I called Cissy to let her know we were on our way. "Don't worry about coming. I'm ok. I have enough people to help me", she said.

When she spoke I heard tension in her voice, the tightness of her vocal cords. Cissy had been very eager for me to bring Rooney, her beloved tomcat, to Athens. She would allow nothing short of a major situation to prevent or delay her reunion with Rooney.

"What's wrong?" I asked.

"You need to talk to Garrett."

"He doesn't have his phone and he hasn't called me. When did you talk to him?"

"Last night. He called after you called me. He's going to call you this morning," Cissy was terse with her replies and volunteered nothing.

It was comforting to hear Garrett had called his sister to discuss whatever was going on. My children's close relationship is something I'm thankful for and I don't take it for granted. Their dad and his sisters have a very distant and cold relationship. For no particular reason, Dick would sometimes go years without seeing or speaking with his sisters. It was not a family tradition I wanted passed down to my children. I vowed early in my marriage, before my children were born, to do all I could to encourage a strong bond and trusting relationship between my future children.

"Where is he?" I asked.

"The Lourdens. He called me from Mr. Lourden's phone."

Garrett has always maintained friendships with some wonderful people, the Lourdens are no exception and I was relieved to learn he was with them. But even with the relief of knowing where my son had spent the previous night, the drive to Athens was almost unbearable. Dick's behavior in the car caused me to recoil and made my skin crawl: he tried to hold my hand, he leaned over and kissed me when we were stopped at traffic lights, suggested we take a drive up the East Coast in September. His behavior that morning was confirmation, another familiar behavior pattern. In the past, when he was caught doing something he shouldn't be doing, he would suddenly morph into a doting and overly affectionate husband. Years ago his transformation had comforted me, reassured and convinced me he was faithful and true. He would tell me I was wrong, insist he could never hurt me and assured me I would never know how much he loved me. Dick would act as if he was devastated that I would give thought to distrust. I had always wanted to believe him, for years I had, but somewhere along the way, I stopped hearing and accepting his confected promises. Now I saw his fake affection for what it was, a manifestation of: **This Is What I Have To Do To Save My Own Skin.** *I silently kicked myself for hanging on so long.*

On the east side of Atlanta, we passed the Sugarloaf Parkway exit on Interstate 85, and I thought of my nephew Justin. I said a quiet prayer for him and his precious family of three. I prayed there would always be truth and mutual respect in his marriage. I prayed he would always be a good and honorable man in his child's eyes; and in the eyes of his wife. I thought of how he too had been hurt by Dick Crisco's broken promises over the years.

The Sugarloaf sign must have reminded Dick of the three as well. "Hey, why don't we stop by and see Old Fuzzy Top on our way back from Athens. Maybe it won't be too late for them to have dinner with us." Dick was suggesting we visit our five month old great-nephew and his mom and dad. Something, under normal circumstances, he knew I would be eager to do.

"I think they're in Waycross this week," I replied.

We drove north on I-85 for a few more miles and entered Highway 316, the long road leading to Athens, Georgia. It was apparent to me Dick believed he would rope me in again, corral me in his rodeo of deception and heartache, because he continued his attempt at conversation, making plans for future activities involving the two of us. I could not pretend to be interested. At the moment I just wanted the truth from him about what was happening in our lives. What was he up to this time? Was it adultery, like before? Had he borrowed too much money again? Was it theft, as his previous employer had accused? I remembered the employer's wife saying to me, "You really don't know your husband at all." I had become upset with her when she insulted my husband. I defended Dick and told the woman I believed she and her husband were wrong. And I did, I always believed Dick. Or at least I wanted to believe him. *I told myself I believed him.* If I had been honest with myself, I would have admitted I was in denial.

Recently Dick had begun complaining about the company he worked for, claiming his regional manager "has it in for me". This was another clue, a familiar refrain he often repeated when he was in trouble. I had worried about his comment. Dick had been terminated from a few jobs over the years and he had always laid the groundwork for me in advance of his firing, by claiming someone was "out for him" or "so and so is trying to get me in trouble by telling lies". Dick had been employed with Pancake Hut* barely a year and had just been promoted to manager of his own restaurant in Cartersville. He had a promising career with them, if he could follow the company rules, something he had been unable to do with other employers. He had promised me it would be different with Pancake Hut*. He said he was older now and no longer had the selfish inclinations he had held in the past. He even admitted he would not have been able to work in the restaurant field in previous years because of all the temptations that had plagued him. His admission had been proof to me that he had matured, and I believed him when he said he had buried his demons and vices. Ironically, after we divorced, I learned my nephew, twenty-five years younger than Dick, had said to his wife, "Dick will be great at Pancake Hut if he can stay away from the women."

Knowing your husband is lying, yet being unable to prove it, is excruciatingly frustrating.

Cissy was moving into an older, but well-kept small apartment community in Athens. When she and I found the apartment last spring, I had been impressed with the tidy yards bursting with vibrant purple Crepe Myrtles and fragrant Gardenias. Hostas and Lambs Ears lined the walkways, Peonies bloomed beneath bay windows. Each apartment had a small back yard and patio, protected from prying eyes with a privacy fence. I thought the apartment would provide a nice, peaceful environment for her. Cissy had recently ended a rough, emotionally difficult two-year relationship and her heart was still mending. I wanted her to have tranquility and peace in her life. Her beautiful smile, the real smile, the one that lights up her whole face, had appeared infrequently for almost two years. I longed to see the light in her sapphire eyes once again. Unfortunately, I would have to wait a bit longer to experience the grace of that beautiful, heartfelt smile. Because unknown to us, that previous spring, when Cissy and I had been out looking for her new apartment and making plans for a new school year, her dad had been lurking around dark places, blowing peace and tranquility to hell.

As Dick and I pulled into the small parking lot of the apartment complex, towing the trailer behind the car, Cissy was stomping heavily across the asphalt, toward a large metal trash bin, her arms were loaded with empty boxes and her ponytail was swinging. She looked at us and quickly turned her head, but not so quickly that I didn't see the fire in her eyes.

"She's upset about something," I said.

"She's a bitch, just like my sisters and my mother," her dad said.

"No Dick, she's not a bitch and I would appreciate it if you wouldn't call our children insulting names. Don't you know your daughter at all? She's angry about something and from the expression I just witnessed, she's angry with one of us. What in the world is going on?"

Dick exploded. "I don't know what the hell you've done, but I haven't done anything! What have you done to her? You've always got to piss somebody off, don't you? You can't ever leave well enough alone! What the hell have you been doing? You've done something to stir up some shit! Garrett's mad, she's mad, you've done something!" And just that easily, without speaking with Cissy, he accused me of being the cause of her frustration and Garrett's anger. Once more, he had twisted things and made the problem mine to own. *I was accustomed to Little Dick Crisco pointing the finger and blaming me for anything that went wrong in our lives, but I never grew accustomed to his audacity.*

Cissy returned from discarding the boxes and walked up to me without looking at Dick. I gave her a hug and she returned it very loosely. "You Ok?" I asked.

"I'm fine."

I didn't believe her, but I could tell she wasn't ready to talk.

"I thought I would shop for your groceries while you guys unload the trailer. Anything you need in particular?" I tried to sound light.

"Everything. And some cleaning supplies," she said.

"Alright, I'll be on my way. If I take your car we won't have to bother with unhooking the trailer. Is that ok with you?"

Cissy gave me her keys and for the next two hours I battled the Wally World "move in day crowd" of parents and students as everyone shopped for last minute supplies and groceries. I recognized hope, enthusiasm, optimism and excitement on the faces of both students and parents. I wanted to feel those emotions too, but I didn't. I was heavy with apprehension. Foreboding draped across my shoulders and hung down my back like a heavy black shawl. It angered me that anxiety and fear lingered where happiness and excitement should be. *How dare he take that from our daughter, our family... again.*

When I returned to the apartment complex Cissy was outside, checking the trailer for items left behind. "Did you get everything out of there?" I asked.

"Yeah."

"Where's your dad?"

"Inside. Sitting on his ass." Her response was quick and tight and it surprised me.

Hesitantly, I asked her, "Are you upset with me about something?"

"No. Not you. Not really. Not for anything you've done. I don't want to talk about it right now. I'll talk to you after you talk to Garrett."

Hot, nervous energy pulsed through me as we unloaded Cissy's groceries and supplies. I didn't want to let go of my embrace as we said good-bye, I had seen hurt and anger in her eyes, her body language, the tone of her voice, and I didn't want to leave her. As soon as the doors to the car were closed Dick said, "Hey Baby doll, I was glad when you got back. Cissy was rude to me when you were gone."

"What happened?" I prepared myself for the "poor, pitiful me" story he usually sold, but tonight I wouldn't buy it. I would never buy it again.

"Well, I sat down to watch TV and she said, 'Get off your ass and do something'. She's been a bitch to me."

"What's going on Crisco? Cissy wouldn't talk to you like that unless she was upset about something. Why were you watching TV anyway? We weren't here to watch TV. There's still tons of work to be done in her apartment. I feel terrible leaving her with so much to do. With your help, she could have had most of her apartment set up before we left."

His face took on an expression I knew too well. When Dick realized his lies were catching up to him he would always take on the persona of the mistreated, misunderstood underdog. When he was playing this role, he always relaxed his facial muscles, the muscles around his mouth would become slack and his voice took on a softer, thicker tone. In the beginning of our relationship and for several years into our marriage, I fell for it every time; hook, line and sinker. No more. Tonight I recognized the expression for what it was: part of the act, an attempt to turn me against our daughter in the same way he had turned me against his mom and sisters. The same way he had tried to turn me against my cousin.

"I ain't done a damn thing to her! I should have known you would take her side. You always take their side on everything! I'm tired of it. I'm your husband dammit, you need to start supporting me! I'm nothing to this family. I never have been."

I had heard enough. "How can you say that Dick? How can you say you mean nothing to this family or that I've never supported you? We've stood by you and supported you through hell and back. For years, you've shown the kids and me how invaluable we are to you! You showed us by screwing every whore that looked your direction. Every time you chose another woman and her kids over your own, you showed our kids how much they mean to you. You've proven to our children how much you love them by choosing to spend time with other women's children. Yet, every time you said you were sorry we accepted your apology as the truth. Our children forgave you for hurting them. Each and every time you've hurt them, they've forgiven you! They believed you when you said it would never happen again. I believed you even when I knew I should not. And *every time* you let us down. Forget about me and what you've done to our marriage, but think for one minute of the many times you've hurt and disappointed our kids. Over and over you left them to be with other women and their kids! You sick bastard! How the hell can you even speak those words? We have never meant anything to you! Take me home!"

"Settle down. I'm sorry. I didn't want to get this going. I just don't know why Cissy is being so mean to me. It hurts me, Baby. I was here to help her and she treated me like that and it just hurts. Let's get something to eat before we get back on the road, okay?" Sit down and eat in a restaurant with him? Was he serious? I couldn't look at him without wanting to puke, I sure as heck didn't want to sit in a restaurant and pretend things were okay.

"Let's just get home."

"No! I'm hungry, I've worked like a dog and busted my ass to get here to help that ungrateful girl and now I'm going to eat!"

We stopped at Five Brothers in Athens for a hamburger. I was anxious and upset, I didn't have an appetite. I knew without doubt Dick was lying to me, covering some other despicable thing he had done. *What would it be this time?* We sat under the bright café lights and I watched as Dick devoured first his food and then mine, he ate as if everything in our world was perfectly fine. I sat before him in disgust, wishing the grease of the fries he stuffed down his throat would cause him a very painful and fatal heart attack. I watched him open his mouth big and wide and shove huge bites of a burger into the space behind his teeth. Grease pooled in the corners of his mouth and I waited expectantly for the cardiac arrest that never developed. Years of lies, abuse and unfaithfulness boiled like a cauldron of hatred within me and I wanted him to drop dead in his chair. *I had a vision of myself getting up from the table, Crisco lying in a heap on the floor. I would step over him and walk away. Perhaps I would look over my shoulder and say, "I think you need to take the trash out", to the Five Brothers' manager on my way out the door.*

My phone rang with the strains of New York, New York, the ringtone indicating my son was calling, and broke me from my dark fantasy.

"Hey Mom. What are you doing"?

"I'm worried about you. What are you doing?"

"Not much, hanging out at the Lourden's house. Cissy said you just left Athens. When will you be back in C'ville"?

"I think we'll be back in town by nine o'clock", I told him.

"Ok, good. Do you want to meet me so we can talk?" he asked.

"Yes, I do. Where?"

"How about the parking lot of the church? Nine-thirty?" he asked.

"I'll be there."

"Ok. It's a date", said my son.

"What did he have to say for himself?" Dick asked.

"Just letting me know where he is and that he's alright," I answered.

"If he cared anything about you he wouldn't make you worry in the first place," Dick replied.

"Leave him alone, Dick. This isn't about Garrett and it isn't about me."

Except for the constant ringing and pinging of Dick's phone, we drove back to Cartersville in silence.

I pulled into the driveway of the church at twenty minutes past nine. Garrett was already there, waiting on his bike. The full moon illuminated him and I noticed his dark hair was curling in the damp night air. And as always happens when I see my children, my heart melted. I parked parallel to him and stepped out of the Kia Sorento as he walked around the bike, in my direction. The rain of the past few days had turned the summer night air pleasantly cool, and in the crazy way that happens in times of stress, my thoughts flashed back to similar summer nights of my childhood, summer nights at my grandparent's house; swinging on the front porch swing with my cousins, counting stars, catching lightning bugs and putting them in jars, listening for the lonely, distant hum of jets flying in the night sky and making plans for the future. Plans that always included my Prince Charming and travel to faraway lands.

"Hey Mom", my nineteen year old boy looked tired...drained, but he greeted me with a smile, a hug and a kiss on the cheek.

"Hey Bud. You had me worried."

"I'm sorry about that. I just couldn't stay at the house."

"What happened?" I asked.

Garrett dropped his head and leaned against the car, he was shaking slightly.

"Are you hungry? Do you want to get something to eat?" I asked.

"No. I'm not hungry."

"Tell me what's going on", I said.

"I don't want to hurt you, Mom. I don't want you to hurt again."

"I need to know", I said.

"I don't understand why I always have to be the one to break your heart." Tears formed rivulets down his face and dropped to the front of his shirt.

"Garrett, you have never broken my heart. I don't understand why God has always allowed you to be the messenger of bad news. That seems unfair and I don't understand it, but you have never broken my heart."

Several long seconds passed while Garrett shed tears without words. When he finally spoke, his voice cracked with emotion.

"He's at it again, Mom. If he ever even stopped. I doubt he ever stopped. I caught him red-handed."

"How?"

"His phone, at first. Then I checked into other things. Why did you marry him Mom? You could have had anybody else. Look at him! He's nothing! He's a pig. He doesn't deserve you! He has never deserved you! He doesn't deserve Cissy! Why did you stay with him all these years? What kind of loser throws away the people that love him?"

My boy's words spilled forth in painful, weeping sobs. He was indeed breaking my heart, though not for the reasons he thought. It was my son's raw pain and his own heartache that shattered my heart. I wrapped my arms around him and tried to comfort him, attempting to ease his pain and wipe his tears. But how do you erase the pain of a little boy, now a young man, who's been hurt and mistreated by his own dad? Time and time again he had been hurt by the one man that should have turned the world upside down to protect him.

The old saying is that time heals all wounds. I'm not so sure about that. Parents should delight in their children, and when emotional pain is intentionally inflicted upon a child, no matter the age of the child, the memory of the incident may fade but it never goes away completely. As long as the memory is there, the pain is there also.

"I thought I was protecting you and Cissy. When he was screwing all those women… you know what kind of trash they were, I wanted to protect you and Cissy from their influences. And from his influence and the way he behaved when he was with them. I thought I could protect you from all of that if we stayed married. If I had divorced him you would have been forced to spend summers, holidays and every other weekend with him and his women and redneck friends. If we were divorced, I would not have been able to prevent him from exposing you to who knows what. Sleazy women and drunken men. Probably drugs too, it seems."

I was the one crying now. I saw my anguish mirrored in my son's eyes, and unbearable, physical pain rippled through my muscles. "I was afraid of the things he would expose you and Cissy to."

"I know you thought you were protecting us, but you didn't. You couldn't protect us from him, Mom. He exposed us, me anyway, I don't know about Cissy, to his women and his friends. I know you didn't know, but staying only made matters worse".

"I wish you had told me", I said.

"I was a kid. He made me promise not to tell. Mom, there are things I'll never tell you about him and what he did. I love you too much to hurt you like that."

"I'm so sorry I didn't protect you from the bastard. You and Cissy deserved so much better than him. You should have never been disrespected that way. You know, I always believed he would do better. When he started attending church and promised us he would never go back to that old life, I believed him. I wanted you and Cissy to have your family intact. I realize now it was just a ruse. Church is what he did to maintain control over me. Over all of us. I should have left him the first time I caught him screwing around."

"But you didn't know, Mom. You did what you thought was best. And it probably was for the best. We'll never know. You're right, who knows what he and his redneck friends would have done to Cissy and me. He wouldn't have cared what happened, that much we know for sure."

"I'm going to divorce him, Garrett. I told him the last time he did this that I would never put up with it again. And you stood before him and told him you would never keep his secrets again. He didn't believe us, or he didn't care. Either way, I'm done", I said.

"You deserve better than him mom. You deserve to be happy. You don't have to put up with it any longer. And you're stronger than you think you are. Just think; you could start dating again." He smiled at me.

"Oh no, I don't think so!"

"Mom, not every man is like that idiot. If nothing else you can go out for intelligent conversation. That's something Crisco could never do... have intelligent conversation."

I laughed. "You're right about that. It's one of the reasons he's always degraded you. He knows you and Cissy are more intelligent than he is."

"It's the reason none of the Crisco's like Cissy and me. They know he's stupid and they know what he does is wrong but they cover his butt! Who supports a son and brother that screws up over and over again? Who stands behind a screw up that treats his family like dogs? Grandma and Pawpaw better not support him this time. I'll be done with all the Crisco's if they do." Garrett's jaw was firmly set, a surefire sign that his mind was made up.

"He's emotionally immature and he's practically illiterate, Mom. Did you know that when you married him? I mean, the guy can't spell simple words. He can't compose a complete sentence. Did you know how ignorant he is? You're an intelligent woman Mom, how could you marry such a stupid man?"

"No, I really didn't know. Oh, I knew he wasn't the smartest guy I had ever dated, but I didn't know the extent of his lack of academic intelligence. He kept it hidden very well. Did you know he told me he had an engineering degree from LSU? I didn't find out the truth until we had been married a couple of years. I learned from his mom. He never went to college anywhere. I was sick at my stomach when I learned the truth. He had lied so believably well. And I had told many people about his days at LSU, because he had made the stories sound so believable. I was a fool. But you should know this about him; it isn't that he's really unintelligent. I believe he can learn when he wants to. He's just too lazy to do the work or put forth the effort. It was just easier for him to pretend than to be self-disciplined and produce the work. Plus, his parents never encouraged their children to do anything with their lives other than get married. Academics were never important to your dad's parents. His mom once told me she didn't want him to go to college because he would only go to have sex and get a girl pregnant."

"He never went to LSU? Oh my God. Everything's been a lie, hasn't it?"

Slowly, I nodded, "A lot of things have been."

"Well, you can start over Mom. We all get a new start, a new life without Crisco yelling at us and trying to put us down and humiliate us. He can be someone else's problem from now on. He fits in just fine with those redneck women he's screwed," Garrett said.

"Speaking of someone else's problem, who was on his phone? Candy, from Pancake Hut"?

"She was one of them. You knew about her?" He looked surprised.

"I suspected her and a couple of others. They call his phone all hours of the day and night. Even on his days off they call. I asked him about them and he told me I was a crazy, suspicious bitch and said he was only trying to help Candy with expenses. Candy doesn't even work in his restaurant. She works at the one near Hobby Lobby and McDonalds, yet he said all the calls and texts were work related. I reminded him that Pancake Hut had conducted a spouse interview with me before they offered him the job and had assured both of us that employees were not supposed to call a manager, or manager trainees in his case, on their days off. Anyway, he had an excuse for it all, just like he always has."

"He can deny and make excuses all he wants. I have proof of what he's doing and he knows it. He can't get out of it this time. He's tried to ruin all of us and he hasn't been successful. And that pisses him off." Garrett took a deep breath, seeming to relax a bit.

"You know this already, but I have to say it. You and Cissy are not defined by who he is. You know that, right?"

"He's the sperm donor, Mom. That's it. He has nothing to do with who I am. I don't ever want to see him again. I hate to even look at him. I know I'll have to see him though because there are some things I need to say to him. But I'll never stay another night with him in the same house. And I want you to leave. He's evil, he's dangerous. You need to leave."

"I can't leave yet, I know he's dangerous, and I'll be careful. I wish you would stay, but I understand why you feel you can't. It's your home though," I said.

My son protested, "It's never felt like a home with him in it. I don't intend to hurt you with what I'm saying, but that's how it is. No matter how hard you tried to make it a home, it was cold with him there. I always knew he hated all of us. He wouldn't have exposed me to the things he exposed me to if he didn't hate me. And I don't know if you completely understand what I'm saying when I say I can't come back as long as he's there. One of us will die; either him or me. One of us will kill the other one. I will never back down from him ever again, and he's not used to that. He's used to kicking me around like a whipped dog, a kid that wouldn't fight back. I've grown up a lot this past year living in New York City and working this past summer in Australia. I'm not the kid that left here a year ago. I've got some things to say to Crisco. I've got years of his insults to get off my chest and when I do, it's probably going to get very ugly because he's used to me taking his crap. I'm going to give it a few days before I confront him, but he is going to hear what I have to say. And it won't be done his way, the cowardly way, over the phone or in a text. It's going to be face to face. I'll never call him 'dad' again. He hasn't earned that name."

"I understand why you have to talk to him. And I think you should tell him how you feel, it will be good for you to get the anger out, get it off your chest. Just promise me one thing; promise me you'll let me be there. I need to be there so I can call the police if he gets out of control. You know how bad his temper is and how quickly he escalates. I promise you I will sit back and say nothing, unless I need to phone 911. I give you my word I won't interfere. If you don't want me there, then have Jack or Jim or Greg or Stephen come over. Just don't do this alone."

The thought of my son and Dick left alone to argue in the wooded solitude of our house was extremely frightening to me. Dick kept numerous knives, pistols, rifles and shotguns in our house and also in his truck. He had always owned lots of weapons, and in a few short weeks, even I would be surprised to learn just how many weapons he owned. To this day, I don't know when he purchased most of them or where he got the money to do so.

Dick's anger is quick and volatile and I knew he would not hesitate to use a weapon on his own son. *It's ironic, really. He used to tell me he could never do anything he wanted to do because I was always "stuck up his ass". Later, after he was gone, I learned he had said the same thing about me to others; "I can't do a damn thing without my wife being stuck up my ass". If that's the case, how did I not know when he purchased his weapons, borrowed money from payday loan stores or went to biker bars? How was it he was in relationships with so many women without my knowledge, if I was "stuck up his ass"? The truth is, I was not 'stuck up his ass' as he claimed, nor did I want to be. I worked full time for a major airline; I drove one hundred and forty-two miles round trip every day for my job. I cared for our children and attended all of their games, school field trips, school activities and extracurricular activities. I kept our home clean and prepared home cooked meals and ran my husband's errands. I didn't have time to be stuck up anything. His negative remarks were intended to make me look like a nagging, complaining wife, while gaining sympathy for himself.*

"Ok, I give you my word I'll let you know when I plan to talk to him, I don't mind if you're there. In the meantime, I wish you would get out of there. People love you, Mom. They'll help you. Go to Nanny's or the Robertson's or Donna's or Sherry's. Angie would let you stay with her and so would the King's. Just get out of there. He's a sick man, capable of vile things. Believe me, I know what I'm talking about, Mom." His lips quivered and became dry as childhood memories formed words in his mouth.

I still don't know everything my son knows about Dick. I still don't know the whole of what he saw and heard. But I know this: My beautiful little boy had his soul tortured by the man who should have loved and protected him, a man who should have protected his son with his own life if necessary. Dick should have sheltered our son from men such as himself. Instead, that sick, pathetic, bile infested little man sacrificed his own child for a few minutes of lust. He used his little boy as a decoy, a pawn, an excuse to be with some of the filthiest women the world has ever produced. Looking back, I believe he tried to break the spirit of our son. But he didn't. Because Dick Crisco is such a weasel himself, he greatly underestimated the resiliency and tenacity of our son.

"I refuse to let him run me out of my home. I've got as much time effort and money invested in the place as he does. It's the same home he promised all of us we would never have to leave and I won't just give it to him. I'll be ok. I'll sleep with a knife under my pillow and the phone beside me." Even as I said the words, I knew it was pure craziness to live the way I had just described.

"As long as he's there it won't be a home Mom. You need to stop thinking of it as a home. It's just a house. I know you're attached to it because that's where Cissy and I have been for the last nine or ten years. But we don't have good memories of Shotgun Road. Crisco ruined every possibility of us ever having good memories there."

I started to ask a question and he held up his hand, "No...don't ask. Just know we don't like it there. Why do you think we both had to get away as soon as we graduated? We weren't running from Cartersville or from you. We were trying to get away from him. It's time to move on, get away from the creep. Go where you've always wanted to go. You've always wanted to live in Hawaii or St. Augustine or Tybee Island. Now's your chance to do the things you've always wanted to do. Go where you want. Live where you want. Cissy and I will come to you."

"I promise you I will start making plans. But what will I do? No money, no income, no income prospects. I will leave and I assure you I will divorce him, but I have to be smart about this."

"I'll help you! I'll do whatever I can for you. Just leave before he hurts you even more!"

"Please understand this: I never want to be a burden to you or Cissy. Until you graduate and begin working, you'll have a difficult enough time trying to take care of yourselves. You've done that for the most part since you graduated high school anyway, but I was able to help some with extra money now and then. That will end. You know he will withhold money from me. It was hard to get him to help either of you before; he will stop all efforts financially once he knows I'm serious about divorcing him."

"I don't want his money. I don't want anything at all from him. I don't want a relationship with him. In the past, when you've taken him back, you've always convinced me and Cissy to maintain a relationship with him. And we have, but don't ask me to try again. I won't. I've tried and tried and he didn't care. He's never cared. I'm done with him, it's over for me," resolution settled firmly in Garrett's voice.

"I won't ask you to maintain a relationship with him this time. Heck, I don't plan on having a relationship with him any longer either. I only asked in the past because I believed it was for the best, I had faith he would change his ways every time he said he would. I know now he doesn't care about having a relationship with his family. I'm sorry I dragged this thing out for so long," I said.

Garrett looked toward the full moon and began to sing, "Well it's a marvelous night for a moondance, with the stars up above in your eyes…"

"Life's going to get better for us Mom, it has to. We've lived in hell long enough." With those words, spoken by my son as he looked me squarely in the face, the last twenty-three years flashed behind my eyes. I saw the foolishness of my efforts to save my family. I saw the disdain in my husband's eyes as he spoke to me. I saw the lust in his eyes when he looked at the teenage girl friends of our teen children. I saw the pain in the innocent faces of my children, pain that became anger as they grew older. *Anger which became indifference toward their dad.*

I had tried to make life comfortable and happy for my children. They had tried to be happy kids. But how could they ever have had a happy, sweet childhood with their dad constantly putting them down; a dad always angry; a dad always speaking to them in a condescending manner? I saw how pathetic I had been, I saw how pathetic I must have appeared to my children. I had unwittingly contributed to their pain and it was killing me. It was all so clear now. Why had it taken so long for me to see the truth?

"Call me when he's at work and I'll come by. Ok?"

Tears constricted my throat so tightly I could not speak, I nodded.

"I'll be at the Lourden's house for a few days. I'll be fine. We're all going to be fine, Mom." He gave me a hug and kissed my cheek.

"I'll call you when I get to their house tonight."

The muscles in my throat relaxed enough for me to speak, "Ok. I love you buddy. I'm so sorry, for everything." I began to cry again.

"You're a good mom. You were always a good mom. Cissy and I are lucky to have you. I mean, just think; Crisco is drawn to whores like a maggot to rotting meat, what if you had divorced him and he had married one of them? Think of what would have become of us if we had a stepmom like one of those women! Smile mom. Life is about to get better. And Mom? You did save our family. Our family is and always has been you, Cissy and me. Crisco never wanted to be with us, we've all known that for a long time. You saved the part worth saving Mom."

Before going home I drove to Pancake Hut to speak with one of the women Dick had been seeing. Garrett had given me some of the details of the text messages and voice mails left by the different women, Candy was one of them. I knew which Pancake Hut Candy worked in and drove there to speak with her myself.

After leaving Candy, I returned to the house and found Dick on the sofa, watching a rerun of America's Funniest Videos.

"Where have you been, Babydoll?" he asked.

"I was with Garrett."

"Oh yeah? What was he havin' to say?" Dick's tone was light and playful.

"He told me what really happened last night. He told me why he left the way he did. He told me about the text messages and the voicemails. All day you've let me worry about Garrett. All day you've tried to lead me to believe that something was going on with him. And all along you've known what's going on because it's about you and your sluts. How could you do that?" I didn't take my eyes off Dick, watching for the signs of his lies to appear. I didn't have to wait long.

"What the hell is that little sonofabitch saying? There weren't any damn messages from any damn body!" His playful tone was quickly replaced with feigned indignation as he raised himself to a sitting position. Dick placed both hands on his knees, one of his fingers twitched against the bare skin of his leg as he yelled at me.

"Stop it Dick. I've spoken to Candy. I've spoken to one of the cooks at Pancake Hut. I know what's going on. I won't fall for your lies again. Never again. I'm finished with your filthy game of charades."

"He's lying to you! But just like always, you believe everyone but me! I ain't done a damn fuckin' thing, and you're going to believe him! I'm sick of this fucking shit!"

That night I finally admitted to myself that Dick would never take responsibility for his actions and would always divert blame to someone else. But our children? Our son? He would throw our own son under the bus and try to make this his problem? I was so disgusted with Little Dick at that moment that I became physically ill. I rushed to the back deck and released the bile that burned in my throat. All the while Dick continued to rant about how everyone was out to get him and blame him for things he had never done.

"Dick, I told you I would never go through this with you again and I meant it. I want a divorce. I want you to leave." Hell's tight hold on me began to weaken as I spoke those words.

"I'm not leaving! I'm not giving you a damn divorce! If you want a divorce, you file. I'm not doing it!" He left the den and made his way to our bedroom. I did not follow him. That night and every night after that I slept in our daughter's bedroom.

The next morning I called my mom and told her the news.

"Oh my God, I thought he was past this nonsense," she said.

"I thought so too. I hoped so. But he's never going to change," I said.

"What are you going to do?" she asked.

"Oh, I'm done. I'll file for divorce and I'll live in a cardboard box and eat cat food before I'll stay married to him this time."

"So you're finally ready to get off this rollercoaster ride?" She had heard unwavering resignation in my voice.

For the next few days I kept a low profile and tried to come up with a plan for my future. I told very few people what was going on in my life, yet people began to post comments on my Facebook page and leave messages on my phone: Praying for you; thinking of you; call me so we can talk, etc. And then, one post really caught me, it was from my friend Missy:

"Wow! That was a powerful letter Garrett posted!"

I responded to her and told her I had not read it, so she forwarded it to me:

Missy: Here you go, Danita. I read it and cried because I could feel Garrett's pain. The pain he felt as a little boy and the pain he's feeling now. I love you and call if you need me.

Fathers, Who do you think you are?

By: Garrett Able

Written yesterday at 4:17 PM, August 4, 2009

Fathers, who do you think you are?

Who are they exactly? Dad, Father, Pops, all these names are talking about the first true hero in our lives, the first real "Man". As kids we are always saying, "My dad can beat up your dad!!!" And the rebuttal, "Well, MY dad can lift that car and put it on your dads head!"

As kids we are so in love with our fathers. As we grow older we become more and more like our fathers because our admiration towards them is more than we can understand. It is so strong sometimes, you take on every characteristic of your dad. And to a loving father, this is the greatest sign of admiration! Of an unconditional Love that runs so deep… the jelly sandwich he made you the night before last was the most amazing bit of food you ever ate. And the one tomorrow will be better even than THAT one. What I don't understand, is why do some wish they had a better life?

I was seven when my dad showed me his better life. Instead of doing what most dads do and leave their family, my dad was sick minded enough to take me along. Her name was Lorraine*, she lived in Pine Log, not far from my house. My "Father", my "Hero", would take me "fishing" but before we got to the lake we would pick up this woman from the country corner gas station. She would then join us and once we got to the lake I would take my rod and fish while my father left me. I was seven. A child. Once he had his fill of filth he would retrieve me. Tell me, 'don't tell mom I had a friend." This continued for the longest time, this secret life I was forced to share with my father, all the while I was there watching, listening and hurting. I was seven years old when I became a bigger man than my father. On the way to tennis practice, we all ended up at the country corner store one evening… my mom, me, my father and Lorraine. I turned to my mom and told her, 'this is dad's friend". She asked me what I meant and hell broke loose in the store when I described the relationship between my dad and this woman. In front of me, my father denied what I said. In essence calling me a liar. My father broke my mother's heart through me because he didn't have the balls to tell her himself.

This happened two more times, (that I'm aware of), the most recent was two weeks ago. I am 19 years old. Except I feel like I have been 25 since I was 12. My father had a wife who would NEVER leave him. A BEAUTIFUL wife, a loving daughter, and me. His "Buddy" he called me. I am successful, smart, funny, talented, loving, compassionate towards others…but he didn't want me enough to stay, or any of us for that matter.

The Love that ran deep has only made a scar. I am nothing like my father. At twelve I knew I didn't want to be like him. My hero died on the beach of Lake Allatoona.

So this is to you fathers out there: If you are faithful, stay that way. You will be rewarded greatly with Love and happiness *and moments where your children want to squeeze you because they love you so much. And kisses from your wife that make you melt like it's the first kiss you ever had. You will see your children grow and look at you like, "There is Superman, he is sitting right there in front of me...across the table and he is my Dad. MY dad." Your daughters will mold who they want to LOVE out of you!!!! You, who cuts the lawn and drinks out of the jug of milk and chokes on it when your beautiful wife comes into the kitchen and catches you. DON'T LET THAT GO!!!!!!!!!!*

To those of you who are not faithful, it's time to rethink the pros and cons. YOU WILL BE DISCOVERED!!!! YOU WILL BE UNVIELED!!!! YOU WILL BE MADE TO LEAVE!!!!! Because you are WORTHLESS!!!!!

But I do Forgive him.

If you are tagged it's because you either already know, can help my mother deal with this, or because I think you should know.

I was in awe of my son's courage, and distressed by his broken heart. His pain was evident in the words he had written. I knew the pain in his message represented Cissy's pain also. Garrett has always worked through hard times with the written word, Cissy keeps her words inside.

In the days following my decision to divorce Dick, I began to torture myself mentally, thinking of the emotional pain my kids had suffered throughout the years. I had stayed in this marriage too long. It had taken me too long to face reality, and now time had stolen the sweet years of childhood from my children. A friend had once asked me, "Do you know where time goes? It goes so quickly."

I had answered her, "Oh, time becomes memories."

Painful questions were staccato lightning bolts to my heart: Were all of my children's memories laced with pain? Would time to come bring better memories? What made me stay with Dick? Why had I chosen to believe him time and time again when history had proven him to be deceitful? Why could I not let go? Why had I refused to admit a monster lay underneath the nice smile? *Why had I never given up on him?* The answer to that last question came more easily than the others: I couldn't give up on him because he was my husband, my children's dad. I had to believe he loved them as much as I did. I had believed he would change. I believed he would stop his foolishness *because* he loved them enough to want change. I believed he wanted their respect as much as I wanted their respect for him. In the end, he did not stop. He never changed. He loved himself and his carnal lifestyle too much to give it up for his children.

And now, we were here. My stupid, stubborn determination to fight for my family, and Dick's determination to destroy us, had ended here on Shotgun Road, Cartersville, Georgia in the year 2009. Too many years had gone by. Too much time had become painful memories.

I thought of the many incidents over the years, incidents that led to this day. Now it was clear as crystal, the many times that I should have jumped ship, bailed out. Throughout the years I had seen Dick 'through a glass darkly'. Until now, I had not recognized my failure to see things as they were. 1 Corinthians 13 has always been one of my favorite chapters in the Bible, and I had tried to apply it to my marriage.

[4]Love is patient, love is kind. It does not envy, it does not boast, it is not proud. [5]It is not rude, it is not self-seeking, it is not easily angered, it keeps no record of wrongs. [6]Love does not delight in evil but rejoices with the truth. [7]It always protects, always trusts, always hopes, always perseveres. [8]Love never fails.

Love didn't fail. The kids and I didn't fail. Dick's inability to love his family is *his* failure, not his children's, not mine. It was obvious to me now, what I had once been oblivious to: Dick would never change. Therefore life with him would never change. It occurred to me that another verse in Corinthians defined my frame of mind during the full length my marriage:

[12]Now we see but a poor reflection as in a mirror; then we shall see face to face. Now I know in part; then I shall know fully, even as I am fully known.

[13]And now these three remain: faith, hope and love. But the greatest of these is love.

In other words, I had not been able to see my husband for the type of man he really was. It was as if I had viewed our lives through a darkened glass. Because of that, I had not been able to admit to myself that life with him would always be difficult. I had been unable to see him for the chronic liar and adulterer that he is. I had been unable to admit the marriage was destined for failure from the start. My faith and hope in love, my faith and hope in Dick, had skewed my ability to see things clearly.

Then I knew in part. Now I know fully. My children had known fully all along.

Reflection was a painful but necessary process for me, one of many 'first steps' toward healing. Dick's rejection had hurt my dignity and my heart. But his rejection of our children was excruciating and ripped my heart to shreds. Finally realizing and acknowledging the pain of my children was so overwhelming, I was unable to think of it all at once. I could allow small increments of memory to surface at a time, nothing more. I would process the memory and then store it back in the dam of heartache trapped in my soul. Several times the dam tried to break and flood my mind, yet I was able to hold it back, allowing only streams of painful memories to trickle slowly into my consciousness, one ugly memory at a time. I could not permit a sudden overwhelming flood of memories of my children's full heartache. I don't think I'm as strong as my children; I would have drowned under the weight of those heavy waters.

In the days following my declaration of divorce, Dick Crisco made my life miserable. If his mission was to humiliate and disrespect me with one final fireworks display of vulgarity and indecency, he accomplished his mission. He left pornography open on the home computer. He wrote the names of his "date matches" from a Cheater's website on notebook paper and left the document on the bathroom counter. He stayed out late and came home drunk and high. When he was home he talked with women most of the night, planning dates with them. He brought women from a local biker bar into our home. This was very different from his past habit of successfully hiding his encounters. His behavior was my confirmation that he knew his gig was up.

I was disgusted by Dick's behavior and I didn't want to be near him anymore than was necessary. When we were in close proximity, I felt as if I had brushed up against something dirty and couldn't dust the filth off, stepped in fresh dog crap and couldn't scrape it off the bottom of my shoes. I wanted a better life for my kids and myself. Brief glimpses of a better way to live began popping in and out of my thoughts, and without much effort, for the first time in more than twenty-three years, I began to envision a life without Dick. And I was excited about it. It felt as if a weight heavier than the University of Georgia's entire offensive line had been lifted from my shoulders. *I knew I had* finally broken free from the burden of an unfaithful and abusive man; my children however, weren't yet convinced of my resolve. Later I learned they had had discussions between themselves of their doubts about my declaration. Throughout their entire lives, I had forgiven their dad when he hurt our family, so their doubts were reasonable and understandable. But I had no doubt; I knew I would never go back to Dick Crisco. The darkness dancing around Dick Wayne Crisco, Jr. had become palpable and frightening. I couldn't get away fast enough.

Apprehensively, I began calling select family and friends, the ones who knew of Dick's history of chronic lies and adultery, and told them of the latest drama he had created. They had heard it before and almost to the letter, each person initially assumed I would be angry for a few days, only to forgive him once again. But before our conversations ended, each said to me, "You sound different this time. You're serious about this, aren't you?" Yes indeed, very serious.

To outsiders, casual friends, those not in our immediate network, and a few close friends, our family life was a beautiful and enviable tapestry, tightly woven with respect and love, the borders carefully and securely hemmed to prevent unraveling. Making the calls to these unknowing family friends was more difficult than calling those who knew the truth. I didn't know where or even how to begin telling them our life had been a dreadful lie. A lie I had hoped to make true is still a lie. We had fooled them and I knew many would be hurt by the deception. Rightly, some would feel betrayed and I would ask their forgiveness. Most were simply shocked beyond belief, it was difficult for them to comprehend, to "pour the thought", as my uncle said. With my enabling, Dick had perfected the image of the classic devoted dad and husband; it would take a while for the truth to settle on folks.

Unburdening myself from the weight of deception and humbling myself before these kind people with the truth was freeing, but I was still tormenting myself with the '*What if's and What I should haves*'. I was still fighting with myself, holding back painful memories and suffering physical pain from the stress of my emotional battle. I wanted to get on with life, was ready to move on, but I felt I had come up against a mountain of fear that I couldn't climb over. The memories haunting me were real and I was fearful of cracking under the ugliness of them, so I kept them at bay. But like any other fear, I realized I would never conquer it until I faced it head-on. I began climbing the mountain, one painful memory at a time.

Reflections of Carnal Discoveries 1994

I love the quietness at the beginning of each new day and hardly anything compares to the quiet beauty of an autumn morning in North Georgia. On this late October day, I woke early and quietly walked to the back patio with a glass of iced water. The brilliance of red, gold, yellow and green glistening with dew in the fall sun nearly took my breath away. A cool, soft breeze gently lifted a few leaves from the trees and carefully laid them on the ground in front of me. I lowered myself to a lawn chair, relishing the peacefulness of the morning, before I had to hand it over to a Saturday of chaos and cartoons. I knew the kiddos would be full of energy today as we prepared for their joint birthday party at the American Adventures Theme Park. They were great kids. I had heard other parents refer to their own children as 'handfuls'. I couldn't say that about Cissy and Garrett. Inquisitive and curious, yes. Active? Most certainly, as they should have been at their ages. But they were obedient and polite children. Sometimes, I found it hard to believe that God had blessed my life with such wonderful little people. I was amazed that He chose me to parent these two precious children. Sometimes I doubted my ability and wondered why I had been entrusted with two of the most amazing gifts in the world. So in the peacefulness of the morning, I offered up a prayer of praise and thanksgiving for my family. I thanked God for my kids and for my husband, Dick. The two of us had weathered many storms in our nearly nine years of marriage, but I felt we were finally on solid ground. There had been numerous upheavals: job losses for Dick, financial losses, the loss of the first home we built, several moves between three different states, countless arguments, two years of trade school for Dick, a devastating health problem for me, without the benefit of medical insurance. The stresses had been heavy and staggering, but we were still standing, and finally, Dick and I both held good jobs with established companies. So this day I said a special prayer of thanks to God for Dick's new outlook and what I believed was our mutual determination to walk, crawl, run or climb our way through the rough spots of life.

For a few more moments I lingered in the lawn chair with my eyes closed, facing the October sky. "Good morning, Mommy. Is it time to leave for the party yet?" It was my little boy, Garrett, speaking with the breathy lisp of a four-year-old. I had not heard him open the door and come outside. He gently climbed onto my lap and gave me a kiss and a hug.

"Good morning to you too, Bud! No, we've got a few more hours before time to leave for the party. Are you excited?" I asked.

"I'm berry, berry excited! I'm going to get Cissy up! Ok?"

And off he went. I looked toward the sky and whispered, "Thank You," before going inside. Once in the kitchen, I pulled bagels and cereal from the pantry and was reaching in the fridge for milk and yogurt when two soft arms snaked around my waist. "Good morning, Mommy. I love you. Is Justin here yet?" Garrett had been successful in waking Cissy.

"Well, Good morning Miss Cissy, I love you too! No, Justin isn't here." We'll pick him up as we leave for the party. He had plans for something else this morning, but he's spending tonight with us." Justin is my children's cousin and they love him like a brother; a party without him was unthinkable.

"Mommy, even though we're having the party today, my real birthday isn't till November. Will I have another party then?" It was a logical question for a little girl almost six years of age.

"No sweetie, but I'll bake a cake on your real birthday, just like I did for Garrett on his birthday in September. Remember? We're having the combined party in October because it's the month in the middle of your birthdays. You both wanted American Adventures to host your party and the park will be closed in November. Remember when we talked about it?" I asked her.

She nodded her head up and down. "Yes, I just wanted to be sure. I'm happy about today, Mommy," she said softly and sweetly.

"Me too," I whispered as I kissed the top of her head.

I walked to the master bedroom to wake Dick and found him on the phone. He looked at me and said into the handset of the phone, "Ok, I'll see what I can do, but my kids are having their birthday party today." He placed the phone and the bedside table and let out a deep sigh. "Sonofabitch", he said.

"What's going on?" I asked.

"Oh, it's work," he answered with exasperation hissing on his tongue. "They want me to come in today because somebody called in sick. On my off day! And they want me there by four o'clock. Damn."

Immediately I was in protective mom mode, my shoulders squared with tension. "Didn't you tell them we've had our children's party planned for a couple of months? It's their birthday party, it only happens once a year."

"Yeah, but they said my job could be in jeopardy if I don't show up," Dick stood with slumped shoulders; helplessness was etched on his face. "I don't know what to do."

I felt terribly sad for my husband and my children. "Dick, you've already worked over forty hours this week. They can't make you come in today. The kids will be devastated if you aren't at their party. When did work call, anyway? I didn't hear the phone ring."

Dick sat down on the side of the bed, looking at the closed blinds of on the window; he didn't answer me. His back was to me so I walked to the other side of the bed and faced him, asking again, "Who called? When did they call?"

"When you were outside. John had one of the guys call me, he said John wanted me to call him in fifteen minutes, said he needed to talk to me about something. I guess I shouldn't have called him back. I should have let it go. Now I don't know what to do."

Something about the tone of his voice and the dull, vacant look in his eyes made me distrustful of what he was saying. On the other hand, I knew Dick had tried very hard to get a job with this company and I knew he wouldn't do anything to jeopardize his job. "Dick, I know this job is important for our family, but our children will be heartbroken if you aren't with us today. You can't be fired for not coming in to work when someone else calls in sick. Employers can't do that." I pled my case.

"I guess I'll call him back and see if I can come in later," he said.

I could see Dick was trying to come up with a solution, a compromise that would work for everyone.

"That's better than not being there at all, but some of the kids are sleeping over after the party and you've promised to make chocolate chip pancakes in the morning. Do you think you can be home in time for that?" I asked.

Dick exploded, "What the hell's more important to you? Huh? A damn birthday party or my job?" His outburst startled me. His temper was not a secret, and he was seldom able to restrain himself from explosive tantrums, but this one was unexpected and seemed unjustified.

"The question is this: what's more important to you? You know as well as I do your employer cannot terminate you for refusing to work an unscheduled shift. Especially since you've already worked more than forty hours." I couldn't withhold my frustration.

"Fuck it," Dick said, "I'll just let 'em fire my ass and then you'll be happy. Happy to have me stuck up your ass just like it's always been. Just like my damn mother! And when we get kicked out of this damn house because I've lost my job you'll be whining again. Fuck you!"

I wasn't going to ruin the kid's day by having an argument with their dad. "Forget it, do what you have to do."

When I returned to the kitchen, Cissy and Garrett were sitting at the breakfast table, silently eating their cereal and yogurt. Their earlier excitement had waned considerably due to the argument they had just overheard. One of them asked me what was wrong. "Well, dad's boss wants him to come to work today and that's upsetting to your dad and to me. Dad wants to go to your party instead of work and his boss doesn't understand."

Moments later Dick walked into the kitchen, smiling, and announced, "Well I think I have it worked out. I called John back and told him I had to be at the party and he said I could come in afterward. And I'll be home in time to make the pancakes! I told him I would have to leave work before six in the morning, no matter what's going on. How's that?"

I thanked him for working out a solution and as each of our children put their dishes away, they thanked him too. Garrett hugged his dad around the legs before he left the room, "I'm glad you'll be at my party dad."

"Me too, Buddy", he said to our son.

"Do you want me to drive the van to American Adventures and you drive separately in the Subaru so you can leave directly from there for work?" I asked.

"No, I'll come back with ya'll and then I'll take the van because the Subaru is acting up. I haven't told you, but it's been stalling out for a couple of days. I need to look at it tomorrow. I don't want to drive it and have it break down with me tonight. If something were to go wrong with it, you wouldn't be able to come get me since all those kids will be sleeping over."

The rest of the day moved at a racer's pace. Even while I stayed busy cleaning the house, preparing bags with party favors for the guests and running last minutes errands, I couldn't shake the morning's incident from my mind and because of it, knots of tension formed in my shoulders and pain throbbed in my temples. Dick's post argument behavior was causing red flags to pop up on my radar. He was being unusually polite and kind, over the top with accolades. Dick was always polite to friends and strangers. He was almost always polite to his family when we were in the company of others. But in the privacy of our home, his demeanor was usually one of indifference. I made excuses to the kids and to myself about his attitude. When there was prolonged interaction between us, if Dick had been at home for an extended period of time, the kids and I usually became a source of aggravation for him. It didn't take much to trigger an outburst of anger from him and he was not one to feel remorse for his behavior. For that reason, his current, overly sweet and apologetic attitude, coupled with his earlier tirade, made me suspicious that something was up with him. At first I told myself his new attitude was an attempt at redemption from the ugly things he had said that morning; a sign of his developing maturity. Still, I couldn't shake the wariness. Uneasiness tugged on me all day.

The birthday party went well, the kids had fun on the rides and filled themselves with pizza, cake and ice-cream. Dick was in his element, he has always liked to be the center of attention, even at his children's birthday parties. Usually his attention seeking behavior was a source of embarrassment for me, but he was in a good mood and I was happy to see him smiling, seemingly enjoying himself, so I overlooked his loud antics. A couple of times he pulled me close and whispered apologies for the ugly things he had said earlier, he said he wished he didn't have to go into work that evening. I chastised myself for having doubts about him.

On the drive home from the party, Dick and my nephew Justin begun singing a country song I had never heard:

Yes I admit I've got a thinking problem
She's always on my mind,
Her memory goes round and round
I've tried to quit a thousand times.
Yes I admit I've got a thinking problem.

Dick sang with gusto and conviction, Justin laughed as he tried to sing louder than his uncle. I sat in the front passenger seat of the van, smiling, while a familiar dark warning began to invade my thoughts. I pushed the feeling aside and silently scolded myself for being suspicious, for allowing the words of a corny country song to place doubt in my mind. Perhaps Dick was right when he said I conjured up trouble.

Dick rushed to the shower as soon as we arrived home. When he emerged he was wearing the dark blue shirt of his work uniform and a new pair of jeans. The uniform shirt, with his name embroidered on the pocket, was unbuttoned at the top and I could see the ribbed collar of a green sports tee peeking out. "Aren't you wearing your work pants tonight? You'll ruin your new jeans and I just bought them last week," I said to him.

"No, John said I'll be supervising the crew tonight, so I won't get dirty. I love you. See you in the morning and be hungry for pancakes when I get home!" He gave me a kiss and a hug and walked out the door. He didn't bother saying goodbye or goodnight to our children.

Later that evening, as I served popcorn and ice cream to the children, I was still troubled. I couldn't shake the apprehension that enveloped me. Life felt off-center. No matter what I did, the feeling wouldn't leave me. After getting the boys settled into Garrett's room and the girls into Cissy's, I cleaned the kitchen and picked up the clutter in the den. I was still wired when I finished cleaning and decided I may as well take advantage of my nervous energy and do a load of laundry. I entered the laundry room and exhaled an exasperated breath, I had been able to teach our children to place their dirty clothes in the laundry baskets, but Dick still dropped clothing on the floors, in the sink, in chairs, on top of the dryer and any other convenient location. I lifted a pair of his jeans from the floor, and a wadded-up piece of paper fell out of a front pocket. Unfolding the crumpled paper, I saw a message written in large, loopy letters, "I love you my funny, sexy man! Kisses, Dawn."

The world grew dark around me, it felt as if my heart would thud to a sudden stop and I heard myself moan, *"Oh my God"*; raw words falling hard against the laundry room walls. I leaned against the cold washing machine, and wondered who Dawn could be. With my stomach cramping from knotted nerves, I walked to the wall phone in the kitchen and dialed Dick's work number. His supervisor, John, answered the phone and I asked to speak to Dick.

"Dick isn't working tonight, this is his weekend off. Dick said your kids were having a party tonight. Is something wrong?" John asked.

"I don't know, maybe" I said. "Dick told me you called him in to supervise the overnight shift tonight."

There was a long troubling pause before John spoke; his silence spoke before his words. "I didn't call him in", he finally said.

Understanding and realization closed around my heart until I could barely breathe. My tongue became dry and thick and it was almost impossible for me to articulate. Rapid thoughts tumbled with bits and pieces of events and conversations from the previous week. An earlier conversation with Dick had bothered me all week and he had become angry when I questioned him about it, and now it was front and center in my thoughts. "John, was Dick honored with a dinner at Longhorns last Friday evening? A dinner spouses weren't invited to attend?" I asked the question haltingly, afraid of hearing the answer I already knew. Still, I hoped I was wrong.

"No ma'am. Dick hasn't been honored for anything," John's tone had become grumpy and rough.

"I see", I said.

"As a matter of fact, Danita, there are many days and evenings we can't find him. He takes off in a fuel truck and we can't get him on the radio. He's already been reprimanded twice. So no, he hasn't received any honors,"

"John, do you know anyone in your office by the name of Dawn?" I asked.

"Yes, I do. Dawn Downs, she works here in accounting. Her husband George is our uniform salesman. Why?"

I told John about the note.

"Well, she's a harmless flirt, Dick and her husband seem to be friends. They carry on and cut up every time George is in the office. As a matter of fact, I know Dick went to lunch with Dawn and George one day last week. I just don't see anything happening between them. I haven't seen anything between Dick and Dawn that looks suspicious. Nothing that would indicate they know each other on any level other than a work related basis. It must be another Dawn. This one is very active in her church, our church. I go to the same church with her and George. It's definitely another Dawn."

I apologized to John for disturbing him and thanked him for his time. Without realizing it, he had confirmed my fear that something sinister was going on with my husband. My mind was reeling and my stomach was churning, I felt sick. I thought about the changes in Dick's behavior during the last few weeks: he had seemed increasingly distant and more easily frustrated, he had gone fishing on the weekends more often than normal, and stayed on the boat longer than in the past. Contrary to his nature, he brought flowers home for no special reason and he had purchased a bracelet for me just to say he appreciated me. His changing behavior had confused and baffled me, but Dick justified it with reasonable excuses. He repeatedly told me he was worried about lay-offs at work, his increased mood swings and elevated frustrations were related to his concerns about the possibility of losing his job. I believed him when he said the frequent fishing excursions were a way to relax and release pent up stress.

The flowers and bracelet had been unusual gestures, something out of the ordinary for Dick, but I had been happy with them and saw them as proof of an increase in his affections for me. But now, with this note from Dawn and a lie about work, I doubted he had been truthful about anything he had said. But why would he bring me flowers and gifts if he were cheating with someone? Guilt? Nothing made sense, yet everything made sense. My feelings twisted with bewilderment while I sat in the darkness on the kitchen floor and pondered the past few weeks. The kitchen was warm, but my body shook with the cold chills of worry, and by two o'clock in the morning, nervousness had sent me on several trips to the bathroom, there was nothing left to come up but dry heaves. I was thankful my children were sleeping peacefully in their rooms, blissfully unaware of my anguish or the turmoil billowing around us.

At some point, I decided to call Dick's work number again. Perhaps John had been wrong, or maybe I had misunderstood. Was it possible another department had called Dick into work and I just assumed it was John from the fueling department? There had to be a logical explanation for everything. Possible scenarios formulated in my mind and I was renewed with hope as I dialed the number. The phone rang several times before being answered by a man who identified himself as, "Malon. Fueling."

I asked to speak with Dick.

"He ain't here, ain't been here all night. Probly' out wit his Ho. Who dis?"

I told him I was Dick's wife and the technician let out a loud whistle. "Oh hell, I done messed up now! Ol' boy gonna be pissed! Don't you go tellin' him I told you nothin'. That boy crazy."

I assured him I wouldn't repeat his name and I asked if he knew who Dick's 'Ho' might be.

"Sho do! It be that Dawn from the office here. She come in here ever day wit her ass showin', Dick be all over that shit!"

Blood rushed to my temples, and had I not been sitting on the floor, I would have passed out. My heart was beating so rapidly it caused my voice to tremble breathlessly, as if I had just finished a long run, "Do you happen to know Dawn's phone number?"

"Hang on jist' a minute, they's a list in the break room of everbodies' numbers."

Seconds later the technician returned to the phone. "Well, it ain't got her phone number on here, jist got her pager number. I been pagin' Dick all day. He owe me ten bucks and I need my money."

Another jolt to my emotions, I didn't know Dick owned a pager. I asked Malon to give me Dick's pager number and he did without hesitation. It was becoming clear to me this man didn't have much respect for Dick, he seemed eager to reveal Dick's secrets.

"Hey, you want Dawn's husband pager number? It's on the list here too. He sells us our uniforms. His name George." Malon gave me the pager number and reminded me, "Memba now, you didn't hear none of this from me. And listen here, your man Dick ain't the onliest one bumpin' Dawn. Most of us here done had a go wit her. Dick the one can't let it go though. That shit ain't that good."

Agony swept through me as I ended the conversation with this stranger, a stranger who had effortlessly revealed horrible things about my husband. Heaven help us, was Dick really being reckless and careless with our lives? This behavior went far beyond his lies about money and bills, this behavior could be detrimental to our health as well as our lives. I was numb, too weak with sorrow to stand up and place the phone handset back onto the wall mounted cradle, so I let it lie on the floor beside me. In the darkened kitchen the robotic voice recording of an operator said, "If you wish to make a call please hang up and try again." Then I heard another voice in the darkness, a sweet voice saying, "What's wrong mommy? Are you ok?" It was Cissy.

"Oh, I'm ok Sweet Girl. I just couldn't sleep, that's all", I tried to sound truthful. "Are you ok?" I asked. "What are you doing up in the middle of night?"

"Oh, I just had to tee tee and then I heard you talking to somebody. Who were you talking to Mommy?"

Always sensitive, inquisitive and intuitive, Cissy's question hovered heavily over us; I could feel her warmth next to me in the darkness. I was thankful she couldn't see my eyes, for I knew she would see the lies in them.

"I was talking to your dad."

"I sure am glad he didn't have to go to work till after the party", she said.

"Yeah, me too", I whispered. "Now you get back to bed. You'll be tired tomorrow if you're up all night. I'm going to bed in a minute. I love you. Night, Sweetie."

"Night mommy, I love you too." I received a precious hug from my little girl before she returned to her room for the night, and that simple, trusting hug drew hot tears out of my deep, cold well of despair.

So that what I had told my little girl would not be a complete lie, I went to the master bedroom, closed the door and crawled onto the Queen Anne Rice bed I shared with Dick. I did not sleep. I sat crossed legged on the bed, clutching the pager numbers in my hand and feeling as if my life was falling down around me. I wanted to be proactive, to do *something*, but I didn't know what the something should be. I decided to call Dick's pager. The act of dialing the pager number made me extremely nervous because it was admitting he had told another lie, kept a secret from me. And I knew there was only one reason he would keep his pager a secret. *Wouldn't a man want his wife and children to have his pager number regardless of whether anyone else had it? Yes, a man who cared about his family would want that. But a man using his pager solely as a way to communicate with his mistress would not want his wife to know about his dirty secret.* I dialed the pager number and when prompted, I entered our home phone number and held my breath, waiting for his return call, a call I knew I would not receive. Dick had kept me unaware regarding the pager, he would know something was going on when he saw our home number displayed on his pager's screen. It had been almost three in the morning when I paged him. I waited until twenty minutes past three and then I paged Dawn's number. I imagined her reaction when she looked at the screen of her pager, realizing Dick's home number was the number displayed. They would realize their secret was out and I wondered to myself if they cared. I imagined them laughing.

I waited a few minutes, giving Dawn time to call. My silent phone mocked me. In time I dialed the pager number of George Downs and entered my home number. Right away, the house phone rang.

"Hello?" I answered nervously, unsure of what I would say to the person on the other end of the line.

"This is George Downs, I received a page from this number." I thought I detected anxiety in the unfamiliar voice and I wanted to hang up. Feeling terrible for the things I was about to say to this man, I began with an apology, "George, I'm sorry for contacting you in the dead of night like this. You don't know me, my name is Danita Crisco, and I…" before I could finish my sentence George interrupted me. "You're Dick Crisco's wife," he said.

"Yes, I am."

"Then I guess you *do* know he's screwing my wife," he said.

For a moment I couldn't breathe or speak, this man had just put into words what I feared but had not yet said aloud. That I was having this conversation was unbelievable to me. George's words were difficult to process. He had just bluntly uttered the ten most sickening words I had ever heard, solidifying the awful things Malon said just a few hours earlier. Before speaking with George, I had still held onto a bit of hope. Those ten ugly words dashed all hope and confirmed my nightmare. Strangely, the sentence flowed off George's tongue as if he was saying something very familiar and common to him. Something he was resigned to live with. I didn't understand how he could sound so calm. Like me, hadn't he just learned of this developing situation? My brain could not yet form a sentence that included the linked together words, 'having an affair' or 'screwing my husband'.

"Hello?"

"I'm sorry, George. No, no, I didn't know. I wasn't certain anyway. But some things have occurred today that forced me to think of the possibility that Dick could be involved with someone. Are you sure?" I asked.

"Oh, there's no doubt about it. They're together right now. She's asked me for a divorce. I can't believe you're saying you didn't know about it. As a matter of fact, Dick told my wife he's going to divorce you and you're ok with it," he said.

"George, I have to tell you I'm shocked and this is very difficult for me. I'm hearing about these things for the first time tonight and I just can't make sense of any of it. I didn't know about any of this. Dick has never mentioned divorce to me. I certainly didn't know anything was going on with him and your wife. He's never mentioned her name, not even in passing when he's talked about work. He once told me the only woman in the office was a "cheap hag", that's how he described her. I can't believe this, any of it."

"I'm not making it up, God knows I wish I was", he said.

"I know you're not lying. Why would you lie about such a thing? But it's something I can't or don't want to believe. How could he do this to our kids? You said Dick and your wife are together right now, do you know where they are?" I asked him.

"No, I don't know where they are. A hotel I guess. Or the back of his work van. He actually fucked my wife in the back of a work van one night. I caught them parked in the cul de sac of the street we live on," he sobbed now, bitterly and painfully.

His words hit me harder than a fist in my stomach.

"Oh my God. How could he do this? Excuse me just a minute," I ran to the master bathroom just in time for my bowels to leave my body in a hot, liquid stream as images of Dick with another woman played like a disgusting movie in my mind. Horrific scenes of their encounter in the back of a dirty work van burned behind my eyes. I trembled, unable to disconnect from the image. When I returned to the phone, George was still waiting on the line. Shaking uncontrollably, I asked, "When did you catch them in the van?"

"A few nights ago. Dawn received a phone call just after midnight, a few minutes later she left the house. I asked her where she was going and she refused to answer me. I knew the call was from Dick and I knew she was going somewhere to meet him. I wanted to follow her, but my little boy was sleeping in his room. He's only eight years old, I couldn't leave him alone and I couldn't wake him because he had school the next day. I watched her back out of the garage and drive to the end of our street and make a right hand turn, leaving the subdivision. I was still standing in the window about five minutes later when she came back down the street with her headlights off. There's no other exit once you pass our house, it dead ends into the cul de sac. So I waited a few minutes, relieved, thinking maybe I had been wrong and she wasn't going to meet Dick after all. Maybe she just needed time alone or something. When she didn't return home after about fifteen minutes I decided to walk to the cul de sac. As soon as I topped the rise in the street I saw Dawn's Camaro parked on the right side of the circle with a white utility van parked next to her. My first thought was that she was in danger. Then I realized the van was a white airport van and that's when I knew it was Dick and I knew they were together. I walked up to the van and opened the back doors. I caught them in the act. It was horrible and vulgar."

I felt his pain because it was now my pain and it hurt like hell.

I asked George if either Dick or Dawn said anything when he opened the van's door; I wanted to know what he had said to them. How does one react in such a situation?

"Well," he said, "I told Dawn she needed to get dressed and go home. She told me she would go home when she was good and ready. Dick was an arrogant bastard and said to me, 'Dawn is exactly where she wants to be. Get your fat ass back in the house.' As if seeing them together wasn't bad enough, Dick added salt to my wounds by insulting me. Do you realize you're married to narcissistic sonofabitch? A sociopath? A bastard without a conscience?"

I had no doubt George was being honest with me, but I yearned for it to be a mistake. A small piece of my heart urged me to hold onto hope; hope that Dawn's lover wasn't in fact Dick. Hope that George was wrong about everything. Hope that Malon was wrong about everything. In reality, I knew there were no mistakes on the part of these men, but distress does crazy things to the mind, even while personal evidence points straight arrows at the truth. Not only could I hear the painful certainty in George's voice, but he had quoted a phrase that was true Dick Crisco. Variations of the phrase, "*your fat ass*," was one of Dick's favorite insults to hurl.

Back in those days, I didn't see Dick as the bully he is. He presented an image of a self-confident man and that's how I saw him. But he is a bully. I see him so clearly now, and like every other bully he is filled with insecurities, self-doubt and self-loathing. Eventually I realized his low self-esteem was the reason he so easily found fault with others. But it would be many years before I would see the genuineness of the demon dwelling within my husband.

Discovering the affair shattered what was left of my self-esteem. By this time in our marriage, I had been insulted, ridiculed and told I was stupid so often that I believed it. At the time, I didn't realize how insignificant I felt. I didn't understand this at the time, and I guess I still don't understand how it happened, but I had accepted Dick's insults as a legitimate assessment of my worth. Almost from the moment we married, he spoke to me the way he claimed his mother had spoken to him throughout his life. He had told me his mom made him feel worthless and stupid as a child, and later in life as well. After we married, he began speaking to me in ways that made me feel like an inadequate and worthless woman. He belittled me and put me down. His affair with Dawn angered me, but more than anything, it hurt me and thoroughly convinced me that what he said about me was reality. Surely, he wouldn't have had the affair if I had been a better person. Mine was a classic case of "not seeing the forest for the trees," As it happened, I didn't realize what his emotional assault was doing to me.

I remember Dick told me his mom used to tell him he didn't "have the sense God gave a goose". I asked her once why she had repeatedly made that comment to her son and she replied, "Because he didn't". I assured Dick I would never tolerate him or his mom saying that kind of things to our children and I meant it. I was willing to take the insults myself, but I would never stand for my children being treated so belligerently. The problem was, and I didn't know it at the time, Dick couldn't have cared less about what was said to our children. For many years Dick and I worked opposing hours because I had never wanted to place our children in daycare. Unknown to me, when I was working and not around to hear, he insulted and emotionally abused our children in the same way his mother had belittled him. He once told me, "I had to move five states away from my mom to keep her from trying to control my life." He may have moved away from her in proximity, but, unfortunately for our family, he brought her legacy of emotional abuse with him.

These days I know that Little Dick boosts his self-esteem by trolling for and obtaining the affections of other men's wives. When he sizes himself up against other men, both professionally and personally, he feels he falls short. So, in a pathetic attempt to boost his self-esteem, he goes after their wives in an effort to convince himself he's better than the other men. It's a game of chase, competition and destruction, and Dick is addicted to the game. When the conquest is made and the adrenaline rush of the competition has dissipated, he grows restless. Outwardly, he hides his discontent and restlessness very well. Buy underneath the surface, there is a fierce storm brewing, and the storm won't subside until he's found one or more married or attached women to conquer. Throughout the 'inner storm', his outward appearance is that of a loving and devoted husband, dad and friend. During the time of my conversation with George, I was unaware of this disturbance in Dick's personality. I was married to him and loved him, and I really thought I knew him. In retrospect, he was a stranger to me. He had never allowed me, or anyone else, to genuinely to know him. It would be years before I finally realized my husband was emotionally wrecked. Dick is incapable of allowing another person to break through the invisible steel walls he built around himself as a little boy. He wants love, but doesn't know how to accept it, or to give it. Dick mistakes lust for love.

Recently, Cissy said this to me about her dad: "Dick is incapable of loving anyone." Hearing her put voice to those thoughts, my soul wept for my daughter and my son, but I was thankful too. Thankful she realized it wasn't just she and her brother whom Dick couldn't love, but everyone, including himself. Unfortunately, knowledge doesn't erase pain.

"I'm sorry to be the one to tell you these things," George said. "Again, I want to emphasize, Dick told Dawn you're ok with all of this. He also told her you had been having an affair for a long time with a friend of his."

I was shocked and disgusted that my husband would invent such a sick lie about me. Any lie for that matter, but one so ugly and vile ripped at my heart. The pain I felt from Dick's betrayal doubled with this disclosure. It was one thing for him to betray me with another woman, but to disrespect me further with savage lies was almost unbearable. Dick, 'Little Dick', as his family called him, knew I would never defile our marriage with adultery. He knew my marriage vows were sacred to me. Many times during our marriage, I had expressed my feelings on adultery; *adultery and unfaithfulness was not only a sin committed against your spouse, but an abomination against your children as well.* How could he fabricate such a life-ruining story about me? This lie, if heard by my children, could cause them to lose faith in me. If they heard such lies, their little hearts would be broken.

It was suddenly and painfully apparent that Dick felt no love or respect for me. How could he put me in that position if he cared anything at all about me? The way I saw it, utter disgust and lack of any feeling would be the only way a man could create such a tale about his wife, his children's mother. A falsehood like that would cause deep heartache for our children. Whether he loved me or not, wouldn't their pain alone be enough to prevent him from conjuring up lies about their mother?

The heartache from his lie hurt almost as much as the actual act of adultery. Both are forms of a betrayal I pray my loved ones never have to experience.

George was curious; he asked how I had learned of the affair between my husband and his own wife. He wanted to know how I had obtained his pager number. Without revealing my source of information, I relayed the events of the day and evening, including details of the conversations between the two airport employees and myself.

"I guess awareness of their deception came to me gradually," George said. "You've been whacked over the head with it all at once. I guess I should be somewhat grateful for small blessings".

George began to tell me of the different ways he had tried to locate me. This was in the days before everyone had computers, so finding a person's home address and phone number was not as simple and easy as it is today. He said he had tried to find our home phone number and had discovered it was unlisted. I explained we had been receiving prank calls and recently had our phone changed to a non-published number.

"What kind of prank calls?" he wanted to know.

"Typical middle-school stuff," I said. "There were calls in the middle of the night, hang-up calls, that sort of thing. Sometimes I could hear breathing and other times the caller would hang up immediately after I said hello," I told him.

"That was probably Dawn, not middle-school kids. She and Dick have a system, a code where one calls the other and lets the phone ring a certain number of times to signal that it's a good time to talk. Then the other one calls back," he said. Instantly, memories flickered in my mind, images of Dick leaving the room or getting out of bed to go to for a glass of milk immediately preceding some of the prank calls. I remembered one night in particular: it was late when the phone rang, Dick answered and swiftly placed the phone back on the table, saying it was another bothersome call and once again he said he needed a glass of milk to help him go back to sleep. When he was gone for an extended period of time, I became concerned and went in search of him. I found Dick in the kitchen, sitting at the breakfast table staring into the darkness beyond the bay window. When I flipped on the light above the table I realized he was talking on the phone and when I asked who he was speaking with he told me he had called the phone company to see if they could trace the prank calls. It was that night he decided to have our number changed from listed to unlisted.

"I doubt those calls were from your wife," I said. These calls happened several weeks ago."

At this point, my understanding of the affair was limited. In my mind, there had been no forewarnings of betrayal because I had made justifications for Dick's behavioral changes. I thought the affair was new, something that had only recently begun. The emotional war unfolding within me was excruciating, I couldn't see beyond what was immediately in front of me. Looking back, I realize I subconsciously tried to protect myself emotionally from the plethora of information I had received in the previous few hours. As a result, I processed the incriminating information very slowly.

"Dawn and Dick have been seeing each other for five months," George said flatly.

Another sharp blow. It was difficult to believe my husband had been unfaithful to me for five months without my knowledge. How had he kept me in the dark for so long? Every word George spoke was difficult to absorb. It was unfathomable that I could have been unaware of another woman in Dick's life. Wouldn't he have slipped up at some point and said her name? Wouldn't he have been away from home at odd times? His demeanor had not changed in a way that would have alerted me to a problem. If anything, he had become more attentive in the last several months. Each day before he left for work he would say, "Baby, I can't wait until my day off so we can snuggle." Walking in the door after work he would kiss me and wrap me in a big hug and say, "I missed you Babydoll, I thought about you all day long!"

"Are you sure of this? I don't see how or when he would have the time. What are they doing? Where do they go? How do you know for certain? We have no extra money for him to spend on your wife; we're broke most of the time. He's usually home when he's supposed to be, when would he have time to be with her?" Questions tumbled off my tongue as a thousand thoughts swirled in my head. Carnal images of Dick and another woman were seared into my thoughts.

"Yes, I'm sure there, are no doubts. Look, do yourself a favor and believe me. I know it's difficult to hear and accept, but it is happening and it's very real. Your husband is a lying, self-centered, low-class snake. He doesn't deserve to be called a man. And to answer your question, I know all of this because Dawn has told me. She's already filed for divorce. I can't believe you didn't have any idea about this. She really thinks you and Dick are soon to be divorced because that's what he's told her. She's already paid the deposit on an apartment for the two of them. As far as where they go, she doesn't give me those details. Like I said before, one night I caught them together in our neighborhood. I know they went to the Renaissance Hotel near the airport another time. I'm surprised he still has a job because they usually get together very early in the morning or late at night. Dick usually works a rotating shift, right? I know he leaves work in a company van to be with her when he works the second and third shift. And when he works first shift they meet during lunch. That's why he's home when he's supposed to be, he risks his job so he can fuck my wife."

I was aghast. The phrase 'I couldn't wrap my mind around it' is overused, but that's exactly the state I was in. The information George gave me was incomprehensible. I was feeling more and more ill, and my heart was beating so hard I could literally feel the pulsation in my ears. My head was swimming with mixed images of our family on Sunday drives and church picnics and Dick in a hotel room with a strange woman.

"We've been looking for land, we plan to build a new house," I said. "How could he be planning to break-up our family? I just don't understand any of this."

"Speaking of your house, do you have a fireplace?" George asked me.

"Yes, we do. Why?"

"Did you and your children go out of town the last weekend of September?"

"Yes, how would you know I was out of town? I took my children to visit their great-grandmother, Dick's grandmother, in Miami, Oklahoma. It was our son's birthday."

"Dick didn't go on the trip, did he?" It was more a statement than a question.

"No. He told me he couldn't take time off work to go with us."

"I believe Dawn was at your house. She told me she was going on a Women's Bible Retreat with some ladies from our church the last weekend in September. About a week later I found a letter from Dick describing to Dawn how he felt when he had sex with her in front of the fireplace. The letter also said 'soon the bitch and the kids won't be a problem', I assumed he was talking about a divorce.

The disclosure of this information was overwhelming, too much to take in all at once. Once more, I became sick to my stomach when George said he believed Dawn had been in my home. How could Dick do such a thing? George had to be wrong about this. I really didn't believe Dick would stoop to that level, to bring a woman into our home and I said as much to George. How could he defile our home, our marriage and our children by bringing another woman inside? He wouldn't do that.

"Twenty-four hours ago you didn't think he would screw another woman, did you?" George asked.

"No. But bringing a woman into our home would be such a personal violation against his family, our children. I can't believe he would do something so reprehensible. Maybe they rented a cabin or hotel room with a fireplace."

"Hang on while I get the letter," he said.

Hot and cold waves of nervousness moved through my body while I waited on George, hoping the letter would somehow prove him wrong.

"Are you sure you want to hear this?"

"Yes."

"Ok then. Here goes, bear with me because his handwriting is very sloppy and most of the words are misspelled."

Dear Dawn,

Thank you for spending the night with me and for driving up here to see me. I can still smell you in the house. Making love to you in front of the roaring fire was the most amazing experience in the world. It felt like we were lost in the woods instead of this godforsaken little town. You're so amazing. You've put life back into my world. I'll do everything I can to make you happy forever and always. I promise you won't be sorry about any of this. The bitch knows she's going to get this house in the divorce, she can have it and that's all she cares about anyway. As soon...

"Stop, please. I really don't want to hear anymore. I'm certain they were here. He's lying to her too though. Aside from the fact that we have never talked about divorce, we don't own this house. We rent from a doctor in Cartersville. So if there is a divorce, I won't get this house or any other house. We don't own anything outright except his old Subaru."

"Wow. All I can say is wow. He's such a liar, and a good one! I listened in on the house phone one night when they were talking. It was about two o'clock in the morning so he must have been working third shift. Dawn asked him how much he was going to have to pay you in child support and he said, 'Nothing. She gets the house and the van and half our savings. The judge said that will be more than enough for her.'"

"Savings? We have no savings other than what I save through my employer. Dick Crisco hates to save money. If he knows I have ten cents saved he will find a reason to spend it plus ninety more cents that we don't have. And what judge? Even an idiot knows you don't speak to a judge until a divorce hearing. Did Dawn actually believe him?"

"Incredibly, yes. She believes every word off his forked tongue."

When I realized Dick had brought Dawn into our home I was outraged. The rage, however, quickly subsided and dark pain took its place. Strangely, when I thought of the two of them in my home, I could only visualize them in front of the fireplace. For the time being, I couldn't picture Dawn and Dick in our bedroom or sitting together at the breakfast table, having toast and juice. Realistically I knew they would have been all over the house. I knew she must have parked in our garage and walked into the house through the laundry room. I knew she would have used my shower, my towels, my soap and shampoo. Later, it occurred to me that I had probably washed the towels she had used, but for the moment I had to mentally compartmentalize and filter the information George was giving me. So in my mind I placed my husband and this woman in front of the fireplace in my home and I built a mental box around them. For quite some time, I would not visualize them anywhere else in my house. I couldn't. Otherwise, I would have to admit to myself my husband was indeed the low down, despicable snake George had described. I wasn't ready to do that, not yet. Call it denial, naiveté' or stupidity if you choose, but it's what I had to do to survive emotionally and to get through the next few days and weeks without falling to pieces. There were still little children for me to think of, sweet babies who needed me to care for them. It was like climbing a very steep and slippery staircase. I had to climb very slowly, cautiously taking one step at a time, pausing on each step to catch my breath and absorb the emotional battering.

As George continued speaking, something the fuel technician had said came back to me. "Has Dawn had other affairs?" I asked. I don't know why it mattered to me, but for some reason it did. Perhaps I thought if she was a skilled 'Jezebel' who had the wherewithal to seduce my husband into an adulterous relationship, then the blame could be placed on her instead of him. By this time, I had become somewhat accustomed to Dick blaming others for his faults and his screw-ups. I wanted to believe him, so it was an easy progression for me to blame others for his problems as well. If the other woman were to blame, it would help to explain how Dick had found himself in this situation. I couldn't bear to think his choice to cheat was because he didn't care for his family or because he was disgusted with me. Right at that moment, I felt like a failure as a wife and mother and I wanted my husband's selfish choices to be about something other than me. *And they were, I just didn't understand yet.*

"Yes, she had an affair a couple of years ago. But it was nothing like this. I don't know what that would have to do with Dick. She didn't claim to be in love the other time. She says she loves Dick. I forgave her for that one and I would forgive her now. I mean we go to church, she teaches Sunday school. I'm in the praise and worship band. I believe marriage is forever. So I forgave her. Now she's doing it again and she plans to divorce me. We talked to our pastor when she did this before and he counseled us. I'm too embarrassed to tell him she's doing this again. I'm betting this isn't Dick's first affair, is it?"

"A few years ago our apartment manager told me he was screwing a seventeen year old girl in the complex. She had no real proof to show me and Dick had a reasonable explanation for everything she had said, so I dropped the matter. He had always said "Jan is evil and lies about her tenants." I thought back to our days in Cheyenne and wondered if he could have been cheating all those years ago.

"Well, don't be surprised if you learn of more women. He's too good at covering his butt for this to be his first spin around the dance floor. He's very smooth with his lies. You know, before I knew he was involved with my wife, I really liked him. We got along well; we talked about hunting and fishing. We even had lunch together one day and later, I learned that on that same day we went to lunch, he and my wife had gone out to the service road by the Ford plant in Hapeville and had sex in her car. You know, during the times I was around him, there was absolutely no hint in anything he said, or did, that would let me know he was even minimally interested in my wife. He's so good at deception it's scary. Last week, after I confronted him about ruining my marriage, he asked if the three of us could meet for lunch and talk. We went to lunch and he apologized to me and told me how wrong it was for him to date my wife. Right there in front of Dawn, he told me it was over. He sounded so sincere. I believed him. I really believed him. That day, I asked him about you, and he assured me your marriage was over. He said he had tried to keep you happy but that it was impossible and divorce was the only answer. His eyes even watered when he said how hard he had tried to please you but nothing he did worked. I believed every word he said. Later that night, Dawn and I got into an argument, she said I was a gullible fool and she was disgusted by me. Dick had told her they needed to convince me their affair was over so I would stop bothering and 'stalking' them."

George and I talked into the early morning hours. Later I sat on the bed in our dark bedroom and reflected on everything he had said, still finding it difficult to believe. Not for the first time, I found myself making excuses for Dick's behavior. In the past, he had accused me of not giving him enough attention. So maybe that was the problem. I was very convincing when I began to tell myself his unfaithfulness was my fault. *Well, I could fix that!* If we could work things out, *I would change my behavior.* I would lavish attention on Dick.

At the time I was working four, ten hour shifts per week. I always prepared dinner before I left for work in the afternoon so that Dick wouldn't have to worry with preparing a meal after he had worked all day. I had asked him to clean dinner dishes so they wouldn't be sitting with dried food during the hours between the evening meal and the time I came home after midnight. He usually failed to remember to clear the table and wash the dishes and several arguments had ensued because of it. So that night, I decided I would no longer fuss over a dirty kitchen. I would clean the dishes and the kitchen when I came home from work. He had accused me of being a nag, and now I could see that perhaps I had been. After all, he worked more days each week than I did. His job was more physically demanding than mine, therefore he was more tired than me, and what right did I have to ask him to help clean the kitchen? Would it really hurt me to do the chore when I came home from work? *I would accept responsibility for my part in this bump in our marital road.*

Dick came home just after eight the next morning and walked in the house whistling, as if he were coming in from checking the mail. I was in the kitchen, preparing breakfast. "Hey Beautiful," he said as he wrapped his arms around me. He didn't mention my calls to his pager. Everything about his behavior was so ordinary I could have easily convinced myself the night before had been a bad dream. But I knew it hadn't been a dream and I knew I needed to confront him with the information George had revealed, but the children and their friends were in the house. I decided I would act as if everything was normal and say nothing to him until after breakfast, when the kids were outside playing.

Time crawled to a standstill before I finally had the opportunity to say, "I paged you. Why didn't you return my call?"

"You didn't page *me!* I don't have a pager!" he denied.

"I called your work and they said you weren't there. And someone gave me your pager number," I could feel the heat rising to my neck and face.

"Whoever said that is a lying fuck! I was at work all night. Just ask John!" Veins bulged in his neck and temples as he screamed at me.

"I did speak to John. He told me you weren't there. He's not the one who gave me your pager number, but he confirmed you were not at work and he said you hadn't been called in to cover for anyone either." I looked Dick in the eyes, searching for the truth that wasn't there.

"I'm sick of this shit! Every time I turn around some motherfucker is lying about me. I've got a good mind to tell him he can shove this job up his ass! How do you like that? You want to mess with me? I'll show you what I'll do. I don't need this damn hassle. And who the fuck gave you permission to call my damn boss anyway? Keep your nosey ass out of my business. My job is none of your fucking business! I kill myself for this damn family and all you can do is gripe and complain. I worked my ass off last night and now I come home to this shit! Fuck you!" Dick spun around and left the house, slamming the front door behind him. He didn't return until much later that afternoon.

I was stunned at the speed at which life had turned and changed. Less than two days ago I was content with what I thought was the peaceful structure of my family life, today it was crumbling around us and I was anguished by the hurt I anticipated my children would feel once they knew of the situation. I wanted to protect them but I felt powerless to stop their dad from bulldozing the landscape of their world.

We had plans to go to a cookout that evening, so I decided if Dick came home in time for the engagement, I would say nothing that would upset him. The kids had been looking forward to the cookout and I didn't want to spoil their evening, nor did I want another scene in front of them. Dick's behavior and the things I had learned from his co-workers and Dawn's husband had to be addressed, but I needed to find the right time to approach him. Dick never liked to talk out our problems, preferring instead to pretend there was nothing wrong. This problem could not be ignored. I had been told by a man I had never met that my husband planned to divorce me and move into an apartment with another woman. This couldn't be swept under the rug.

Dick was scheduled to be off work the next day and I felt I could wait until then, while the kids were at school, to broach the subject. Meanwhile, I was as nervous as a cat on caffeine. And I was angry. I was angry with Dick's selfishness and disregard for our marriage and our children. I wanted to pick up a spiked steel rod and beat him with it, causing him physical pain equivalent to my emotional pain. Somehow I think I knew even then, subconsciously, of Dick's inability to feel remorse or emotional distress for anyone other than himself.

Dick came home in time for the cook-out and his attitude had improved greatly. He actually seemed sorrowful over his behavior, "Hey Mamacita, I'm just going to hop in the shower and then we can leave for Lynn's house. Do you have the kids ready?" He asked the question and he gave me a kiss, as if nothing was wrong.

"Yes, they're ready to go. We've been waiting on you," I said to him.

He hugged me tightly but gently, "I'm sorry about the last two days. I spent time alone today, praying, and I realize I overreacted. You are the most beautiful woman in the world and you are the best thing that ever happened to me. I never want to hurt you again the way I hurt you when I said those things this morning. I don't ever want to see pain on your face like that again. I hate to think what my life would be like if I had never met you. Do you forgive me?"

I returned his hug and nodded my head up and down, eager to forgive but knowing I couldn't let it go until everything was in the open.

"I love you", he said as he strode to the back of the house for a shower.

Dick had been in the shower for a brief period of time when the phone rang. I answered the call and George Downs spat rapid words, "Dick and Dawn have been together the last couple of hours and they plan to meet again tonight!" It took a minute for his words to register with me. How could I reconcile this news with the tender moment I had just experienced with Dick? I couldn't paint the two scenarios onto the same canvas.

"Are you sure?" I asked. "Dick told me he was alone all day. He said he was praying. Do you know this for sure?"

I felt certain George was mistaken, Dick had seemed so remorseful and apologetic. Different scenarios tripped through my head and I felt perhaps Dawn was lying to George. Maybe she wanted to get her husband's attention and in some sick, messed up way she believed this was the way to go about.

"I'm sure, without any doubt. I bought a recorder that connects to a phone line. I've recorded two days' worth of calls between them, but I just had a chance to listen to the tape a few minutes ago. They talked about their plans in detail. I know they met today in a park behind Mt. Zion church. My Lord, that's where we go to church. Dawn has reserved a room for them at a hotel for tonight. I don't know what to do anymore." George sounded defeated.

"This is all so unreal," confusion mixed with heartache and frustration and settled in me again, adding to the nauseous heat I already felt. "So you're saying they spent last night together and then they were together again this afternoon? And they have plans for tonight as well? And all of this was on the recording?"

"Most of that information was on there. Dawn told me some of the details herself after I confronted her this afternoon. She isn't trying to hide the affair anymore because she believes Dick is leaving you and she believes, as do I, they will live together soon. But she tries to keep the details of their activity secret because she knows I'll interfere if I can. This morning before church the phone rang and she answered it very quickly. When she got off the phone she said she would drive separately to church because her friend Mia needed to talk to her about something. When I finally got to listen to the tape I realized the call was from Dick rather than Mia. He told Dawn he only returned to your house this morning to tell you to 'kiss his ass' and get some clean clothes. He said he informed you he would be spending the rest of his life with her. Then he told Dawn he had to see her this afternoon or he would lose his mind. On the recording, Dick told her, 'I can't go more than a few hours without your beautiful body otherwise I go into withdrawal like an addict coming off cocaine'. She gave him the address of the park and told him what time to be there. When she came home I told her I knew she had been with him and she admitted it. She doesn't know about the tape recording and she's curious about how I found out about their plans.

She thinks I listened in on another line." George spilled this information in a rush, anxious to get relay the news.

George continued, "I can't believe he told you he was praying. That's despicable. Believe me, he was on his knees but he wasn't praying. Come to think of it, Dawn was just as bad. She played the tambourine for the praise band at church this morning."

I told George we were about to leave for a cook-out and I felt certain he was mistaken about Dick meeting his wife later that evening. I could not imagine Dick disappointing our children again. Nor did I want to believe his earlier apology was not sincere.

"I'm not mistaken", he said. "I don't know how he plans to do it, but he's planning to stay in a hotel with her tonight. I seriously doubt he would let her pay for a hotel room and then not show up to use it with her."

I heard the water in the shower shut off and I told George I would get back to him later. I was positive George was wrong or had misunderstood the plans between Dawn and Dick. Maybe they were making plans for another night, but not this night. The people we were cooking out with had a large playground and sandbox built in their yard and Dick had seen and heard the excitement Cissy and Garrett had about the cook-out there. Not only that, he had abruptly cancelled a planned trip to a pumpkin farm the week before, with the same family. He would not cancel plans and disappoint the kids again. That much I felt certain of.

We secured Cissy and Garrett into the van and drove onto the two-lane country road leading away from our house. Cissy was sitting behind her dad playing with a Polly Pocket doll and Garrett was sitting on the third-row bench seat, caught up in a dinosaur fight. We had driven less than two miles when Dick looked at me, reached for my hand and said, "Has anyone told you that you look beautiful today Sweet Baby?" He lifted my hand and kissed each of my fingers before speaking again, "Oh, I forgot to tell you, I have to work third shift tonight. The boy that called in sick last night is still sick. There's nobody to take his place but me. I hate it, and I tried to get out of it, but it's what has to be done. At least I'll have some good overtime on my next check."

A knot formed in my stomach and anger stung my eyes, I could not back down any longer. "You're lying to me", I said through gritted teeth. "I know exactly what you're plans are. You're not working tonight! You're going to be with Dawn Downs!" *Could he really believe I would fall for this story again?* My head ached and my stomach churned. I felt like I had lived a lifetime in the last twenty-four hours.

Before I knew what was happening, Dick backhanded me across my left eye. Clearly, I now understood what it meant to see stars. The vision in that eye went black with flashes of bright white light popping in sequence to the throbbing pain behind my eye. Reflexively, I covered my eye with my left hand and Dick grabbed the hand and yanked it away from my face. Quickly, he snatched my wedding rings off my finger, scraping my knuckle as the rings came off. Dick wrapped his fist so tightly around the rings they bent out of shape; rapidly he rolled down the window and tossed them out. He slammed on the breaks so forcefully we were all slung forward. I was vaguely aware of a maroon colored van stopping in the opposite lane, the driver yelling at Dick. My concern was for Cissy and Garrett. I turned around and looked in the back of the van to be certain my precious children were okay. Both had stopped playing and were looking at me with terror filled eyes. Dick spun the van around in the middle of the road and drove back towards our house. Once there he jumped out and got into the Subaru, almost knocking me down as I stepped out of the van. "Get the hell out of my way!" he screamed. Then he was gone. Again.

A month before I learned of the affair with Dawn, Dick had flown into a maniacal fit and hit me. Returning home from dropping Cissy off at school, I had been surprised to find Dick standing on the screened porch, staring vacantly at the creek which ran beside our house. Garrett was in my arms, resting on my hip as I walked up the steps to the porch.

"What are you doing home? Why aren't you at work? Are you sick," I asked him.

"It's none of your damn business why I'm not at work! I can stay home when I want to. Get off my fuckin' back"!

I felt Garrett become tense and hold to me tighter as his dad's temper exploded around us.

"We can barely pay our bills when you work a full week. I just don't understand why you aren't at work if you aren't sick. If you're sick, I understand," I said.

As my left foot landed on the top step, Dick's fist came through the screen of the door and caught me on the cheek. I grabbed the railing as I stumbled backward to the step below, successfully preventing both Garrett and myself from falling to the ground. Without another word I walked to the car and strapped Garrett in his car seat. We drove to my mom's house in Waleska where we stayed until time to pick Cissy up from school. When we were a safe distance from our house, Garrett said, "Mommy, I'm sorry dad hurt you. When I get big I won't let him do that anymore." Neither Garrett nor I said a word to my mom about the incident. She thought we had simply dropped in for a surprise visit.

To this day, Garrett has not forgotten that he was in my arms when his dad hit me hard enough to knock us off the steps. Forgetting is much harder than forgiving.

Now this, another assa[...]
had to get out of this mess[...]
where would we go? I slid[...]
the ignition. "Mommy, wh[...]
told her their dad was hav[...]
him. I hated myself for lyin[...]
arrogant selfishness, but th[...]
would hurt them too much [...]
at protecting them would only [...]

"Well he's scaring me," [...]

I apologized to them an[...]
out. Both nodded their head[...]

Making small talk, pasti[...]
deceptive excuse for Dick's a[...]
out. But watching my two inn[...]
a good time with their friend[...] ...wrenching. Both tried to hide their sadness and both made valiant attempts at having fun, but their grief was apparent to me. Knowing their dad was in a hotel room with another woman was killing me. Didn't he care about them at all? Forget me, how could he toss his children aside? What kind of man does that? I vowed to myself I would fix the problem or I would get out once and for all.

That night, I thought back to the difficulties in the early days of our marriage. I had made excuses for Dick's behavior even then. In reality, our good years as a family had been as fleeting as a summer wind and I had held on to the memory of those good times for dear life. I asked myself why I was still in this marriage. I should have left Dick the first year we were married but I had held high hopes for us. My commitment to marriage was for life, not something to give up on easily. Two innocent children were in the picture now, children that loved both parents. I still had hope and a dream for our future, I believed Dick could and would change.

In the early 1990s, my dreams of an orderly and happy family life were not yet completely crushed, because I had not yet fully seen the sleazy monster behind my husband's nice smile, nor did I understand the depth of his depravity and his ugly private life. Nowadays, this is the advice I would give any newly married person: *At the first sign of lies and deception, GET OUT. He/she won't change. If they don't respect you enough to tell you the truth then they don't love you enough to be faithful to you. Love and Respect go hand in hand. A selfish person doesn't understand forgiveness. Rather than feel thankful for the grace and mercy of forgiveness and the opportunity of a*

*...vantage of the forgiver. He sees your ability ...es bolder with his deception. Forgive and move ...meone out there who will love you and respect you ...r she hurts you physically? Call the police and pack ...hat. The backhand across my eye was not the first time ...me, nor would it be the last. Pride can be a dangerous thing. ...t prevented me from reporting Little Dick to the authorities for ...as too embarrassed to let anyone know what was going on in my ...d others to think I had a perfect marriage. I wanted everyone to believe ...ic image Little Dick crafted and presented. And I had come to believe I ...weak. I believed there was something wrong with me, that I didn't deserve ...nything better than what I had. Little Dick blamed me for the physical abuse, he said I caused it. His constant accusations led me to believe I was at fault. I silently accepted the blame and my self-image deteriorated until I saw myself as ugly and useless. One time, in the beginning, I told Dick's mom about the physical abuse, believing she would help me. Instead she said, "You must have done something to deserve it". She confirmed Dick's accusations; **it was my fault**.*

It's very difficult to verbalize my mindset during those times. The first time he hit me, he told me I was worthless. After he knocked me to the floor he kneeled over me with his cocked fist drawn back level with his shoulder, and screamed like a maniac; he screamed that I was an ugly bitch. He screamed, "I can kill you! I could kill you with one blow!" I believed him.

Without realizing it, I began to believe I had nothing to offer anyone. These days I realize Dick is insane, but in those days I was unaware of his insanity and the mental disorder of his maternal grandmother. Dick and his mother said I was crazy. He told me everyone knew I was crazy. *Would the police believe me if I reported his abuse?* He said they wouldn't. He said law enforcement would laugh at me because it was obvious I was crazy. I realize now that low self-esteem caused me to act stupidly, even crazily. I was indeed crazy; crazy for staying in an abusive relationship. The more time I spend apart from Dick, the more clearly I see the absurdity of trying to maintain a family life with a lunatic.

Dick was not home when we returned from the cook-out later that evening. I had hoped and said a silent prayer that he would be there, that he would have had a change of heart about his decision to spend the night in a hotel with Dawn.

"Dad's not here, huh Mom? I'm sorry you're sad Mommy," Garrett hugged me, his sweet, breathless little boy voice fell against my cheek and filled me with grief for him and his sister.

"Thank you, Bud. No, he isn't here, but we'll be ok. Hey! It's late and it's time for you to hop in the tub!"

Walking down the hallway, I saw Cissy lying stomach down on her bed, looking toward the wall. "Hey Sweetie, are you feeling alright?" I asked.

"Mommy, why does Dad always get so angry? I don't think he likes us anymore." Her eyes were filled with sadness beyond comfort.

"He loves you and Garrett as much as I do Sweet Girl. He just has a lot on his mind right now."

To protect them from his disgusting behavior, hoping to protect their emotional health, I was still lying to my children and it made me so angry I wanted to scream. I was furious with myself for lying to them, but I justified it was better to lie than to hurt them with the truth. *And what if I tell them the truth and then we work things out? They would have been hurt for nothing.* This was the lie I told *myself.* Dick was pursuing selfish pleasures and he believed he was entitled to them. He probably wouldn't have cared if our children had known the truth about what he was doing, but I did. Sitting beside my precious child and hearing the distress in her voice, anger rose in me and I wanted to slap Dick. I wanted to hurt him the way he was hurting us. But how do you hurt a hollow man?

It was almost noon the following day before Dick came home. I was in the kitchen preparing sandwiches and soup for lunch, when I heard him pull into the garage and enter the kitchen through the laundry room. I didn't look up when he came into the room or when he sat down at the breakfast table. Several long minutes passed before words were spoken. "Can you sit down? I need to talk to you," he said.

Dick looked pale and weak. I expected him to say he wanted a divorce and was leaving permanently.

"I'm sorry. I'm sorry for everything. I don't know what came over me. I don't know why I've been so stupid. I met with her last night and I told her it's over. I hope you can forgive me. I love you and the kids more than anything in the world. I want to keep my family together. I hope you'll let me stay. Will you ever be able to forgive me?" Dick's lips trembled as he spoke. In all the time I had known him, I had never seen him like this, so vulnerable. "I'll do whatever it takes if you'll keep me. If you'll let me stay, I'll make it up to you. I'll work till my dying day to make it up to you and the kids. I'll be the husband you deserve and the dad the kids need. Will you please keep me? Will you ever be able to forgive me?"

Tears of relief and forgiveness rained down my face. "I already have, I've already forgiven you," I said.

Dick leapt out of his seat and fell to his knees in front of me. Tears flowed freely from his eyes as he laid his head on my lap and wrapped his arms around my waist. "I can't believe you're my wife. I don't deserve you. You're the best thing that ever happened to me. You and our kids mean more to me than anything. I have to tell them how sorry I am, I hope they will forget how stupid I've been."

The next week Dawn was terminated from her position at the airport. According to Dick she was fired for stealing from her employer. Two weeks later, Dick was terminated for reasons unknown to me, but I had my suspicions.

Less than a week lapsed before Dick found employment, his termination began to seem like a blessing in disguise. Dick's new job was in the town where we lived, previously he had driven over sixty miles each way to work. Not only would we save money on fuel, but I believed Dick's stress levels would drop dramatically once he no longer had to deal with Atlanta traffic. Another benefit to working in Cartersville, Dick would be free to attend more of our children's activities. The week we shared between his termination and the start of the new job had given us time to reconnect. We had long talks about how, when and why things went wrong. Dick and I agreed to work daily on improving our marriage. We started to communicate and share with each other in ways we never had before. We began to build a protective, impenetrable wall around our marriage. In some ways, it seemed the affair was the best thing that could have happened to us. I eventually found peace and contentment in our renewed marriage, I was thankful for the restoration. My happy, laughing children brought me much joy. I began to find pleasure in the simple things again, even in everyday, mundane chores. A Roy Campanella quote became my constant companion:

"I asked God for strength, that I might achieve. I was made weak, that I might learn humbly to obey. I asked for health, that I might do great things. I was given infirmity, that I might do better things. I asked for riches, that I might be happy. I was given poverty, that I might be wise. I asked for power, that I might have the praise of men. I was given weakness, that I might feel the need of God. I asked for all things, that I might enjoy life. I was given life, that I might enjoy all things... I got nothing I asked for but everything I hoped for. Almost despite myself, my unspoken prayers were answered. I am, among men, most richly blessed!" **Roy Campanella**

Letters from Dawn began filling our mailbox. Each letter expressed her love for my husband. She sent me copies of letters and cards Dick had written to her during their affair, letters telling her how much he loved her, how much he loved her body. Letters saying he had never loved me. When I showed Dick the letters he told me they were written when he was "out of his mind". He said they meant nothing, he had only told her what he thought she wanted to hear. I chose to believe him. I refused to allow the letters to disrupt our newly discovered love, respect, compassion and passion.

One day I was ironing a pair of Dick's jeans, reflecting on how far we had come in the weeks since the affair, when I suddenly felt compelled to write Dawn a letter. I tried to push the thought away, but the notion wouldn't leave me alone. Several days later, still unable to shake the idea of the letter, I settled myself at the table in the bright, sunlit nook of our kitchen and composed a letter. This is how it read:

Dear Dawn,

Please forgive the intrusion of this letter. I realize it must seem strange, receiving a letter from me. The thought of contacting you was strange to me at first, but I feel strongly it is something I have to do. I hope you'll read to the end, this letter isn't intended to hurt or condemn you.

Dawn, you and I have much in common. We're wives, mothers, daughters, employees and sisters. And we've loved and been hurt by the same man.

Your affair with my husband hurt me to my core. You could have physically ripped my heart from my chest and I doubt the pain would have been worse than the heartache I felt upon learning of your affair with Dick. My marriage crumbled in a broken heap around me and I blamed you. Rationally, I knew Dick was as much to blame as you, but I was irrational for a while. After the passing of a few days I looked at the problem in whole and began to see that I was more to blame than either one of you.

I came to realize there were times I had been neglectful of my marriage. Up until "the affair", my focus had been on work, homework with the kids, afterschool activities, house cleaning, grocery shopping and all the other things that make up daily living. My marriage had been placed on the lowest rung of the priority ladder. Dick's relationship with you opened my eyes. Our marriage is better now than it's ever been in the past. And in many ways, I have you to thank.

My heartfelt wish is for you and George to have a restored and renewed marriage as well. I know he loves you with his whole heart. And so does your little boy. My guess is your marriage had been suffering just as ours had. Why else would one disregard his or her children and spouse and employ the risks associated with an affair? My prayer is for you and George to find a way to repair the damage and move forward to a beautiful and fulfilling marriage.

You know, the other day Dick said to me, "Your first family is your only true family. No one else could ever replace that." What he said is true. Our families deserve to know they're first in our lives.

I have forgiven Dick and I forgive you as well. May you and George find everlasting love, peace and forgiveness between you.

Sincerely,

D. Able

Before writing the letter to Dawn, I reflected on the stages and events of my married life. Specifically I thought of all the mistakes I had made as a wife and how each mistake had been a stepping stone toward the affair. For years my husband had blamed me for the choices he made. In the beginning, I fought Dick and his mom when they insisted or insinuated I was the reason he lied or spent too much money. I had argued we are all responsible for our own choices. Dick and BJ were relentless, never giving up their stand that he would not make poor choices if not for me. Bit by bit, they wore me down and somewhere along the way I had come to believe them. With the affair, came full acceptance of my responsibility in Dick's choices. I vowed to correct my mistakes and never allow my marriage to become a victim of my own carelessness ever again. *I was stupid for allowing them to break me down. I was very stupid. But this frame of mind, an overhaul of one's personality happens when you hear something over and over, day in and day out. Eventually we believe what we're taught.*

Remembering the early days of our marriage was difficult. I was forced to admit weaknesses in myself and I didn't like it. I was uncomfortable admitting my faults. I also saw weaknesses in my husband that I did not like, but I told myself he was correct, his weaknesses were made worse because of me. It was easier for me to accept accountability for his actions than to admit he was a complete screw-up. In some crazy, mixed up way, it was easier.

*I want to be clear here: In a rational state of mind, I knew I was responsible for myself only. I knew I was not responsible for Dick's actions. But for a long time, I was not thinking clearly or rationally. My emotions and my desire to make my marriage work clouded my intellect. I was willing to do, say or believe anything to have the 'perfect little family'. Underneath my irrational thinking was a foundation of fear and doubt. Mix it all together, and I was a mess. It's insane to live that way. Don't do it to yourself or your children. Don't allow it. Run. While you're still thinking with your rational mind, run. Today I recognize the times I should have left. Times I should have left for good. I **knew** even then I needed to leave, and now it's bizarre and odd to me that I didn't. At the time I thought the power of love was enough to change a man's empty heart. It is not. Love does not change the core of a corrupt man.*

Symbolic Violence

February 1986

Sunday, February twenty-third, was a beautiful, bright winter day. The previous day, our wedding day, had been cold and wet. A dreary drizzle of moisture had fallen from dark clouds throughout the day, and I couldn't stop thinking God was trying to tell me something. Along with rain, my wedding day had brought with it an ominous feeling. More than once that day I thought about not showing up at the church. I talked myself out of it, blaming my feeling of dread on wedding day jitters. *Besides, what about all the people in town for the wedding?* Two of my bridesmaids had traveled long distances and spent small fortunes on wedding attire and activities. I couldn't let all those people down, so I forged ahead, blaming my unease on the cold rain. The day after our wedding, the sun and leftover raindrops created a dazzling brilliance in the trees and on rooftops; seemingly a perfect day for beginning a new journey, but my uneasiness had worsened. My wedding night had given me more reasons to worry than to be happy.

For our first night as newlyweds, my father-in-law had reserved a room for Dick and me at a nice hotel north of Atlanta. Alcohol had not been served at our formal reception and this was not something Dick's family was accustomed to. The hotel reserved for us had a ballroom with a bar and a disc jockey, and the plan was anyone who wanted to continue the wedding celebration would meet at the hotel after the formal reception, sort of an 'after the reception party'.

The previous evening, nearing the end of the official reception, we changed out of our wedding attire and ran through tossed birdseed toward our decorated vehicle. On the drive into Atlanta, the rain began again.

"Well, we did it!" I exclaimed excitedly, smiling over at Dick.

"Yeah, and I'm starving! I didn't eat anything. We paid for all that food and all I got was one bite of cake because you were dragging me around to talk to everyone."

A chuckle escaped my lips as I glanced across the seat at Dick; I thought he was joking with me. He wasn't.

"Why did you do that to me? I haven't eaten all day!" His face was red with fury.

"I didn't plan for us to go without food, it just happened. I thought your dad said you and he ate at the mall when you picked up your tuxedo. I'm sorry Dick, I just thought we needed to make an attempt to speak to everyone at the reception. Many of our guests drove a long way and brought expensive wedding gifts for us. It isn't every day we get married and they wanted to congratulate us! It would have been rude not to speak with them. We can get something on the way to the hotel if you want."

I had hoped what I said to him would calm him down, but my words only caused him to become more irritated.

"Hell no I'm not stopping for food! I just paid a shitload of money for that food back there by God, and I won't pay for anymore tonight!" His face was red and puffy as he screamed at me. I couldn't believe we were arguing, only a few hours after our vows were spoken. Actually we weren't arguing, Little Dick was having a one-sided screaming fit. This fight was ridiculous. How could this be happening? Dick was blaming me because he had not eaten. Until I saw him at the altar, I had not seen him nor been with him all day, I had no way of knowing he had skipped meals. But here he was, somehow making his hunger my responsibility. Greeting our guests and visiting with them as they congratulated us had prevented him from eating during the reception, because of that he was angry with me. Very angry. I needed to fix this problem before we got to the hotel, I didn't want our friends to see him like this. How would I explain his anger? Would anyone believe he was angry over food? I could hardly believe it myself.

Suddenly, I remembered something one of my bridesmaids had said earlier that day. "Hey, Jayta told me she would box up some food from the reception for us. She said when she and Terry were married they didn't eat much at their reception, so she would prepare a package for us and give to your mom. Hopefully your mom will have it with her tonight."

We drove in silence the rest of the way to the hotel. I couldn't believe this was my wedding day reality. Since I had been a little girl, I had daydreamed about my wedding: *It would be a fairytale day with lots of friends, family, smiles and laughter. My groom and I would look dreamily at each other across a crowded reception hall, content with knowing we would be spending the rest of our lives together.*

My wedding day had not been at all like my dream, and what was left of the dream was about to become a nightmare.

I was heartsick. As Dick and I entered the hotel lobby, I felt as if I had a twenty-pound weight in the pit of my stomach. A raucous round of applause erupted as we crossed the threshold into the hotel's ballroom, holding hands and smiling; picture perfect. On cue from one of the groomsmen, the DJ played an old Buck Owens song, *Tiger By the Tail.* The message was for me, but I didn't get it:

I've got a tiger by the tail it's plain to see,
I won't be much when you get through with me....

Dick ignored the hor d'oeuvres table and made a bee line for the bar. Some of the guys trailed after him, with a lot of back slapping and corny jokes. *I remember watching him interact with the men, marveling at how handsome and calm he looked.*

I mingled with Dick's grandmother and other family and friends, and after a short time, the beginning strains of Chicago's *You're My Inspiration* filled the room, and the DJ announced this dance was for the bride and groom only. Hand in hand, we made our way to the center of the dance floor, we looked as close and together as the fused couple on top of a wedding cake, but an invisible wall of tension separated us. As we danced, Dick nuzzled my neck and kissed my cheek, smooth dance moves belied the friction between us. For just a second, it seemed Dick was beginning to relax. During our first dance, he pulled back a bit and smiled lovingly as he spoke to me. To everyone watching, it may have looked as if he were speaking words of love. What he actually said is, "If I don't get something to eat I'm going to tear this damn place apart." Then he leaned down and appeared to kiss me on the cheek. In reality, he bit me, hard. I dug my fingers into his neck and told him he was hurting me. Dick looked at me with a drunken look of disgust and a lopsided grin and said, "I didn't hurt you." The song ended and we walked off the dance floor with our arms around the others waist, smiling.

Twenty-five years and four months after our wedding night, he would speak similar words to me, this time regarding our children.

"Cissy and Garrett need to call me dammit! Why the hell won't they call me?" He had called me from Cheyenne, Wyoming, his new home.

"You know why they don't want to talk to you, Dick. You've hurt them. For years you hurt them," I said to him.

"What the hell are you talking about? I never hurt them! They've hurt me, but I've never hurt them!"

The morning after our wedding I had a small bruise on my cheek. Dick Crisco tenderly rubbed the bruised place with his thumb and said, "I'm sorry, baby".

I didn't realize it at the time, but he had already sized me up. He had known I would not make a scene when he bit me during the dance. He knew the appearance of happiness and perfection was important to me and he used it against me. If only I had exposed him then and there, on the dance floor.

"*If*, is the largest word in the dictionary", my mom likes to say, and it's true.

There is a photograph someone took of us during that dance, Dick's arms are wrapped lovingly around me and I'm gazing adoringly up at him. I've always been tempted to rip the photo to shreds but I was never able to let myself destroy it. The photograph was part of the 'perfect couple image' I wanted so badly. For years I felt angry with myself every time I looked at that picture. Others who saw the photo made comments about how sweet and in love we looked, but it always made me sad and angry. To this day, I haven't been able to toss it out, but I have a different reason for keeping it these days. The photograph reminds me of how deceiving an image can actually be.

By the time we made our way to our hotel room on our wedding night, Dick was so intoxicated he could barely walk. My wedding night was not one of wedded bliss…for now I'll leave it at that. The following morning we woke and made our way to a nearby IHOP for breakfast. Dick, a non-coffee drinker was hung-over and ordered black coffee in the hope of bringing clarity to his dark and muddy mind.

We sat in awkward silence and waited for our pancakes to arrive. I tried to think of something I could do to help redeem the terrible start of our married life. Suddenly, our Honeymoon popped to mind. In the disturbing hours since our ceremony, I had not once thought about our Honeymoon. Tension and the stress of wedding planning were over and in a few hours we would be somewhere enjoying our Honeymoon. The Honeymoon would be our fresh start.

In the months leading up to our wedding, Dick had refused to tell me where we were going or what we were doing for our honeymoon. Each time I asked, he would tell me I would just have to wait and see. No matter how many times I explained I would need to know what and how much to pack, his answer was always the same; "You'll be fine."

"Where?" I asked now, with a smile I couldn't contain.

"Where what?" Dick responded absently, he was looking across the restaurant, trying to grab our server's attention.

"Where are we going for our honeymoon? Aren't you going to tell me?" I couldn't believe he was still dragging this out, the anticipation was killing me.

"I don't know. Where do you want to go?" He still hadn't looked my way.

"What do you mean you don't know? You said if I would plan the wedding you would plan the honeymoon," I thumped him teasingly on the shoulder, I wanted to believe he was playing. I thought he would say: *Had you going, didn't I?*

Instead, he said, "Well, I don't have much money so we can't go too far".

All this time, I had believed he was planning our honeymoon, a surprise, but he had planned nothing at all. That was the surprise: no plan. I felt betrayed. Not because there was no trip, but because of the deception. Not once had Dick indicated he had no plans. He had fooled me all along, always indicating he was making plans.

"Seriously?" I asked incredulously.

"Why are you always so damn dramatic? What's a honeymoon anyway? We've already wasted enough money on this damn wedding. All you want to do is spend money! I'm not made of money! If you wanted a big honeymoon you should have married that son-of-a-bitch dentist! Don't tell me you can't believe this! You know I don't have the money for this shit!" He lost it right there in the middle of IHOP. While Dick hissed and bellowed at me, his faced turned red and his eyes bulged like a big bullfrog. I was embarrassed and humiliated, but more than anything, I was frightened. Dick instantly recognized my fear and it made him feel powerful. He sneered at me as if I was the most disgusting thing he had ever laid eyes on and then quickly stood and walked outside.

I could feel the eyes of the other patrons burning through me as I reached for my purse, I didn't want to look up. Someone gently placed a hand on my shoulder, "Ever thang alright, Sweetie"? It was our waitress, her voice thick like soft southern velvet. She placed her hand on my chin and tilted my face toward hers, I almost cried when I saw the compassionate way she was looking at me.

"Yes, I'm ok. If you could give me the check I would appreciate it. If our food is almost ready, could you put it in 'To Go' boxes, please"? My throat was tight and my voice cracked when I spoke, heat burned my face from the inside out.

In a few minutes she returned with our food, boxed and bagged. She didn't offer the food right away, instead she placed it on the table and cupped her thin brown hands around my face. "Honey, you gots yo'self a gut lookin' man there, but don't you let him be treatin' you like you nuthin'. A man that don't respect you ain't a man. Don't care how purty his face be. An another thang, you hold that purty head high. Don't let me never see you lookin' down like you done somethin' wrong. You ain't wrong. He is though." She had seen right through Crisco. She was strong. Why wasn't I?

As I paid the cashier I worried that Dick had driven away, leaving me at the restaurant. I needn't have worried. I found him waiting outside, standing by the car, fuming mad. It was then I remembered he had handed me the car keys before we entered IHOP.

"I want to explain something to you...," I tried to say to Dick. He held his hand up in front of my face, indicating he didn't want to hear what I had to say. I pressed on. "You need to hear what I have to say. Please listen to me." He gave me a disengaged look but I kept talking.

"When I said 'I can't believe this' I wasn't exactly talking about our honeymoon. I was saying I can't believe you led me on for so long. What I can't believe is you weren't completely honest with me. I would have understood about the money. But you led me to believe you had a big surprise for our honeymoon. Why didn't you just tell me the truth? The truth would have saved a lot of trouble. Did you think it would be better to tell me today rather than six months ago? It's the deception I'm upset over. It isn't about going someplace or not going someplace for a honeymoon. We can have a honeymoon at home."

For a moment he didn't respond, I could only hope he was listening to me.

"Get in the car. Where do you want to go?" he asked.

"If we don't have the money to go anywhere, let's just go back to the house and unpack our wedding gifts. We can go somewhere later, in a few months."

"No. We'll go somewhere for a couple of nights," he insisted, calmer now.

"Well, what about Charleston or Savannah? They're both only a few hours drive, and I've never been to either city. I've lived in Georgia all my life and have never been to Savannah, that's pretty sad." I began to feel a twinge of excitement about visiting either of those two historical cities.

"I hate the beach," Dick says dryly.

"It wouldn't really be going to the beach," I say. "We could tour the city. Sure, the beaches are nearby, but both cities are supposed to be romantic and beautiful."

"No, we're not going there. I don't want to go there," Dick responded.

"Ok, you decide. Where do you want to go?"

"It's *your* honeymoon. You decide. Let's go where you want to go." There was not the faintest glint of interest in Dick's eyes when he spoke to me.

"It's our honeymoon," I say, trying to ignore the tone of his voice and the implication in his words. "It should be someplace we both want to go."

"I don't really care where we go, so you decide. I'm just not going to Savannah or Charleston."

"Why don't you like about Savannah or Charleston? I didn't realize you had been to either place."

"I haven't and I don't want to either. Now, where are we going? Where do you want to go?" He was getting frustrated with me.

"St. Augustine would be my next choice, but since you don't like the beach or historical cities, what about Nashville? That's only four hours from Atlanta and we could tour the Grand Ole Opry. Did I ever tell you I fell down the steps of the Ryman when I was four years old and got to go back stage?" Dick loved country music so I thought for sure he would like the Nashville idea. Meantime, I couldn't believe we were actually sitting in the parking lot of IHOP, the day after our wedding, trying to decide on a honeymoon location.

"What's in Nashville? I don't want to go to Nashville."

I suggested a few more places and Dick didn't like any of them. Finally, things became crystal clear to me: it didn't matter what city I named, he would find it undesirable. Silently, I decided I would make no other suggestions. He could choose or we would go home. "I have no other ideas, I guess we could just go back to the house," I said.

"No, we have to go somewhere," Dick said.

"Ok, you decide, I'm out of ideas."

"How about Gatlinburg?"

"Fine," I say.

I was disappointed with his choice but said nothing. He knew I wasn't a fan of Gatlinburg and looking back, I believe he expected me to complain about his selection of honeymoon destination. Previously, I had mentioned to Dick my wonder at the fascination with Gatlinburg, Tennessee. Yes, the mountains are beautiful, if you can look past the tacky souvenir shops. But it's one of those places where one trip in a lifetime is adequate. Both of us had been to Gatlinburg numerous times, but never together, however.

A few hours of silence later, we had almost made it to Gatlinburg when we passed a roadside sign that said: Cades Cove. Dick got excited and turned the car in the direction of the arrows. For two hours we drove around Cades Cove looking for deer and stopping to snap photos when we saw their white tails in the fields and forest. The entire time we drove the loop around the cove Dick kept saying, "I wish I had my gun with me!"

The only photos from our honeymoon are of white tail deer and a woodpecker.

Shortly after our tour of Cades Cove, we were checked into the loosely termed "honeymoon suite" of a rundown motel in Gatlinburg. By the time we were settled in our room, snow and ice was forming a blanket on the ground. Our motel had no restaurant, so I suggested we have dinner early to avoid driving in the quickly accumulating ice. We had not eaten all day, our IHOP pancakes were still in the take-out boxes, untouched.

"Ok, let's go eat then," Dick was ready.

"Maybe we should stop by the front desk and ask them to suggest a restaurant for us," I suggested.

The front desk was actually in a small glass and rock building detached from the motel. Our motel was the kind with the room doors facing the parking lot.

"Ok, you wait in the car, I'll be right back." Dick said.

When he returned he said the clerk recommended a place within walking distance, a couple of street lights past the motel. Then he said, "You won't believe this. Jackson Orley is staying at this hotel. I went to high school with him in Baton Rouge. Remember me telling you we played football together at Broadmoor?"

"How do you know he's here? Did you see him in the front office?"

"I saw his name on the registry. Baton Rouge was the address next to his name. There can't be that many Jackson Orley's in the world, and I know he's the only one in Baton Rouge," Dick said.

Twenty-two years later we were visiting Dick's sister and her family in Baton Rouge, Louisiana. While there, Dick decided he wanted to look up a few of his old friends. Jackson was one of them. Admiring vacation photos on the bookshelves of Jackson's den, I happened to think of that honeymoon night in Tennessee and I mentioned it to Jackson and his wife.

"No, that wasn't me. Couldn't have been me. We were living in London at that time. I know there isn't another Jackson Orley in town. Guess I need to see if someone's been using my name all these years!" *By this time in my marriage, I was well aware my husband was a liar and I have no doubt he lied about seeing Jackson's name on a motel registry in 1986. Why would he lie about something so mundane? Just because. Dick needs no reason to lie. It's who he is, it's what he does. Deception comes more easily to him than the truth.*

We easily located the restaurant, a quaint chalet style cottage perched alongside a slow moving creek. Outside, snow was falling heavily. Inside, the crackling fireplace and candlelight warmed the dimly lit dining room and created a romantic ambiance. After being seated, Dick reached across the table, held my hand and asked, "Has anyone told you today how beautiful you are?" For the first time since our wedding ceremony, I felt like a newlywed in love.

The moment was fleeting. Within seconds of glancing over the menu, Dick said loudly, "I can't afford this, let's go." So without another word, we stood and left the restaurant. Humiliation burned in my chest, rose up my neck and colored my cheeks as we walked across the dining room toward the door.

"Where do you want to go now?" Dick casually asked when we stepped outside, embarrassment and disappointment seemingly emotions he was incapable of feeling. I shook my head from side to side. "It doesn't matter", I told him. "We should just go back to the room, save our money."

"Like hell! I'm starving!" said Dick.

We walked back to the motel, and as I opened the door to our room, Dick said to me, "I'll be back in a minute, you go on inside." Half an hour later he returned with a grocery bag filled with bread, peanut butter, grape jelly and a quart of milk.

Sometime during the night the electricity went out in the motel and we woke the next morning to a cold room. "Baby, let's just shower and get out of here and go home," Dick said to me. "I can't stand to see you cold like this." I was comforted by the gentleness in his voice.

While Dick was in the shower, the power to our room was restored. I turned the thermostat up to heat the room, thinking Dick would appreciate the warmth when he stepped out of the shower stall. After a long shower and several minutes spent shaving and grooming, Dick opened the bathroom door and stepped into the room, "What do you have the heat on? You tryin' to burn us out of here? Turn it down."

Rummaging through his suitcase, Dick said he thought we should get back to Georgia as soon as possible in case the snow and ice worsened. Without warning, he suddenly flipped his suitcase upside down. "Fuck! My stupid sister didn't pack any underwear for me! Mom told her to pack my suitcase and now I don't have any socks or underwear! She's so damn stupid mom had to remind her to wash her own ass most of the time! I don't know why mom would have Vee pack for me instead of doing it herself. She probably did this on purpose. I guess she thought it would be funny. Stupid bitch!"

Tension was strung tightly across the small motel room. Dick's anger was electric and his sudden outburst was frightening enough to keep me quiet, but the unasked question burning my tongue was, "*Why didn't you pack your own suitcase?*"

The next few weeks were difficult. Dick was distant and angry most of the time. His inattentive behavior and distant attitude worried me. When I asked him if something was wrong or bothering him he would lash out at me and tell me to stop whining and mind my own business.

"If something is bothering you I want to know. I'm your wife, we're a team. We're supposed to work together on problems, we don't have to deal with them alone and independently," I said. Dick remained unwavering, whatever was bothering him was sealed within.

From the very first night we lived together as a married couple, Dick never came to bed when I did. My feelings were hurt by his avoidance of me and I was confused by his sudden detachment. When I asked him why he stayed up late he claimed he was never tired, that it took him time to wind down.

One night, a few weeks after our wedding, I lay in bed, wondering why things were so messed up. I could hear the television blasting in the living room, so I decided I would try to talk with Dick one more time. I got out of bed and walked to the living room where I found him watching television. He was masturbating.

"What are you doing?" I asked, shocked.

"I'm not doing anything! Stop snooping and bothering me and go back to bed! If you think I'm going to pamper you and treat you like a baby you're wrong! You're nothing but a damn, snooping bitch. Just like my fucking mother!"

What? Where did that come from? I just wanted to understand what was going on in our lives. Yet, in a matter of seconds he managed to divert attention from the act I caught him in and transform it to my problem. *Whining and bothering...?* My husband's behavior and accusations confused and rattled me.

Twisting the truth, turning the tables and displacing blame were skills he had obviously perfected many years before we met. *In the months leading up to our divorce, I learned Dick had been addicted to pornography since he was a young teen. He had become very adept at keeping his addiction concealed. Secrecy was second nature to him. For more than half his life, pornography and masturbation had been as much of his daily routine as brushing his teeth.*

In the early days of our marriage we constantly argued over what I saw as irresponsible behavior. During our engagement, we had purchased land with a dream of building a home on the property. We needed to save money for the down payment and we had agreed to cut back our spending where ever possible. Frequent dining in restaurants was one of the first luxuries to be cut. Every work day I packed our lunches so we wouldn't be tempted to eat out with co-workers. Every evening Dick would come in and tell me, "The lunch you made me today was delicious!" One evening he arrived home before I did, our rented house had a very narrow driveway so I parked behind his truck. I exited my car, arms loaded with work bag, purse and a bag of Florida Oranges a co-worker had given me. As I passed between the tailgate of his truck and the front bumper of my Honda, I smelled rotting food. Looking in the bed of his Ford I saw every lunch I had packed for him during the past two weeks. Rotting bananas, oozing yellow-green secretions, were scattered about the pick-up. Pickles were swollen in plastic sandwich bags. Turkey sandwiches, slick with rot, were black and green. Strewn about the truck bed were sacks and cups from various fast food restaurants. In the mix of trash and rotting food were several plastic cups filled with paper napkins and tobacco spit. Numerous empty tins of Copenhagen were scattered and mixed with the other trash. The stench was powerful and insulting. The trash and discarded lunches represented wasted money.

When I walked into the house I found Dick reclining on the sofa, watching a fishing show. I was furious and unable to hide my anger when I asked him why he had lied about eating the sack lunches I had prepared for him and spending the money we had agreed to save. He immediately jumped to his feet, yelling and screaming, throwing his weight around, accusing me of snooping in his truck. He ran to our bedroom and slammed the door. I assumed he wanted to get away from me for a few minutes and cool off, but that wasn't the case. I heard drawers opening and feet stomping. "He's preparing to leave," I thought. But then I remembered he kept his clothes in the spare bedroom. The closets in the old house were so small they could barely accommodate the clothing of one person, let alone two. I stood behind the bedroom door for a moment before I opened it, unsure of what I would find. Cautiously opening the door, I discovered Dick had pulled all of my clothes from the closet and drawers and thrown them onto the floor. He was simultaneously ripping them and furiously stomping on them, still wearing his dirty work boots.

His behavior frightened me. It also hurt me deeply. The way he was treating my clothing was insulting and I remember thinking, "At least he has self-restraint and is ripping and stomping my clothes rather than stomping me." Even as those thoughts rolled through my mind, I knew I should get out of the marriage. But, I knew I would stay. I also knew I would not tell anyone about Dick's behavior. My pride would not allow it. Writing this, I can't believe I didn't pack my things and leave. But that's what pride does, it confuses the rational mind. Pride convinced me a failed marriage meant I was a failure. And separate from the pride, I actually believed this was temporary behavior for Dick. *I just needed to know what was causing his problems so I could fix things.*

When he noticed me watching from the doorway, he lunged toward me and fastballed the shoe he had been erratically folding and squeezing in his hands. I backed away and ducked to the side, and the shoe missed its target, landing on the floor behind me.

"Don't you ever go fuckin' snoopin' in my truck again! That's my g**damn truck and you will stay out of it unless I'm in it with you! Stay out of all of my shit! My shit does not belong to you!" His face was twisted and demonic, obscenities rolled off his tongue.

"Dick, this is nonsense. You're acting crazy. I wasn't inside your truck. I was walking past it and smelled the spoiled food. Why would it matter if I had been in your truck anyway? Why should I have to defend myself against it?"

In a split second, Dick was standing a mere two inches in front of me. He hunched his shoulders and lowered his head so that we were eye to eye, I felt the heat of his angry breath and his spit sprinkled my face as he screamed more degrading obscenities.

"You're a g**damn fucking snoop just like my g**damn mother! She snooped through every damn thing I ever had and you're the same way! Stay away from me and my shit!" Dick picked up another shoe, a black sandal with three inch heels, and slung it against the wall. Then he left the house, slamming doors and rattling windows on his way out.

For a while after he left I stood in the middle of the foyer, trembling more from fear than from the cold temperature of the old house. Over and over the scene replayed in my head. The argument had begun about one thing: my discovery of the discarded, uneaten lunches and the subsequent revelation of Dick's lies and deception. Yet it had ended with Little Dick's accusations of snooping, and comparisons to the mother he despises. Seamlessly and effortlessly, he had quickly twisted the argument until it no longer resembled the initial issue.

I was becoming increasingly aware of Dick's ability to deflect attention when he was caught up in an uncomfortable situation. Dick Crisco is a master of manipulation and is capable of fluently twisting any situation or argument that may cast a negative light on himself. Painlessly, he points the finger of blame toward an innocent party. With Dick, it's always another's fault. Whether it's his termination from a job or an affair with a woman, Dick never accepts responsibility. The problem is forever the fault of another. At least that's always his argument. Unfortunately, this argument over the lunches was early in our marriage and I didn't have a history to fully assess his behavioral problems. All I knew was our arguments always ended in unresolved, frustrating blow-outs with the burden of fault resting squarely on my shoulders. *And I thought our problems were temporary.*

Numerous times in our marriage, I caught Dick in bold lies. Early on, I tried to talk to him about the problems his deception created in our relationship. Eventually I realized the futility in confronting him with the untruths. When it comes to defending himself, Dick's mind is nimble and quickly spins another believable web of lies to argue his defense. He is masterful at twisting words and every argument ended with me defending myself against false accusations. Sometimes he would bring up previous arguments; anything to deflect attention from himself.

So I say to anyone in this type of relationship: LEAVE. If your significant other is never willing to take responsibility for his actions, walk away from him or her. This behavior was learned and developed long before you entered his life. He's not changing. She's not changing. Get out. It gets worse with time, never better.

A constant state of developing crisis is how I would describe my newlywed life. An ongoing sense of dread and fear took root in my thoughts, yet I made excuses for it. My stomach would begin to ache on my way home from work, anticipating Dick's dark mood. I walked as if broken glass was beneath my bare feet when I first approached him at the end of a work day. Optimistically, I continued to believe his moodiness was the result of adjusting to living as a couple. I convinced myself all newlyweds experienced a rough phase.

My mother-in-law told me I expected too much from her son.

A friend told me it would take a year to work out the kinks. So, with quiet hope, I began to eagerly anticipate our first anniversary, even though we had been married less than a month. *"If we can just make it a year"*, became my silent mantra. I still believed in happily ever after.

Usually, Dick left for work before I did every morning and arrived home after me in the evening. We were pinching pennies and I was extremely conscientious about shutting off every light and the furnace before leaving the house. Yet every day, I came home to find several lights on and the furnace burning. The house we rented was more than one hundred years old and there was no insulation behind the plaster walls or underneath the old plank floors. Heating the house was a difficult and very expensive task. We had agreed to use the furnace only while we were home, and even then, we closed off the rooms we weren't using. So

I was alarmed one day when I came home and found the furnace going full speed and the lights "burning a hole in daylight" as Dick light to say. The first time it happened, I mentioned it to Dick and he blamed it on our elderly landlord. "That old bitch must have come over here during the day while we're working. You know she doesn't want the pipes to freeze. She thinks the furnace will keep the pipes from freezing up."

"I think I'll go ask her about it," I told him.

"Don't worry about it, I'll talk to her tonight. She has a room she's thinking about putting crown mold in and she wants me to come over and give her a bid on it."

After dinner Dick visited our landlady, fifteen minutes later he returned to our house. "That was quick," I said.

"Yeah, she decided not to do any work to the room."

"What did she say about the lights and the furnace?"

"Just what I told you, she thought the pipes were going to freeze so she came over."

"I don't understand why she didn't talk to us about it first. Why did she turn on the bathroom and kitchen lights? The thermostat is in the front foyer. She knows we're trying to conserve our resources, this seems very unusual." Dick responded by shrugging his shoulders.

"This makes no sense to me, I'm going to call her and ask her to please let us know when she's coming inside the house. True she owns the house but our rent doesn't include utilities and her carelessness will cause our electric and gas bills to increase. Anyway, I don't think she's legally permitted to come inside just because she feels like it."

"She doesn't want to talk to you. To avoid miscommunication, she only wants to deal with one of us and I told her it would be me. You know how old people are. She's going to do what she wants to do. But just to shut her up I told her we would leave the furnace on low."

Almost every day the lights and furnace were burning when I came home. During our two-decade marriage Dick never got in the habit of turning off lights or the central heat and air of our homes.

Our arguments continued and became more intense but our days were sprinkled with tender moments and intermittent hours of love and laughter, joy and fun. Small portions of happiness; just enough to keep me hopeful.

Feelings of failure, helplessness and worthlessness tugged at the corners of my mind. Self-doubt followed me like a dark rain cloud as Dick's episodes of symbolic violence continued: he tore at my personal belongings, kicked the furniture, punched the walls, broke lamps and slammed doors. Dick called me a crazy bitch every time we argued, and without realizing it, I had begun to believe him. His words cut me to the bone but somehow I continued to hold on to the hope that this was an adjustment period, a phase of early married life that would soon pass.

Before long, the symbolic violence became the real thing.

The Grand Illusion

During our courtship, Dick had told me mind boggling stories about the escapades of his Cajun friend from Louisiana, Sambo Boudreaux. There were tales of bar room brawls and broken hands, fights with husbands of dancers and battles with brothers of girlfriends. One of the fights resulted in Sam's subsequent need for a partial set of dentures to replace his missing front teeth. In the retelling of every story, Dick portrayed himself as an innocent observer up until the moment he had to rush in and rescue his friend from yet another potentially fatal encounter of some kind or another. BJ hated, despised and abhorred Sambo Boudreaux. According to BJ, Sambo never failed to bring trouble and strife into Little Dick's life. So I was a bit surprised and somewhat aggravated when, less than two months after our wedding, Dick told me his mom had called to say Sambo was interested in moving to Atlanta and she had informed him it would most likely be just fine if he moved in with us until he could find a job and an apartment.

"Why would she take it upon herself to tell him it would be ok to stay with us? She said she despised him and he was 'nothing but trouble'. Why would she want to add more stress to our lives?" I believed Dick would understand my point of view. I was astonished when he pointed his finger at me and shouted, "Piss on you! You can't think of anyone but yourself can you? You're nothing but a selfish bitch. When my family sees somebody in need we help them. Sambo needs my help and he's going to get it! After mom called, I called Sambo and told him it would be alright to stay with us. He'll be here tomorrow night and I don't want to hear another word about it! To hell with you!" Dick yelled as he slammed his way out the front door.

I couldn't believe the joke our marriage had become. Just two weeks prior to Sambo's stay in our home, Dick's sister and her husband had been living with us, they had been our houseguests for several weeks. Barely two weeks after our wedding, my mother-in-law called to say her daughter's husband had lost his job in Baton Rouge and because of the building boom in Atlanta, were moving to Georgia to seek employment.

"He doesn't have a job lined up yet, but it shouldn't take him long. Can they stay with you till they find a place of their own?"

"Yes, of course," we said. What else do you say when your mother-in-law calls to ask for your assistance with her daughter? I had misgivings, I was very concerned about the kind of impact another couple sharing our small, one-bathroom house would have on our struggling marriage. But I was very much aware I would be damned by the Crisco family if I voiced my misgivings. Even if I explained my hesitations weren't personal, or because I didn't want to help, but because Dick and I hadn't yet figured out how to live with each other, the Crisco's would criticize me and never forgive my insensitivity.

So my sister-in-law Vee, and her husband, moved in and we made it through a few weeks without too many problems. Dick and his sister had never been able to get along and there were a few disagreeable moments while they lived with us, but there was never a reason to be concerned about their influences on Little Dick. I realize now that even then, in the early days, I knew Dick was a follower, a weak minded person. I was always concerned about the influences others would have on him. *Another big red flag I chose to ignore.* If anything, I felt Vee and her husband were good influences on Dick. My former brother-in-law is a good man, a homebody, and he treated his wife and Dick and me very respectfully. Money was tight and tension was high, but there were no extra personal worries created by the two in-laws. Dick's temper toward me even subsided quite a bit during the time his sister stayed with us. Unfortunately for Vee, he diverted his anger and insults to her.

Sambo would be a different type of houseguest and I was very concerned about his influence on Dick. According to previous conversations with my mother-in-law, Sambo was not a good person. The impending arrival of Sambo Boudreaux stirred up anxiety and fear within me. I felt powerless in the direction my marriage was taking. For a few minutes after Dick slammed his way out of our house, I stood in dumbfounded silence, unsure of what to do. A dark, sick feeling took root in my gut and fueled more worry. After a while, I decided to phone my sister-in-law and apprize her of the developing situation.

"My mother would not encourage Sambo Boudreaux to stay with you and my brother! She hates Sambo. He's an alcoholic and a drug addict! Probably even worse than that! Dick stayed in trouble when he hung out with him. My stupid brother is lying to you! My mother would not want Sambo to stay with you!" Vee was emphatic.

"Vee, I spoke to your mom. She told me Sambo called her and talked to her about moving to Georgia. She said she didn't think we would mind so she gave him our phone number."

"Then all I can say is my mother has lost her damn mind! I'm going to call her and see what's going on. I'll call you back."

A short time later Vee called me, and she was hot with anger, "Mom says you called her and told her you thought it would be a good idea if Sambo came to stay with you, and my mother would not lie to me! Why in the name of hell would you make up something like that about her?"

I was aghast, "Hold on just a minute Vee, think about that for a second. Why *would* I do such a thing? In the first place, how would I even know Sambo was moving to Atlanta? Dick didn't invite him to our wedding because he didn't know how to get in touch with Sambo. He didn't have a current phone number for him. This is crazy. Your mom is lying about this. You can ask Dick, she told him Sambo called her."

"I don't know what's going on. Mom says you don't really care about Dick and she feels you're out to destroy your marriage because you gripe all the time."

I felt penned in by my mother-in-law's lie. What was she doing? What were her intentions? Was she trying to create more stress in our fragile marriage? I didn't have a lot of time to dwell on it before Dick walked into the house carrying a case of beer and several bags of chips and nuts. This was a first, we didn't have extra money for this extravagance.

"What's that for?" I asked.

"Sambo. Haven't you ever heard of being hospitable to your guests?" He sneered when he spoke.

"You didn't do it for your sister and her husband", I said.

"Just shut your mouth and leave me alone."

The next afternoon I arrived home from work and was greeted with evidence of Sambo's arrival: A truck with Louisiana plates was parked on the grass in the front yard. Dick's truck and his green canoe were missing. Our front porch was piled with boxes and plastic garbage bags, presumably filled with clothing. Inside the house, tennis shoes and boots were strewn about the foyer. More garbage bags and clothes were piled loosely on the bed in the second bedroom. An open gallon of milk was sitting on the kitchen table, the cap discarded on the table. The fridge was stocked with more Budweiser and Miller Beer. Dick and Sambo were nowhere in sight.

The late afternoon became evening and evening crept toward the darkness of midnight, with no word from Dick. I was angry when Dick missed dinner without calling. By midnight I had become extremely worried, I was concerned for their safety but didn't know where to search. Dick's canoe was missing from the side yard, so my assumption was they were fishing. But there are numerous lakes, rivers, creeks and ponds in the area and the two men could have fished any of them. Anxious with fear, I allowed my mind to wander to the fishing death of a man and his two sons from a few years back. His wife and daughter had stood on the shores of Lake Allatoona and watched the horrible scene play out a few watery yards in front of them. The wife, nine months pregnant, had delivered a baby boy the same evening of her husband and son's deaths. Those thoughts made me sick with worry, and when I could stand it no longer, I phoned my sister-in-law.

She answered groggily, "Hello."

"I'm sorry to wake you, but Dick and Sambo haven't been home all night. They were gone when I came in from work today. I'm afraid the canoe has capsized or something. What if they're dead on the bottom of Lake Allatoona or the Etowah River?"

"They're not dead. I knew this was going to happen. They're out drunk somewhere. One thing you need to know about my brother, he does what his friends do. He cannot walk away from trouble. It's why Mary's mom didn't want her to date him. That woman saw what kind of trouble my brother would bring on her daughter and she made damn sure her daughter knew it, because she didn't want Mary's life screwed up. Everybody in Baton Rouge knows what kind of man my brother is. Everybody but mom. He's a follower not a leader. My whole life my mom has acted like he's this and he's that. She blamed everyone else every time Dick got in trouble, never him. I guarantee you it was always his own doing that got him in trouble. He's a follower. That's why he gets himself into trouble so much. He may be my brother but that's the truth." Vee was speaking more bluntly than I had ever heard her before. I felt sick.

"Do you want me to come over there?" she asked.

I thought of the consequences, the rage Dick would have if he knew I called his sister. I was tired of the arguments. "No, that's ok. I'll call you tomorrow. Sorry to wake you up. Wait! What do you mean, 'he gets himself into trouble'"?

"Never mind. I've said too much all ready. Talk to you tomorrow."

With a cramping stomach I sat on the sofa and watched the clock on the mantle above the old coal burning fireplace. At twenty minutes before three in the morning, I heard tires on gravel. My instinct was to get up and run to the front door, but I forced myself to remain seated, unsure of what to expect.

The home's original skeleton key door was still hanging on the hinges of the original doorframe. Even on a good day, it was difficult to get the skeleton key to turn in the door's keyhole, and from the sounds of swearing and fumbling coming from the other side of the door, it was obvious the keyhole was not cooperating. I realized I probably needed to open the door for Dick and Sambo, and as I walked into the foyer and turned toward the door, I heard a strange male voice loudly say, "Shhhh! You best be quiet for' you wake yo' old lady up!"

"Fuck it! It don't matter no damn way," Dick's voice echoed across the front porch and into the house. I was getting used to his disrespect, but I had never heard him sound so backwoods country before.

"Hey woman!" Dick said when I opened the door. "What are you still doin' up?"

A strong odor of alcohol and tobacco entered the door with the two men. "I couldn't sleep because I was worried," I said.

"Worried? What the hell you got to be worried about? Every time you start worryin' something bad happens! You ain't figured that out yet?" Dick was still talking like a redneck and it sounded foreign coming from him.

Sambo had been quiet up until now, "Hey Boo! Give ol' Sam a hug. Sha, you jes a purty as my podnah say dat you is. Come a give dis Coonass a big hug!" Sam's stringy yellow hair was greasy, his hands were dirty and his bloodshot hazel eyes jumped when he spoke. I did not want a hug from him.

That night was the first time Dick Crisco physically fought me. We argued after going to bed; I asked where he had been and he hissed it was none of my fucking business. He said he would do what he wanted, when he wanted, and he didn't have to consult with me about it. He said I was his "fucking wife not his g**damn mother" and he would not answer to me the same way his mother had wanted him to answer to her. "She tried to stay crawled up my ass and I'll be damned if you're goin' to do the same thing!"

Lying awake in the darkened room, listening to the sounds of his drunken snores, I vowed to myself I would leave Dick. Before morning broke I had talked myself out of it. I reasoned excessive alcohol consumption had caused his behavior the night before. In his right frame of mind, he would never react so violently.

Dick refused to get out of bed the next morning, claiming he had a headache unrelated to a hangover. "Close the bedroom door when you leave, I'm not working today," he said.

Sambo walked into the kitchen as I was packing my lunch for the day. I was too embarrassed to make eye contact with him. The bedroom he slept in was separated from our bedroom by only a thin wall of plaster, and I had no doubt he heard our fight the night before.

"Sounds like you two lovin' birds had a fais-do do last night," Sambo said.

"We had a fight, not a party," I said.

"Ah beb, it don matta. The ol' man be hisself after he sleep da drink off. Hey, where you hose pipe at? My truck needin' some water."

Sambo followed me outside when I left for work and I showed him where he could find the water hose and some other tools he said he needed. When I came home from work that afternoon the two men were gone again. Like the day before, Dick's truck and canoe were missing. When they came home after midnight that evening, I didn't bother getting up and I pretended to be sleeping when Dick finally came to bed. The next morning Dick was in the bathroom, leaning against the linen cabinet, when I stepped out of the shower. He said Sambo was gone for the day, on a search for employment. *What did he want me to say?* I didn't respond as I reached behind him and removed a towel from a hook on the side of the cabinet. In order to avoid another fight, I didn't ask Dick any questions regarding the previous night, I didn't ask where he had been or what he had done the night before. I didn't realize my silence was irritating him.

"Talk to me! What the hell's going on with you?" he insisted.

"Why did we get married Dick? I feel like you want a roommate instead of a wife. We've been married such a short time and between your parents showing up every weekend and your sister and her husband and now Sambo staying with us, we've had no time alone. How are we supposed to learn to live together if we have your family and friends living with us all the time?"

"What's there to learn? Huh? What's there to figure out?" he wanted to know.

I continued, "And now you're staying out half the night acting like you're single. Did you just want someone to cook and clean for you and help you pay the bills? Is that why we got married?" I was furious, screaming words at him. With a lightning quick move Dick slapped me across the face. Before I could react, he knocked me to the floor and grabbed me by the ankles. He began to run, rage roaring from his lungs. He ran backwards through the old house, dragging me by my feet and ankles. I tried to protect my head with my arms as he made quick turns around the doorframes of each room and between the boxes of Sam's unpacked belongings. As a result, my arms were later covered with black and blue bruises. When Dick finally stopped his assault against me, my back was covered with a rough red carpet burn. My legs were banged up, scraped and bruised. Purple and blue stains in the shape of Dick's fingers wrapped around my ankles.

The attack ended as suddenly as it began. Dick left me in an injured heap on the dining room floor and casually walked to the bathroom to shower. When I heard the water running in the shower, I gingerly lifted myself from the floor, and as quickly as the pain would allow, I dressed. I left the house on East Main Street and drove to the lake. I felt lost, helpless and worthless as I sat on the hood of my car, watching the waves gently lapping against the clay shore line. I don't know how long I sat there, hours it seems now, trying to figure out how things how turned out so terribly. What happened? How did this happen? Was I really married to a monster? How could I have so badly misjudged this man? I wanted to marry a man who would genuinely love me and our future children, a man who would protect us against the evilness of the world. We would love and cherish each other equally. Until the day of our wedding, I thought I had found him. But too many emotionally difficult upheavals had occurred in the few weeks since we married, I now felt I was living in a never ending nightmare. I wanted help. I wanted to get out of the marriage, but how? I was embarrassed to admit I had been fooled, but I realized I had to admit it and face it. The way I saw it, my only choice was to leave him. I had no plan other than to go home and start packing, I would figure out the details later. Facing the disappointment of my family would be difficult, but I would do it and move on.

I pulled my sore and bruised body into my car and drove back to East Main Street. My heartbeat quickened when I came into view of the house and saw Dick's truck sitting in the yard. Pulling into the driveway, I noticed Sambo's belongings were no longer piled on the front porch. When I opened the old wood and glass door, I was hit with the strong and familiar scent of pine cleaner. Sambo's other items, the boxes and bags of clothing and shoes were nowhere in sight.

Dick entered the foyer from the living room as I stepped across the threshold. Tears streamed down his face as he came to me and gently wrapped his arms around me, "I'm so sorry. I don't know what got into me. I don't want to lose you. I don't know what I would do if I ever lost you. Please forgive me. I promise nothing like this will ever happen again."

I tried to speak, to interrupt him, but he stopped me. "Don't talk yet, ok? Let me finish. I need to say these things to you. It's been so hard to adjust and I don't know why. But I promise I'll get past it. You're the best thing that's ever happened to me. You're the best part of me and I realize that now. I won't be able to live without you. Please give me a second chance."

Relief washed over me as Dick's apology caressed forgiveness into my heart. I returned his kisses, I told him I loved him and promised I would forget the last two days. The dissolution of my marriage was not something I truly wanted and I was more than willing to give it another try.

Most of the time, a clock holds no special distinction, but is merely a tool to measure duration, minutes ticking away on a timepiece: one hour to bake the cake; fifteen minutes on the treadmill; ninety minutes to play a game of soccer; eight hours in a work day. Unless we're waiting for something to begin or end, we don't give much thought to time, allowing it to pass unnoticed, quietly stealing life from us. More specifically, we don't recognize the significance of the individual moments in our lives, the life changing, split-second decisions or long-contemplated choices we make while the clock ticks. If only the clock's alarm would buzz a loud warning when we waste precious moments or make poor choices. Like the moment I extended forgiveness to Dick. In that moment there were no sirens or alarms shrieking out a warning, alerting me that the moment would change the course of my life. Other than the relief and warmth I felt after hearing Dick's apologies, there was nothing extraordinary about the ticking seconds. But when I remember this time in my life, its significance is clear. This is the moment I taught my husband how to treat me. This is the hour I began to lose perspective. This is the day I stepped through the looking glass and began to lose myself, the night I began to disappear. Years would pass before I would resurface. Sadly, during all that time, during all those years, I didn't even realize I was missing.

The day I sent a letter of forgiveness to my husband's lover, almost a decade of lies and secrecy had slipped between Dick and me. I still didn't realize what I had put in motion all those years before, on that day in 1986, when I had accepted his kisses, apologies and promises with an embrace of forgiveness. Incredibly, ten years later, I still held out hope for a happily ever after ending. As far as I knew, until his affair with Dawn, Dick's promise of love and faithfulness had been honored and I could say I was happy I had chosen to stay in my marriage.

I was content, convinced we were on the right track and thankful my marriage and now my family had survived another storm. Convinced we had beaten the odds, I placed the letter to Dawn in the drop-off box at the Cartersville Post Office with a solid belief that Dick's affair was a once in a lifetime transgression. I had no doubt his apologies were sincere.

This letter to Dawn, an offering of forgiveness, symbolized an ending and another beginning.

It was true Dick had gone back on his promise to never hit me again, and that bothered me. Years had passed in between the two incidents and I found myself making more excuses for his latest transgression: the stresses of a growing family, bills, car troubles, and the stress of work. I reasoned these things, along with the guilt I imagined he felt because of the affair, had caused him to lose control. He wouldn't do it again. He promised me he would never hit or shove me again.

Several months passed without incident. The kids were busy with sports and scouts and various other extracurricular activities. Our marriage was on solid ground and I felt we were closer than we had ever been. We made time for date nights, we went dancing again. Dick would surprise me with sweet notes left on the bathroom counter or in my Daily Agenda. Every now and then something would trigger a painful memory, and despite my best efforts, I would remember the pain of betrayal. I would express my feelings to Dick and ask him to help me work through the pain. He had never been one to listen to what he called 'whining', but after the affair I had told him it would take me a while to recover from the anguish. One of the ways I process emotional pain is to talk about it. I explained there would be times I would need to talk things out with him and he promised he would be patient and listen.

I never felt more love from him than I did during those talks. While I poured myself out to him emotionally, Dick would cradle me and tell me how much he loved me. He would say he had been wrong to put the family through so much heartache. Sometimes he cried with me. He promised to never hurt us again and I believed him. Our kids believed him. We believed him and forgave him and he betrayed us again.

The next betrayal was much more sinister than the first, and could only have been conceived by a man without conscience.

To the public eyes of Cartersville, Dick was a model citizen, husband and dad. Dick was first in line to volunteer for a community project, a church outreach or a school function. Other moms at Cartersville Primary and Cartersville Elementary would tell me they wished their husbands were as attentive as Dick. Dick basked in their praises. But where it really matters, in our home and in the eyes of his children, especially Garrett, Dick was a skunk. Unknown to me, Dick had sunk to a depth of depravity to which only the vilest of men will sink. He used our little boy as a scapegoat, a pawn in his sick game of lies and adultery.

Revelations 1996

"Mommy, when we finish our dinner will you please give Cissy and me each a quarter, so we can have our fortunes read?"

Our family of four had spent a nice summer day exploring the creeks and mountains of Northern Georgia and had stopped for dinner at a Calhoun, Georgia barbeque restaurant, the kind of locally owned establishment that tapes photos of local high school sports teams on the windows, places collection jars for kids with cancer next to the cash register, and serves thick, rich BBQ and sweet iced tea. As far as I was concerned, we were closing the day perfectly. Exhausted with the good kind of tired you get from exploring the outdoors with children, I remember having a sense of peace, feeling very happy and content with life. We didn't have a lot of extra money but we had two very healthy children and we had good jobs. There was much to be thankful for.

"I think I can spare fifty cents," I laughed as I rubbed Garrett's buzz-cut hair. Almost seven years old, he loved talking about life in the past as well as thinking of life in the future. He dreamed of inventing a time machine that would allow him to travel back in time to revisit history and forward into the future, so he would know what awaited him. He possessed every ounce of faith needed to believe a time machine was possible. So, when he and Cissy saw the electronic Fortune Teller's machine in the restaurant, he had no reason to think it would tell him anything but the truth.

Anticipating all the wonderful mysteries the fortune teller would reveal, Garrett could hardly contain his excitement during dinner. After paying the cashier, the four of us walked to the arcade corner of the restaurant and read the operating instructions, as neon lights danced brightly around the machine. "Place the palm of your hand here. Insert coin here," the instructions read.

Garrett was first in line. He placed his little hand in the designated spot and I inserted the quarter. "You can be an astronaut or a rock star!" the machine promised.

"Did you hear that Cissy? I can be an astronaut someday! Now see what it says about you!" His blue eyes beamed with exuberance as he stepped aside to give his sister space in front of the magical box. Nine-year-old Cissy placed a sweet hand decorated with sparkly purple nail polish on the outline, and I inserted another quarter. Lights blinked and chimes dinged before the machine blurted, "You are destined to be a famous movie star!"

"Did you hear that Ciss? You're going to be a movie star!" Garrett hugged his sister and danced a little jig.

"Mommy, does that machine really know I'll be a movie star?" Cissy asked softly.

"You can be or do anything you want, Sweet Girl," I answered.

"Dad! Get your fortune told!" Garrett jumped up and down and clapped his hands as he encouraged his dad to peek into the future. Dick stepped up to the machine, placed his hand on the designated spot and popped a quarter in the slot. More lights blinked, some chanting from the fortune teller and then a drum roll. "You have two hundred and twenty-five girlfriends!" the machine shrieked. *Of all things,* I thought, *it had to say that?*

Dick laughed at the absurdity of the mechanical clairvoyant's announcement, and in that moment, I noticed something had sucked the air out of Garrett. My son appeared to deflate, as a balloon does when it's been pricked with a needle. His head dropped, his little shoulders slumped and he gave his sister a look that made my soul cry.

I said to him, "Oh Buddy, that machine doesn't know anything. It's all pretend."

Cissy's big blue eyes were filled with love and compassion as she placed an arm around her little brother's shoulders, "Brub, it's ok. It's not the truth. There's not really a fortune teller in there. That's just a silly old machine."

Sadness settled over him, and during the thirty-minute ride home, Garrett was silent. Dick tried to cheer him up with the crazy jokes Garrett usually loved, but he was having none of it. I knew my little guy believed the fortune telling machine was legitimate, and my heart ached for him. Dick tried to persuade Garrett by explaining the functionality of the machine, "There's a recorder inside which randomly tosses out comments and fortunes. Even if your mom had put her hand on the stupid machine, it would have said she had two hundred and twenty-five girlfriends," Dick insisted.

From the backseat, Garrett stared coldly through tear rimmed eyes at the back of his dad's head, but he remained silent.

Not for a few more weeks would I understand why my little boy had such faith in the words emitted from a piece of machinery. At seven, Garrett had already been a victim, used by his dad in unthinkable ways. When his life should have been swimming in the innocent sea of ballgames and bugs and bikes, Garrett had already been exposed to the slimy soul of his dad. Unlike me, Garrett knew firsthand his dad would stoop to the lowest pits of hell to fulfill selfish desires. Garrett knew his dad thought so little of him that he would use him as an excuse to spend time with another little boy's mama. My precious boy had seen behavior from his dad that I could not yet imagine. At seven, Garrett knew his dad was a selfish liar. Of course he trusted the voice coming from a box of plastic and aluminum more than he trusted his dad. Dick had proven himself to be untrustworthy. At seven years of age, Garrett understood his dad did not love him enough to protect him from pain or guard his innocent heart and mind from vulgarity. He knew his dad had no respect for our family. At the sweet, tender age of seven, Garrett privately acknowledged what I refused to admit: his dad was a heartless, womanizing liar.

I was unable to forget Garrett's reaction to the Fortune Teller; the message had troubled him deeply and that bothered me. His sadness was still apparent a couple of days later and this was not normal for my usual happy-go-lucky little boy. As I prepared dinner on Tuesday night, I mentioned my concerns to Dick. Quickly, he became agitated and snapped, "You're always looking for trouble! If you keep looking for trouble you're going to find it! He's just a kid for God's sake! What does he know? You can't really believe his mood swing means anything!"

Mood swing? Garrett didn't have mood swings and I reminded Dick of this.

"You're spoiling him Danita! You pamper and coddle him too much!" Dick was screaming, red in the face.

"How am I pampering him? Don't you know the difference between concern and pampering?" I asked. I was concerned for my little boy because something was bothering him. Why wasn't Dick concerned as well?

"Let it go and drop it! Now shut your damn pie hole! I don't want to hear any more about it!" Dick ran to the door and made a quick exit to his truck. He drove away without a word, his reaction left me in a state of disbelief.

While he was gone I began to reflect on the changes in Dick's behavior during the last several weeks. First, Dick had begun phoning me before I left work every afternoon to see if I was leaving at my scheduled time. When I asked why he had suddenly become so interested in my schedule, he said he just wanted to know when to expect me home. He said too many accidents happened on Interstate 75 between Atlanta and Cartersville and he was just worried about "my baby" being in Atlanta traffic. My heart was warmed by this change in his attitude. Dick had never been one to worry or express concern, not for me or anyone else. At first, I saw the expressed concern and questions as proof of Dick's growing commitment to our family and our marriage. It made me happy to know he was thinking about me and took time from his busy day to check on me. His disregard of our son's feelings didn't pair well with the growth I felt I had seen in Dick. His concern about my safety during my drive home and his indifference to our son's sadness didn't line up. The way I saw it, his love and concern for my well-being should extend to our children.

I thought of the *calls*. Not long after the onset of Dick's afternoon calls to me, I began receiving hang-up calls. Initially, the calls brought back hurtful memories of the affair with Dawn, but I mentally reprimanded myself and brushed it off. Dick couldn't be that callous. *Our family had come too far.* The frequency of the hang-up calls increased and started occurring all hours of the day and night. Our home phone would ring, I would answer and someone would hang up. As before, I noticed Dick never received the hang up calls. When he answered, there was always someone on the other end of the line. I mentioned this to him, "Oddly, no one ever hangs up when you answer." He didn't respond and I took it a step further, I pointed out the similarity of these calls and the calls that came to the house when he was involved with Dawn.

Dick became furious, "I can't help that people hang up on you! God knows how many enemies you have! Everyone hates you and it's probably someone you've pissed off! People from work call me and I can't help that they're on the phone when I answer! Why don't you get Caller I.D.? Then you'll know who is calling, and you'll get off my back!"

Dick's comment about people hating me hurt on many levels. The comment was another red flag, another reason for me to worry. It was the kind of thing he had said to me when he and Dawn were having their adulterous affair.

Every morning my alarm sounded at three-thirty, so I could get to my job at Atlanta's Hartsfield International Airport by five o'clock. I hated leaving our house at the very quiet, early morning hour of four, leaving my family sleeping in darkened rooms. With eagerness, I looked forward to my days off so I could linger in a drowsy, half-sleep, half-wake state during the pre-dawn hours. Those early hours had become the best time for Dick and me to catch up on life and reconnect with each other. Lately though, my off-day mornings had been disrupted with calls from the wife of one of Dick's employees. The bedroom phone sat on a night table on the side of the bed where I slept, so I was usually the one to answer. The wife would announce an emergency of some kind before requesting to speak with Dick: her husband was already at work and one of her kids was sick; he had a flat tire and needed Dick to get him; he was terribly ill and wouldn't be in today, or his car was broken, and he needed Dick to give him a ride in. Dick would end the calls with the wife and say to me, in a despondent or aggravated tone, "Well, I've got to go in early, that idiot is having another problem. I don't know why his hag of a wife can't take care of this shit".

During this time, Dick worked as a maintenance manager for a scrap metal recycling center, and he had five or six men under his supervision. I knew the names of most of the men, but the name the woman gave when I first answered her call was new to me. Dick said the man was a new employee. Separate from Garrett's reaction to the Fortune Teller and the hang up calls, I would have chalked up the early morning calls as nothing more than a bothersome employee; even though in the year Dick had worked for the recycling company, no other employee had ever called our home.

From the tone of her voice and the language she used, I could tell the woman was from the south, but she didn't speak with the soft, gentleness of a southern lady. Her grammar was lazy and careless, her country accent was laced with the harshness associated with nicotine abuse, her tone was fused with rudeness, therefore I wasn't surprised with her continual, inconsiderate wake-up calls. Prior to her early morning calls, I had started believing Dick regarding the hang-up calls, contributing them to wrong numbers or kids playing games. But combined, the phone incidents began to meld into a single problematic situation. I just didn't know how to begin to connect the dots. When asked if there was a problem, Dick profusely denied any wrongdoing and told me I was going to force him to do something wrong because I continued to ask him what was going on.

"You're just like my damn mother! She wouldn't shut up till I finally did what she accused me of doing!" It was a familiar strain from his old song, the song of an adolescent.

That evening, while Dick was still away, I completed dinner preparations. The kids were playing on their trampoline in the backyard, I could hear their laughter and squeals of delight as they jumped and flipped. I paused in the middle of chopping cucumbers to watch them. My nephew Justin was staying the night with us. He was older, taller and heavier than Cissy and Garrett, his high jumps bounced the two younger kids around like basketballs on hardwood. I stood at the kitchen window and marveled at how beautiful their love for one another was, yet my heart was heavy and I tormented myself emotionally, 'Was I really creating something from nothing? Was I making harmful, unfounded assumptions against my husband?' The kitchen phone rang shrilly and tore me from my thoughts, I answered and a female voice said, "You don't know a thang' about your husband." Before I could respond, the line went silent.

Within a few minutes of the strange phone call, Dick pulled into the driveway and made his way into the house through the garage. A horrible stench came in with him.

"Where have you been?" I asked.

"Driving around. I had to get away from you and your damn crazy ass nagging." His insulting words were more evidence of the problem I feared most.

During his mean stages, Dick loved hurting me with his words. Why I put up with it is a mystery to me still. I wish I could say I allowed his words to roll off me like water on oil, but that would not be true. I absorbed his spoken words; they sank into my soul and slowly murdered my spirit.

I decided not to respond to his comments and instead told him about the call I had just received. "Who could that be? Do you have any idea what she was talking about?" I asked him.

"How the hell should I know? Fuck, you're probably making the whole thing up anyway!" Once more he turned and walked into the garage, slamming the door behind him. From the window I witnessed a surreal scene unfold before me: As Dick pulled out of the driveway, my nephew ran behind the truck, calling Dick's name, waving at his uncle's back. Dick never slowed down and never looked back.

Uneasiness and dread churned in my stomach as I finished cooking dinner and called the kids to the table. The three chatted lightly, their usual giddiness subdued. "Where did dad go? He almost ran over Justin," Cissy asked the question.

"He probably went to work," I said.

"Yeah, right," Garrett said.

Later that night, my mind worked overtime and kept me awake. I almost, but not completely, had myself convinced that Dick was right about me, maybe I *was* inventing a disaster of the mind. Before falling asleep, I decided I would at least find out where the hang up calls were coming from: I would order the Caller I.D. service from the phone company and I would not tell Dick about it. Very few phones came with Caller I.D. built into them at the time, a separate Caller I.D. box had to be purchased separately and connected to a phone line.

The next day, after calling the telephone company and ordering the Caller I.D. service, I drove to Radio Shack and purchased one of the Caller I.D. display boxes. I connected the identifying box to a phone in my little girl's room and slid the box underneath her bed, out of sight. It didn't take long before I received a hang up call. I answered the kitchen phone and said hello twice before the caller disconnected. Immediately I went upstairs and pulled the box from its hiding place, the LCD screen showed a seven-digit number and displayed "Pay Phone" on the screen. I waited a while before dialing the number. No one answered.

Later that day, my cousin Jayta called. We chatted for a while before she said, "I pulled into the Country Cupboard on Tennessee Street yesterday thinking I saw Terry's truck there and it was Dick." Terry was my cousin's husband. "I never noticed before that they have the same exact truck! I saw the truck in the parking lot when I was coming back from the bank. I was wondering what on Earth Terry would be doing all the way up on Tennessee Street during his lunch hour. I went in the store and low and behold it was Dick in there paying for gas."

"I've never noticed their trucks being similar either," I said. "Dick goes to that Country Cupboard to purchase bottled water for the guys at work and I think the company has a fuel account there too."

"Well, I just never noticed before that they have the same truck! Same color, make, model everything," she said.

After my conversation with Jayta, I called Dick, but I didn't mention the call from my cousin. There was no reason to bring it up; there was nothing unusual about Dick purchasing fuel and water at that location. "Do you still plan on going to tennis practice with the kids and me this afternoon? Practice is at five-thirty," I reminded him.

"I wish I could go, but I can't," he replied. "I have to stay late tonight and get things set up for inspection tomorrow. And I won't be able to eat with ya'll either. Just go on to Ryan's without me. They're ordering in pizza for us to eat here. They don't want anyone leaving until everything is ready to go."

I told him I was disappointed he wouldn't be able to have dinner with us. The kids always looked forward to piling their dessert plates with cookies and ice-cream when we dined at Ryan's, each of them liked to see if they could eat a bigger mountain of ice-cream than their dad. "Hey", he said, "it'll save us a few bucks. Look at it that way."

Ending the conversation with Dick, I turned to walk into the den and was startled to find Garrett standing behind me. "Mommy, why didn't you want to talk to me the other night when you were working?" he asked, referring to the nightshifts I had worked the previous week.

"When, Buddy? I always ask to speak with you and Cissy when I call from work," I assured him.

"Uh-uh. Sometimes you call and dad says you don't want to talk to us. I asked to talk to you and he said you didn't want to talk to me." Pain, confusion and a little bit of anger swirled in my little boy's unblinking blue puddles. "Why, Mom?"

"Oh, Bud, there must have been a misunderstanding. I always want to talk to you and Cissy when I'm away. I miss you when I'm away from you. Especially if you guys are home and I'm working. Maybe you asked to talk to me exactly when I had to take care of a flight. I bet that's it."

"Nope. It's happened a bunch of times. You didn't want to talk to me. Dad said it." Solidly, my seven year-old stood his ground.

"I promise you, I always want to talk to you. I would never refuse to talk to you unless I absolutely couldn't. Even then, I would call you back at the very first opportunity." I hugged and kissed him and tried to reassure him but sadness and doubt were written clearly in his expression. Garrett's behavior had become a huge concern to me. Something was obviously troubling him.

"Do you want to talk to me about something, Bud? Is everything okay at school?"

"Everything's okay, Mom. Hey, I was wondering, can I have your big brown purse to use for my detective bag? Josh and I need it for our detective business." He intentionally and quickly moved the conversation away from my line of questioning.

Garrett may not have known how to reveal the horrible source of his heavy burden, and I'm certain he felt powerless under the weight of his dad's heinous secrets, but that would soon change. Unknown and unseen to all parties involved, fate was unfolding around us, arranging a time and a place for an abused little boy to innocently shed light on a dark secret.

While we piled tennis rackets, tennis balls and ourselves into the van, I told Cissy and Garrett their dad wouldn't make it to practice or dinner that night because he had to work late. Cissy asked, "Why does dad have to work so much now? He used to never work this much." I explained the responsibilities of his position and she seemed satisfied with the answer at first, but then she said, "He acts weird sometimes when you're at work."

"Yeah, really weird," Garrett echoed.

"How so?"

Neither child answered me.

We talked about their day as we drove into town, crawling along at a snail's pace in the afternoon traffic on Tennessee Street. "Hey, there's dad's truck up there! Yay! He gets to come to practice after all!" Cissy's bright smile reflected in my review mirror.

I looked ahead at the traffic in front of me as Dick was making a left turn into the Country Cupboard convenient store. His words, "they don't want us to leave" rang in my ears. Immediately my heart began pounding a familiar rapid beat against my chest, it happened every time I caught my husband being untruthful. Thoughts and questions rushed through my head: *Why is he going to the store again? Wasn't he just here yesterday?* I could feel the jumbled pieces of the jigsaw puzzle of my life coming together, creating an ugly picture.

Without thinking about it, I flicked on my left blinker and inched the van forward in traffic, toward the entrance of the store's parking lot. By the time I turned into the lot, Dick was already inside the store.

I parked the van in front of the windows and I could see Dick standing at the counter, he appeared to be talking to the young female cashier. As I exited the van, I asked the kids if they wanted to go inside with me. Garrett decided he would go with; Cissy wanted to stay in the van.

When Garrett and I walked into the store, I was struck by the foul reek of stale coffee and cigarettes mixed with unwashed body odor. I recognized it as the same stench I had smelled on my husband's clothing lately. Immediately upon entering the store, I sensed tension. My awareness was elevated and worked without effort, trying to understand the scene before me: There were two women at the counter, the skinny, older one looked frail; she said hello. Strangely, the other one, the one talking with Little Dick, never looked at me. She appeared to be staring at something on the back wall of the store. The younger clerk's indifference and apparent attempt at becoming invisible forced my attention on her. I noticed she, unlike the older attendant, was not wearing a store uniform. Her tightly fitted shirt was cut low, and was splattered with food stains down the front. Her denim cut-offs were short and tight. Her partially exposed, stretch mark scarred stomach bulged above her waist band and hung over the front snap of her Daisy Duke shorts. Her frizzy hair was several shades of brown, red and yellow and fell in disarray around her freckled face, and hung loosely below her thick shoulders; it was unwashed and matted with oil at the scalp. The acrylic nails on her fingers were long and painted hot pink. Decals of flowers and butterflies adorned the tops of the pink polish. Every finger, including her thumbs, sparkled with tawdry costume jewelry.

"Hey girl, what are ya'll doin' here? Thought the kids had tennis practice tonight. You're going to be late, don't you think?" Dick thumped a tin of Copenhagen between his thumb and middle finger as he asked the question, unblinking.

"We saw you pull in and thought maybe you were going to be able to go to tennis practice with us after all," I replied, barely mindful of the words I spoke.

"No, I'm just getting' some things to take back to work with me."

As Dick spoke, I became aware of Garrett standing at the sales counter, looking up at the frizzy haired clerk, waving his little fingers in greeting. Somewhere in my cloudy consciousness, I realized he recognized this person. Confusion swirled about me.

"Hey." I heard my little boy say to the stranger.

Swiftly, my focus traveled from Dick to my son and back to the woman. She was ignoring Garrett and still had not taken her eyes off the back wall. She appeared to be frozen in place, a smile stitched across her yellowed teeth. Long, dirty hair fell across one eye, and I remember thinking I would be bothered by hair in my eye, unable to leave it hanging there.

Seemingly in slow motion, I watched Garrett stand on tip-toes and reach further across the counter, another attempt at getting the clerk's attention, something he would not do with a stranger. I was vaguely aware of the older clerk watching my son's interaction with the younger clerk, an odd expression played across the older clerk's craggy face.

"Hey", Garrett said again, this time a bit louder. There was still no response from the clerk, she remained motionless, fascinated with the back wall. Dick retrieved a pack of Skittles, Garrett's favorite candy, from the countertop display rack, and offered the candy to our son. *My awesome little boy showed no interest in his dad's silent bribe.*

How does Garrett know this woman? The entirety of the situation unfurling in the store felt unnatural, uncomfortable. It was as if I was watching a movie that had been split and spliced back together, out of order and out of focus. Time moved slowly it seemed, but things soon became clear. Nonsense began to make ugly sense. Red heat crawled up neck.

"Who is that Garrett?" I asked.

"Oh, that's dad's friend, Clara Faye. She goes fishing with us."

"Damn!" The grungy woman finally moved and found her voice. She slammed the store's counter with her fist and laughed out loud. She looked at Dick.

"That's not true! He doesn't know what the hell he's talking about!" Little Dick yelled and screamed, his fingers twitched.

"Yes I do," Garrett said, without looking away from his dad.

"What the hell!" Frizzy Hair was giving Dick a look of shocked disbelief. Her next sentence was directed at me with a shake of her head, "You better listen to your boy!"

The notion that we were standing in the mix of this absurdity, that we were actually a piece of it, infuriated me. My child did not deserve this. I took Garrett's hand and walked out the doors of the Country Cupboard. Dick followed us; he got into the van and sat in the passenger seat. I asked him to get out and he refused.

"I'm not leaving till we get this settled! Garrett she didn't go with us! You know she didn't go with us! She just happened to be at the lake when we got there. Don't you remember?" Dick was glaring at Garrett.

Garrett slowly moved his head from side to side. "No dad, we picked her up at the other Country Cupboard. The one by our house. You said 'don't tell mom I had a friend'. Don't you remember?"

Of the two males before me on that beautiful, warm Spring day, the only man in my presence was the seven year old boy who refused to back down from the red-faced, screaming bully.

"Fuck it! Fuck all of you! Nobody cares about me anyway!" Dick slammed the van door and walked back into the store.

"What happened in there?" Cissy's eyes were wide with fear and curiosity.

I tried to think of something to tell her, something that wouldn't hurt. I could think of nothing. Garrett spoke first.

"Dad was talking to his girlfriend, the one he told me not to talk about. *That's what happened.* Now do you believe the fortune teller?"

We were still parked in the store's parking lot; Dick was back inside the store. I could see him in there with the clerk and it ripped my heart out. When I put the car in reverse I noticed a pay phone attached to the outside wall of the store. On a hunch I decided to check the number printed in the center of the dial. I wrote the number down and when we returned home I compared it to the number which had appeared on the Caller I.D. box a few nights earlier. It was the same number.

Dick didn't come home that night.

For the past several weeks I had been on low doses of chemotherapy which required weekly trips to Piedmont Hospital in Atlanta. Dick had not accompanied me to the appointments, I had not asked him to go with me because the appointment was a full day's event and we couldn't afford for him to miss work. But the week prior my physician had requested someone accompany me on the next visit and Dick had offered to go. The day after the encounter with Clara Faye was my appointment, we were scheduled to leave our house at nine o'clock the following morning. The upheaval of the day prevented me from sleeping that night; I was upset over the turn our lives had taken in the past twenty-four hours. I fluctuated between wanting a divorce and wanting to work our marriage out. In the end, I felt that keeping our family together was the best thing for the children. I had never seen the first mistress, Dawn Downs, but I knew she was a woman who did not value family. This time, I had the displeasure of seeing, hearing and smelling Clara Faye and I knew I could not allow my children to go near her. What would happen to them if I divorced their dad? I couldn't tolerate the idea of my innocent babies spending time with her.

Throughout the night I conversed with myself over the possible reasons for this second round of infidelity. Recently I had read an article which claimed many men cheat when a spouse becomes ill. Although I was functioning at ninety percent, my health was in a grim state. So, I came to the conclusion that my health was the reason Dick had been unable to remain faithful. His fear of losing me had pushed him to another woman; this is the lie I convinced myself was true. It sounds foolish to me now, but at the time it made perfect sense.

With no word from Dick by eight-thirty the next morning, I called his employer and asked to speak with him. I waited several long minutes while Dick was called in from the junk yard.

"Hello," Dick answered the phone in a hurried tone.

"Hey. Are you still going with me today?"

"No."

"But you said…"

"I don't give a damn what I said."

Silence.

"Where did you stay last night?"

"That's none of your damn business." Abruptly, he ended the conversation.

In that moment I was finished with Dick and our marriage, all my reasons for staying were gone. And if Dick's behavior wasn't enough to convince me to leave, Clara Faye put the final straw on the camel's back a few minutes later. She called me and seemed to take pride in relaying some of the details of the times she had spent with my husband. She informed me he had taken a vacation day a week before; they went to breakfast at a nice restaurant in Atlanta, afterward they had spent the afternoon in an Atlanta hotel. She said he had taken another day off work and had taken her and her boys to Dave and Buster's for lunch. Another time he treated them to Six Flags tickets. She described the sheets on my bed and the perfume on my bathroom counter. She told me how Dick had instructed her to wait on the road near our house in the middle of the night and watch for me to leave for work so that she could park in my garage and use the key he had given her to enter my home and go up the stairs to our bedroom; while my children slept in their rooms across the hall. She told me he had spent the previous night with her and her boys and had prepared his "special Jambalaya" for dinner. Clara Faye told me she had asked her husband to leave more than a month ago, in preparation for Dick moving into her home. And her husband had obliged.

I thanked Clara Faye for the information and told her she was welcome to my husband and all of the problems that come with him. "He's yours. You can deal with the bastard and all of his lies. I'm done," I said.

Brimming with pain and fear of the future, I called to cancel my doctor's appointment and then I called my cousin Jayta. I told her Dick was having an affair with the woman Jayta had seen him talking to the day before.

Jayta thought I was playing a bad joke on her.

"I'm not teasing or joking. I'm serious."

"That girl in the Country Cupboard is nasty, there's no way Dick would be interested in her. Besides, he just wouldn't do that to you. He loves you! Everybody talks about how they wish they had a relationship like you and Dick. He's so attentive to you. He's more attentive to you than Daddy is to Mama and I never thought that was possible. You're wrong about this," she said.

Like everyone else, Jayta was unaware of Dick's earlier infidelity. My desire to keep his affair a secret had protected his image and wrapped a safe cocoon around him. His outward and open display of attention toward me created a loving photo for the world to behold. I had helped him develop such a believable lie, I was afraid no one would ever accept the truth.

I presented her with the details and left nothing out. I included the conversations I had just had with Clara Faye and Dick as well as some details of the Dawn affair. It felt good to finally tell someone the truth about the lie I had been living.

When I stopped talking, Jayta was convinced, she knew I would never make up stories so cruel. "You could knock me over with a feather right now. I would have never thought he would do something like this. And yesterday, well there was nothing in his demeanor that gave the slightest indication that he even knew that girl in the store. And boy! Was she ever nasty! And uglier than a rat that's been beat with an ugly stick! Man! He sure fooled me and you know I'm suspicious of most men! Heck, he was the one man I thought had redeeming qualities. If I wasn't sitting down right now I think I would fall over," she said.

"Do you think you could help me find out where she lives?" I asked.

"Why do you want to know where she lives?"

"I intend to take his clothes to her house."

We live in a small town and the rural community we lived in was even smaller. It didn't' take long for my cousin to get the information I had requested. Garrett had known her name and we knew where she worked, so it was as simple as making a single call. It turned out, my Aunt Mae, Jayta's mom, babysat for Clara Faye's best friend. With a call to the friend, Mae learned everything we needed to know about Clara Faye: Clara Faye was married and had two small children; she had recently "kicked her old man out" so Dick could move in; the older woman working with her at the store was actually her mother and was very much aware of the affair; Dick had recently hired Clara Faye's stepdad to work on his maintenance crew; Clara Faye lived less than five minutes from our house; Clara Faye and Dick had been involved for eight months.

I suppose a trusting relationship with a good man is a wonderful thing. Trusting a man like Dick is similar to running an obstacle course in a pair of stilettos while holding the sharp tip of a knife pressed against your throat. It's only a matter of time before you're seriously injured.

It's really difficult to write about my trust of Dick without being angry with myself. I knew better than to trust him, but I wanted to believe in him. A marriage without conviction was not the way I wanted to live. Admittedly, there had been incidents in the past few months that stirred doubt about his faithfulness, but when I voiced concern Dick accused me of "having a problem" or "being crazy." Eventually, I resolved to believe him until proven otherwise. So onward I marched with trust, blind faith and hope, into a mine field otherwise known as Little Dick Wayne Crisco.

Dick's affair with Dawn was barely over when he began the affair with Clara Faye, that realization knocked the wind out of me. He had taken advantage of my eagerness to make our marriage work; my desire to make him happy. Now I felt foolish, broken and betrayed. I decided I was done with this mess of a marriage. My husband's lies, and selfish arrogance, were too much to bear any longer. His abuse and neglect of our family was taking a toll on everyone.

Later that morning, Jayta came over and we loaded her car with Dick's clothing. Armed with Clara Faye's address and five garbage bags filled with Dick's belongings, we drove the short distance to Pine Log Road. Driving slowly by the address, I spoke haltingly, "Oh… my… God, this can't be it. *Can it?* We need to double check the address, there is no way he would move in to this place."

"Well, this is the address Stacie gave Mama. Maybe she tried to throw us off by giving us the wrong information. A stray cat wouldn't live in that place, much less sleep in there! No ma'am, this can't be the right place," Jayta said.

But it was.

Driving west past the house and circling back around, we were able to view a car parked behind the house. I had seen the same car parked at the Country Cupboard.

To say I was aghast, and shocked by the filth before me, would be an understatement. My husband usually took two showers a day and claimed to loathe dirty people and unkempt homes. If he wore a tee shirt or a pair of jeans for five minutes and then decided to change into something else, he would discard the barely worn clothing as dirty laundry, believing the clothes to be soiled. The dreadful condition of this place was appalling and appeared to be everything Dick claimed to hate. (Years later, and based on several things that had occurred during his life, Garrett would hit the nail on the head when he said, "Crisco loves what he hates"). I could not envision Dick spending time in this yard or inside this house, the waste was overwhelming. With the car windows down, Jayta and I could smell the offensive stench of rotting trash and dog feces that was scattered about the property, and we were sitting idle on the road in front of the house, not parked in the yard.

The structure was more a dilapidated shack than a house, and it had not seen a paint brush in years; it leaned slightly to the right and sat a mere fifteen feet from the road. Thick layers of dirt and grime covered the windows; shingles were missing from the sagging roof and the front porch was missing several planks. Worse than the appearance of the house was the junk and trash surrounding the property and covering the porches. Garbage was strewn about the yard, having spilled out of a heap of ripped and torn trash bags which had apparently been accumulating beside the house for months (ironically the county maintained a trash-recycle-dump station for household trash less than one hundred yards from the house). An old washing machine and a filthy and torn box spring mattress was on the side porch, two large bags of dog food, a soiled and tattered sofa and what appeared to be a car's engine added more disorder to the porch. A hairless dog, covered in open and scabbed wounds, was tethered with a link chain to a tree in the front yard. The dog was undeniably one of the most pathetic creatures I had ever seen, and from his pacing pack and forth, had worn a circular rut in the red clay beneath the tree. (Later I learned the dog was a thoroughbred Chow suffering with mange. Clara Faye had treated the mange by dipping the dog in kerosene, hence the lack of hair on the dog).

Clara Faye watched from the front doorway as Jayta and I dumped Dick's clothes onto the trash covered yard. As we were getting back into the car, Clara Faye stepped onto the porch and entered the front yard. We sped away, covering her in a swirl of dust as she ran behind us down Pine Log Road, screaming obscenities and throwing rocks at our vehicle. When I returned to my house a few minutes later, the phone was ringing. Answering the phone placed me on the receiving end of a maniac's verbal assault. I refused to listen to Dick's madness and ended the call. Immediately it rang again.

"I will not hold this phone and listen to you scream. If you have something to say to me, speak in a normal tone or I'll hang up again," I said to Dick when I answered.

"Why did you take my clothes to that house?" He was breathing heavily and I could tell he wanted to continue his verbal assault.

"Because that's where you're going to live from now on. You want that nasty redneck? You can have her. You can have her full time, not just while I'm at work or during your lunch hour. By the way, now I know why you've been talking like a country redneck. You sound just like your whore."

"I don't want her and I'm not moving there! You're believing a lying whore! What has she told you? I've never been with that woman! I've just helped her family out because her stepdad told me they were on welfare and about to be kicked out of their house. I felt sorry for them and helped them! That's all g**dammit! I don't know why she's lying about this shit! Probably cause' she wants to live in our house. But I swear to you, no one could ever take your place!"

"Dick, she described our bathroom and the sheets on our bed. She told me what time I leave for work every morning and what time I come home. And I haven't forgotten that our little boy knew her. Do you really expect me to believe you were helping her out financially when we're struggling to make ends meet ourselves? Where did the money come from? Is she the reason you claim to have nothing left of your check after 'you take care of everything'?"

"I haven't spent a damn dime on her or her kids. I got donations for that from some churches! And I still don't know why Garrett made up that story, but that's all it is! A damn story! And that woman's been stalking me! Every time I go to Lowe's she's there. When I go to Wal-Mart, she's there. When I go to Ross's Diner, she's there. All I can say is she must have broken into the house when we weren't home and that's why she can describe things in the house. I don't know what to tell you, but I didn't do this! I'm being blamed for something I didn't do!" Dick was relentless in his argument of self-defense and his blame of others.

"Dick, do you really expect me to believe this? She knows too much about you and our family. Besides, your attitude a little while ago spoke more truth than you're speaking now."

"I just acted that way because I was angry with you for not believing me. I'll tell you where I was last night! I was parked behind the Holiday Inn, sleeping in my car, trying to figure out why my wife never believes anything I say!"

"I don't believe you," I said.

"See! That's exactly what I'm talking about! You never believe a word I say."

"Dick, you've lied too many times over the years. It's hard to trust someone after they've lied numerous times. Trust is something that is earned, you know? Maybe you don't know. All I can tell you is this: I trusted you after the Dawn incident and I believed you when you told me I would never have to doubt you again. But you've lied over and over. I questioned you about some of the lies and you said I was crazy. Most of the time I ignored the lies just to avoid an argument, but I can't do this anymore. I'm finished. You've never been happy being married. You've never been happy being a parent. Now you're free. Go. Do what you want with your life but I'm getting out of this horror show and the kids are going with me."

"Fine! I haven't been screwing that whore, but since you don't believe me anyway I'll sure as hell start! That will make you happy, won't it?"

"No Dick, that won't make me happy. Honesty and faithfulness to the kids and me would make me happy."

We were renting the house we lived in and a few minutes after speaking with Dick, our landlady knocked on the front door. She informed me we were two months behind on our rent. "Dick has been promising me for three weeks he would catch the rent up. Now he won't return my calls," she said. She assured me if she didn't receive rent money within three days she would begin the eviction process. With this news, one more precarious wall of my world caved in. All pretenses fell away as I had an emotional meltdown in front of the woman. I told her Crisco was having an affair and the kids and I would be moving out of the house. She apologized for her bad timing and said she understood because she had just gone through a separation as a result of her husband's infidelity.

After the landlady left, I made some tough decisions. Then I made a call to a friend in Alabama and once again called my cousin. "Jayta, I'm going to move out of the house. I'll put my things in storage and the kids and I will stay with Mama and Daddy till I figure something out. But for the next few days we're going to visit Connie in Florence. Do you think you can help me round up some people to help pack up the house? I want to be out of here before Crisco gets off work today."

"Today?! I'm sure I can get somebody to help but I don't know about today."

"Well, let's try. I don't want to stay here another night if I don't have to. I've got to make some more calls and rent a storage unit. Please call me and let me know if you have any luck. I'll call Tunk and Amy and see if we can use their truck."

Before leaving the house I called Crisco's aunt, who lived nearby, in Canton. I told her what was going on and asked her if she could pick up Cissy and Garrett for me that afternoon, she agreed. She said they could play with her boys and she would feed them dinner, they could spend the night if needed. Then she said, "I was wondering when you would finally have enough of his nonsense. His uncle has said many times that he's surprised you put up with Dick this long. He said Dick has always been careless and irresponsible. You know you deserve better than this."

I called a couple of friends, my aunt and uncle, and a neighbor. All agreed to help and promised to meet me at my house within an hour. Everyone said they would bring boxes and packing supplies. When I returned from renting the storage facility I was shocked to see my yard full of cars and trucks. There was also a truck with a trailer hitched to the back, a very large flatbed truck and a van parked on the road in front of the house. Jayta had sprung into action and already had the crew of friends and neighbors packing up the kitchen, loading boxes into the trucks and breaking down beds. I was overwhelmed at the willingness of people to help me, some of them strangers.

Within two hours the contents of the house were packed up and relocated to the storage unit. The only items left in the house was a stuffed deer head (which somehow found itself on the back lawn), a mounted turkey and Dick's hunting equipment. A canoe was the only thing left in the garage. His remaining clothes were tossed onto the front yard, where they were urinated on by a five year old friend of Garrett's. The little boy had watched our furniture being loaded onto trucks by the movers and asked his mom why we were moving. She told him the truth. His dad had recently had a very public affair and the pain of it was still very new and real to the child. Urinating on the clothing was the only way the little guy knew to express his anger toward Crisco. It was his way of defending his friend Garrett.

Late that afternoon I retrieved my children from their great-aunt's house, from there we drove to Florence, Alabama and retreated to wooded privacy. A friend for many years, Connie and her husband lived with their two children in a secluded section of woods in North Alabama. In this part of the state, creeks and rivers meander through tall pines, creating a landscape of serenity. For me, Connie's home would be a peaceful place to regroup; I could rest in the comforting presence of a friend who would listen without judging. For my children, it would be a fun, carefree weekend, something they sorely needed. The drama and trauma of their dad's adultery would be removed from their lives for a few days. My mind and body ached with sadness for my sweet children. Their dad was puncturing their hearts and it was so unnecessary. Was it too much to expect him to consider the well-being of our kids?

A few miles from the Alabama state line, my cell phone rang. It was Dick. I did not answer. For the next twenty minutes my phone rang constantly. Eighteen times in twenty minutes. Eventually I called my mom. "Crisco is calling nonstop so I'm going to shut my phone off. I don't want you to worry if you call and I don't answer. I'll call you when I get to Florence."

"You don't want to talk to dad, do you Mom?" Cissy asked from the rear seat.

"Not right now, Sweetie. Maybe later."

"I think he has a cell phone that you don't know anything about," she said. In the rearview mirror she was looking directly at me, watching my reaction.

"Why do you think that?"

"Because when you're not home he goes to your room after I go to bed. When your bedroom door is open I see him reaching for his hat that he keeps on the top shelf in his closet. He pulls the phone out of the hat and calls someone. He always puts the hat back in the closet and goes downstairs. Then the house phone rings and he talks on it for a long time. He takes the hat with him when he leaves the house because he has the phone in it."

"Thank you for telling me Sweetie, but why did you wait until now?"

"Because I didn't want to get in trouble. Dad gets so angry with Garrett and me when you're not home," she said. My stomach knotted and tears caught in my throat when I looked at my child's battered expression. I apologized to her but I knew my apology would not put a healing balm on her tattered emotions.

When we arrived in Florence I powered on the phone so I could call my mom and tell her we had arrived safely. My phone indicated the mailbox was almost full; fifteen missed messages, all from Little Dick. The first two messages were filled with profanity and threats to have the phone shut off if I didn't return his calls. The last few messages were apologies and promises to never mess up again; claims of lies against him and lessons learned.

Once the kids and I were settled in at Connie's house, I excused myself to return Dick's calls. He answered on the first ring.

"Why did you leave?" he asked.

"I want a divorce, Dick. You've pushed me past my breaking point. I'm broken. You pushed me over the edge and watched me fall. I can't take this anymore. You've made this choice for us."

"I don't believe you. You don't mean that! I'll kill myself if I lose you and the kids. Don't do this! Where are you? Come home and let's talk about this! Please! I love you more than anything. You have no idea how much I love you. This is a nightmare. Don't give up on me, on us. I admit I've made mistakes but all of that is in the past. I'll never do it again. I promise you if it takes the rest of my life I'll make it up to you. Just come home, please!"

I wanted to believe him, but he was saying some of the same things he had said previously. He was making the same promises he had made and broken after the Dawn Affair.

"I've heard this before, Dick. I refuse to be fooled again."

"I was stupid, a fool. Clara Faye followed me around and I lost my will because I was stupid. I didn't think you loved me anymore after Dawn. That's why I fell so easily for her seduction. I swear on my life it won't happen again! Give me one more chance! Please!"

I told him I needed a day or two to think without interference from him. He promised he would allow me time to sort through my emotions. He broke that promise too. He called every half hour until I shut the phone off.

During the night I thought about the things Dick had said. His apologies and promises sounded earnest and heartfelt and I wanted to believe him. By the next morning I was allowing myself the slightest bit of hope that Dick was sincere this time. More than anything else, I wanted my family together. What if Dick was seriously ready to make a permanent change? Could I ignore the possibility?

The kids and I stayed in Alabama a few more days. They enjoyed their time playing with Connie's children but I could tell pain and worry lingered in their spirits. On the drive home to Georgia, I decided to ask their opinions of our family situation: *Did they want their dad and me to work things out? Did they want the three of us to strike out on our own?* They were young, but I wanted to know what they were thinking and how they felt. My choices would impact their lives and I felt they deserved to be part of the decision process.

Neither child immediately responded to my questions regarding their dad. After a few moments of contemplation, Cissy spoke first.

"I guess we could try again. But I don't want you guys to argue anymore. Will dad stop having a girlfriend?"

"I would only want him to stay with us if he no longer has a girlfriend. He says he was stupid for having a girlfriend and that he knows he was wrong," I told her.

"Well, I guess we should give him another chance then," Garrett said.

"I want to talk to him first. Before we get home." Cissy said.

I handed my phone to Cissy and she dialed her dad. After the initial greetings she said, "Dad, we're going to give you another chance. But you can't do what you've been doing. Do you promise me you'll stop and won't ever do it again?"

A pause…

"Ok. I love you. Bye."

"He said he's sorry and won't ever do this again," she informed us.

The remainder of the drive to Georgia was uneventful. We had lunch in Scottsboro, Alabama and afterwards both Cissy and Garrett fell asleep. I began to have doubts about my decision to stay with Dick. I wanted to believe him but given his history, it was difficult. I wanted to keep our family together but I didn't want my children to go through this heartache again. If I left him would I second guess his truthfulness for the rest of my life? Ultimately, I decided trying to work things out was the best option. I thought of our little family returning to a normal routine and it comforted me. I began to look forward to our reunion with Dick; imagining how happy he would be to see us after coming so close to losing us.

Our reunion was sweet and Dick seemed genuinely happy to have us all together once again. In the den, he sat before the children and me and vowed to "never be so stupid ever again". He told each of us how much he loved us and asked for our forgiveness. We gave it freely.

Within a few days, we had the furniture moved back into our house, and life settled into an easy rhythm once more. Dick was very attentive; he brought cards and flowers home to me, and comic and coloring books for Cissy and Garrett. I told him he didn't have to supply us with material things to express his apologies; his commitment to our family was the best apology he could give us.

One afternoon, about two weeks after the reconciliation, Garrett and I were traveling up Highway 411 after dropping Cissy off at a Girl Scout meeting, when I noticed a small, blue car in my rearview mirror. The car was coming up behind me at a very fast speed and did not slow until it was a few inches from my bumper. The car belonged to Clara Faye and she was behind the wheel, an elderly woman sat beside her in the passenger seat. Clara Faye slowed down a bit and then sped up again, steering her car into the oncoming lane of traffic. Quickly, she changed lanes again and pulled her car in front of mine. Once she was in front of Garrett and me, she slammed on her brakes; almost causing a collision of our vehicles. Even with his seatbelt strapped across him, the sudden braking of our car caused Garrett to lurch forward in the backseat and it frightened him. I slowed my speed to a crawl, to create distance between Clara Faye's car and mine. There was a gas station a mile or two up the road and if Clara Faye didn't turn in, I had already planned to stop and purchase gas. I also needed a breather; the encounter on the highway had left me nervous and angry. *How dare this crazy woman endanger my child?* I needed a few minutes to gather my wits.

Clara Faye drove past the entrance to the gas station.

"Hey Buddy, I'm going to stop for gas. After I pump would you like to go inside with me and get a Coke or an ice-cream?"

"Sure, Mom. But what's wrong with that lady? Doesn't she know dad likes us again?"

"She knows Garrett, and I think she's angry about that," I told him. "We're ok now. Wait inside the car till I pump the gas, then we'll go inside the store together."

"Can I unbuckle while you're pumping the gas?" he asked.

As soon as I began pumping the gas into my car, Clara Faye's Ford roared into the parking lot like a bat out of hades. For an instant, I feared she would ram her vehicle into my Toyota, with my little boy still inside; I had quick and vivid images of Garrett and me being pushed into the gas tanks. But the little blue car squealed to a sudden stop within a couple of feet of my car. With a flurry of motion and in a screaming fit, Clara Faye jumped from her car was soon standing before me.

"Bitch! You think you got it all worked out don't you? I got news for you! You don't know nothin' and you ain't got a damn thang worked out! He may be back at your house but he's still coming to mine! He never did stop seeing me! Even the day he moved back in to your house he came to see me! Remember when he went to the store to buy milk? Yeah? He got milk alright, but not any you gonna drank. You can't keep him in your bed. If you wuz half the woman I am you might be able to keep him! But you ain't and you never will be! I got your man, bitch! You ain't got nothin' to hold him down and you ain't gonna be able to keep us apart. My old man done accepted it and you might as well get used to it your own self!"

Until the grandmother spoke, I had not noticed her standing to my left. "No, you ain't ever gonna hold him. Like she jist tol' you, you ain't half the woman she is. If you wuz, you would a never lost him. You can't keep him from her. He done had her, you won't ever have im' agin cause he can't be the same once he had her." As she spoke, snuff spittle trickled out of the side of the grandmother's mouth.

Briefly, I stood frozen in stunned silence. When my tongue loosened itself, I told Clara Faye she should call me or meet with me privately. "I won't have this conversation in front of my son", I said.

"Are you talkin' 'bout that little brat in the backseat of your car?" She motioned violently with her head toward the rear of my car.

I followed the nod of her wild-haired head and saw my sweet, beautiful, hurting little boy with his soccer-shorts clad derriere pressed against the back passenger window, wiggling his backside from side to side. He was shaking his butt in her face. My heart broke for my brokenhearted little boy; it was his way of telling Clara Faye what he thought of her.

My troubles with Crisco and Clara Faye did not end with that encounter. Crisco steadfastly maintained he was no longer involved with her and once again I chose to believe him. For several more weeks I received harsh calls from Clara Faye or her friends. I chose not to answer her calls, but she left ugly voice messages. Sometimes she called from an unknown number and would blurt out a vulgar insult as soon as I answered. During those days technology had not advanced to blocking specific incoming callers from phones, or if it had I was unaware.

Clara Faye didn't limit her harassment to telephone calls. When I shopped, she *coincidentally* appeared in the same grocery store. Several times she appeared in my rearview mirror, following close behind my car. One day she approached me in K-Mart and with the language and attitude of a thoroughbred redneck, informed me Dick was trying to kill me. She used her entire body when she spoke, shaking her head and flipping her hair while she gestured wildly with her arms and hands.

"He's trying to kill your sorry ass and his mama is hoping he does it too. He tol' me that she tol' him she would help him hide your stinkin' body. Why you thank he's always wantin' to know where you at? He told me if I would run yo' ass off the road, wouldn't nobody ever know it was me that did it. I know you leave in the middle the night to go to work an' I know what back road you take. Why you thank I know all that? Huh? How you thank I know?" Clara Faye looked at me expectantly, anticipating a reaction. I did not give her what she wanted. I thanked her for her information, wished her a good day and casually walked away, praying my calm demeanor belied my eagerness to run away from her. Before the previous weekend I would have chalked Clara Faye's message up to the ramblings of a lunatic. But her words were unsettling and they held a hint of truth.

Early on the previous Sunday morning, Dick had asked if I wanted to go for a drive in the North Georgia Mountains. Cissy and Garrett were spending a few days with their grandparents in Arkansas; we had nothing else planned for the day, so it was an appealing idea. It was one of the rare times during the last few months Dick had asked me to share a day with him, and his invitation lifted my spirits. A spontaneous mountain drive seemed like a good way for us to reconnect.

Our Sunday drive started out like others we had taken. Dressed in jeans and tee shirts, tennis shoes for Dick and flip flops for me, I grabbed the camera and we hit the road. As usual on these types of outings, we stopped by a roadside fruit stand and picked up a breakfast of peaches, apples, bananas, nuts, honey buns for Dick and bottled water. Our conversation was light. We made frequent stops by creeks and flea markets. We browsed antique stores and visited with the shop owners. Before morning became afternoon, we had crossed over the Georgia state line into Copperhill, Tennessee. We followed the Ocoee River through Ducktown and beyond, enjoying the site of kayaks, canoes and rafts floating on the bubbly water. We traveled slowly on the sun dappled mountain roads, stopping once or twice to watch the river's activity from high up on the ridge. From a viewing area, I watched in wonder at the spectacular site of nature and man working both in unison and opposition. The last time I was in this part of Tennessee, I had been sixteen years old and at that young age I had not appreciated the tranquil, natural beauty of the Volunteer State. Dick and I sat in comfortable silence above the river and I felt complete inner peace for the first time in weeks. I wanted to linger, I would have been content to stay in that spot for the rest of the day, but Dick grew tired of the river and became restless; he suggested we resume our drive.

Around one o'clock I mentioned I was hungry.

"There is a little café just up the road here. They sell hamburgers and sandwiches, we'll get lunch there", Dick said.

"Really? How do you know? Have you been up this way recently?" I asked.

"No. I remember it from the last time Steve and me were up here". Dick's voice had a hint of frustration in it.

"That must have been more than ten years ago. The place may not be around any longer," I said.

Dick didn't respond to my comment. He had spoken with great confidence when he mentioned the store's location and now he was silent. For the first time that day, I felt uneasy. I had become adept at detecting Dick's lies, and to avoid confrontation, I seldom confronted him. Sometimes when he lied, I could pick up on a slight change in his demeanor. His words sounded truthful, but a barely perceptible change in behavior betrayed him. As soon as he mentioned Steve, I saw the change and my thoughts began to race. I assumed he had spent a secretive day in Tennessee with Clara Faye.

Dick Crisco angers quickly, he loses control of his senses. I didn't want him angry behind the wheel of the car, so I knew dropping the subject was my best bet. Besides, I wanted to believe Clara Faye was in our past. I knew Dick would never admit he had traveled with her anyway, why waste energy on an argument? Still, unsummoned feelings of betrayal surfaced as images of the two of them together played out in my mind. Questions I was unable to ask darted around my thoughts and struck my heart: When were they up here? Did they raft the river? Did they hike the trails beside the river? *I would never know because Dick would never admit the truth.*

Dick's mood had turned dark and I expected him to change his mind about having lunch with me. But soon he said, "There it is. I told you it would still be here."

As we walked into the café, Dick put his arm around my shoulders. "Let's try to have a nice lunch," he whispered in my ear. And we did, we even managed to laugh a little. He made small talk with our waitress and asked her if she could believe his "beautiful wife" had given birth to two children. "She is as beautiful as she was the day we met, maybe even more beautiful," he said to our server. Midway through lunch, Dick reached across the table and held my hand in his while he told me how thankful he was that I had not given up on him. I desperately wanted to believe him. I wanted to believe we had turned over a new leaf in our marriage.

We left the café hand in hand. "Are we going back home now?" I asked.

"Why would we go home now? There's plenty of daylight left and I wanted to drive a little more, see more of this area. We don't get to have days like this very often," he said.

"Okay, that's fine with me. I was just wondering what the plan is."

Once we were in the car, Dick's mood changed again. He became very quiet and seemed frustrated with my small talk so I sat in silence, trying not to upset him with my chatter. The sudden change in his behavior bothered me; I tried not to read too much into it. Quietly, I sat in the passenger seat and watched the green hills of Tennessee whiz by. Dick was focused on the road and had ceased his usual commentary about the nature and wildlife we saw outside the car window. We drove in solitude for another hour. I was anxious for his mood to improve and I was growing tired of seeing the same type of scenery mile after mile. Seemingly, we were driving with no apparent destination so I suggested we turn around and drive south, toward home.

"No, let's drive on a little more. What else do we have to do? Aren't you enjoying spending the day with me?" He shot me a sideways glance, his expression bothered me.

"I always enjoy spending time with you," I replied.

"Then act like it," he said.

We had driven another fifteen or twenty miles when Dick began to slow the car, I thought he was looking for a side road where he could turn the car around. From the corner of my eye I saw him use his middle finger to pull the blinker signal, indicating we were making a left hand turn. He stole a glance in the rearview mirror and very casually turned off the main road onto a single lane of asphalt. It occurred to me Dick was familiar with the road, aware of its existence. He had applied his brakes and clicked on the turn signal before the narrow road had come into view.

Initially, when he used the car's turn signal, I assumed he was going to turn around and head south toward Georgia. But instead of turning around or making a U-turn, we stayed on the road, driving deeper into the woods. Before long, the road turned from asphalt to gravel, eventually becoming a narrow strip of dirt and rocks. When Dick continued to drive into the forest, a sense of foreboding crept through me.

"Where are we going?" I asked him.

He didn't answer.

"Dick, let's turn around. Where are we going?"

"We're just driving. Let's see what's down here," he said.

"There's nothing here but thick woods and we're probably on private property. This Tercel isn't designed for backwoods, hills and dirt roads. What if we get stuck? We're miles from the nearest house or store."

Without looking at me, Dick said, "You worry too much."

"You don't worry enough! I don't like this, it scares me. Let's go back."

Dick ignored my pleas and I became even more anxious as we drove deeper into the densely wooded hills. We were already several miles from the main road and with each turn of the wheels, the road we traveled became less friendly. Rain had washed away most of the gravel and formed deep ruts and gullies in the dirt. Again, I expressed my misgivings and questioned the ability of the Tercel to handle such rugged terrain. I implored Dick to turn back.

"Just be quiet and enjoy the ride, will ya?"

In time we came upon another narrow, makeshift road fingering off to our left. Dick turned onto the road and drove the car down a steep incline. Tall oaks, pines and maples created a dark canopy over the craggy area. Scattered dapples of sunlight penetrated the darkness through small openings in the forest ceiling and caused the creek's water to glisten, creating a peaceful, picturesque scene. But I felt no peace. I sensed something was not right, my apprehension heightened and turned to fear. It was more than a fear of getting our car stuck in the middle of the woods. I felt intense fright.

Dick brought the car to a stop in an open area several feet from the creek's edge and turned to me, "You ready to take a hike, Babydoll?"

Blood and fear rippled rapidly through the veins in my neck, my heart drummed heavily against my chest. I struggled to sound calm when I spoke, praying my voice wouldn't betray me by revealing my fright, and desire to flee. "No, I think I'll stay in the car, these flip flops would make hiking a bit difficult."

"Come on baby, I'll help you. I want you to come with me. I want to spend time with you", he caressed my left thigh while he spoke to me, his touch was warm and easy, but his eyes were void of emotion.

I wanted to go with him. The part of me that always gave him a second chance wanted to believe him when he said he wanted me with him, but I sensed an overwhelming presence of evil and there was no way I was stepping out of the car.

"I really don't think I should go", I said.

His sudden interest in hiking baffled me. That he wanted to hike in a remote location concerned me. Dick Crisco and I had not hiked together since our first date back in 1983. In the years since, when I asked him to hike or walk with me he would say hiking was for "granola crunchers". "You can go by yourself, I walk enough at work", was his usual reply. Eventually, I stopped asking.

Questions and memories popped around in my head like soccer balls. Was my fear unjustified? Was I overreacting? Was Dick simply attempting to do the things I had wanted him to do for years? Was I insane, as he had previously accused? I didn't think so. God gives us intuition and basic instincts for our own protection and my instincts were warnings of danger.

"My flip flops are inadequate for hiking, I'll slip right out of them and I bet there is a mass of poison ivy in here. You know the reaction I have if I get near the stuff, right? I'll just stay here. You go on and enjoy yourself, I'll be fine." I smiled at him as I reclined the seat slightly, another attempt at appearing calm and casual. Dick studied me for a long moment before he exited the car. I was confident he had seen the pulse throbbing in my neck.

I watched Dick walk toward the creek and marveled at the changes in his girth. Dick was six feet tall, one hundred and seventy pounds when we first met. He had been very muscular from the construction labor of his job, and much too thin. Within days of our wedding, Crisco's mom began making comments about his weight. She took advantage of every opportunity to say he was too skinny, a result of my poor cooking skills. Over the years he began to put on weight, yet BJ continued to claim he was too skinny, and accused me of not preparing well balanced meals. When Dick reached a beefy two-hundred and forty-five pounds, BJ finally stopped insulting me about her son's thin frame.

Although Crisco had lost several pounds during the last few weeks, he was still pudgy. His arms and legs remained muscular and powerful, but his stomach was big and spongy and draped over his belt. I watched it wiggle as he walked at an angle away from the car. His timing and coordination were perfect, 'sure-footed' as my grandma would have said. Despite the extra weight, he was still quick and light on his feet.

I kept my eyes on Dick while I slipped my left hand into the Tercel's center console and pulled out my spare keys, the set with the pepper spray attached to a spiraled wrist band. I slid the band upon my wrist like a bracelet, and watched Crisco step onto a large rock in the center of the creek. Creek water slapped his shoes while he turned as gracefully as a ballerina on top of the wet rock. When he faced me directly, he stopped turning and stood stark still, staring at me from his perch. Dick was still handsome but his facial features were no longer sharp and defined, as they had been when we first married. His face was now thick and fleshy, the skin around his light eyes was soft and crinkled and contrasted sharply with the intense, cold look he offered me. He watched me from the rock for a couple of minutes before leaping back to the bank. When Dick began walking toward the car, I removed the keychain from my wrist and placed it beneath my right thigh. He walked slowly and deliberately and he never removed his eyes from me. He didn't blink, not even once.

By the time he reached the car I was trembling with fear, because while Dick stood on the rock and watched me, an image as vivid as a movie played in my mind's eye. The scene in my mind was not a thought I conjured up nor was it an idea that had ever crossed my mind before. The image appeared without forethought or warning: *Dick and I are walking up a sloped, moss covered hill, into the woods. We step over large rocks and fallen tree branches as we climb higher up the hill and deeper into the darkened forest. Dick is walking a couple of paces in front of me. Swiftly and suddenly he spins around, his movements have the fierce characteristics of a wild animal. There is a menacing look in his eyes as he throws me to the ground. My head lands inches from a rock. Dick Crisco uses his powerful arms to lift my head and slam it sideways against the missed rock. Dick Crisco stays with me until I stop breathing. Then he walks away.*

Dick didn't look at me when he got into the car. He fired up the engine and quickly put the car in reverse before throwing it into a forward lurch. I silently thanked God as we sped out of the woods, I don't think I took a breath until we were back on the main road. Not a word was spoken until Crisco said, "You thought I was going to do something to you back there". It was a statement. I didn't respond.

"Didn't you!?"

"No. I told you the reason I didn't get out of the car. Flip flops and poison ivy. That's all", I lied.

The ride back to Cartersville was awkward and uncomfortable. Dick was quiet and sullen, his expression blank. When I spoke he turned the volume of a country radio station as high as it would go and opened his window. It was my clue to shut-up.

There is an old Hillbilly saying, "The water won't clear up till you get the pig out of the creek". On that day, the pig was still in my creek, my water still muddy, I couldn't see things clearly. So I sat silently in that car, on the ride back to Cartersville, and berated myself for overreacting. Even before we rolled across the Georgia state line I had apologized profusely to my unresponsive husband.

There should be no fear in a husband and wife relationship. Love doesn't generate fear, where there is love there is contentment and a sense of safety. The fear I felt in the woods was genuine, I'll never forget the intensity of the sinister force I felt that day, and I should have hit the ground running as soon as I made it safely home. But I was still confused, battling an inner war with heart and mind, conflicted by what I thought was the best thing for the children and a long list of 'what ifs'. In retrospect, I clearly recognize there was no love in Dick Crisco, but at the time, I had imprisoned myself with a desire for the Cleaver's version of the American Life. Unfortunately, Dick was more similar to a threatening version of Al Bundy from *Married With Children* than Ward Cleaver.

"What's wrong with me?" I wondered, on the drive home. *"Why can't I just accept that Dick wanted to spend time alone with me? Why did I have those horrible, sinister thoughts about him? Why did I ruin what could have been a perfectly lovely day?"* I accepted his blame. Sympathy for Dick welled up in me and I tried to express remorse for my behavior.

"I'm very sorry about today," I said as we pulled into our driveway. In a flash Dick unleashed his temper, "Just shut your damn mouth! Will ya? I try to do something nice for you and you make me feel like shit! You have to ruin everything! See if I do anything else for you!"

Within a couple of days, we were back on good terms, the mountain incident was all but forgotten until my encounter with Clara Faye. Trembling like water in the wind, I left the store and drove immediately to Dick's workplace and relayed the confrontation to him. He brushed me off, "She's crazy, you know she's crazy. You can't pay any attention to what she says. Now drop it because I'm tired of dealing with this shit!"

So I dropped it and I kept quiet. I could see I had easily played into Clara Faye's schemes. I felt ridiculous for fearing Dick and his reminder of what friends and family would think if I mentioned my feelings to them, put things into perspective. "They'll think you've lost your ever-loving mind," he said.

I really just wanted to forget the whole miserable summer and move forward, but I knew we had to deal with our issues. Layers of deception and pain lay piled on top of us like a mound of heavy quilts and we would need the professional help of a marriage counselor as well as individual counseling to help us climb from beneath the weight of it all. I knew Dick thought counseling was a frivolous profession and a pointless endeavor. So with trepidation, I approached him with the idea of marriage counseling. His reaction didn't surprise me, he said he knew what his problem was and he didn't need to pay "any head shrink" to tell him what to do. I didn't want to give up that easily, I knew our family was in serious trouble and I wanted help. I called BJ and asked if she would be willing to help persuade Dick to seek help. She had been telling me for years I needed to see a therapist, so I thought she would see the need in her son as well. I was wrong. Just as she had many years before, BJ told me I was her son's only problem.

"This is just another way for you to waste money," BJ said. Dick and his mother frequently accused me of spending wastefully; it was something they had done for years. The accusations were non-founded, even ridiculous, considering I wore the same clothing and shoes year after year and most of the furniture in my house was either given to us or purchased by my parents.

As it was, I had no support from Dick's family in getting him to therapy, and at the time, my pride prevented me from asking anyone else. So, I tarried on, trying to maintain a semblance of normalcy for my children, yet feeling as if I was bound in a straightjacket while walking barefoot on broken glass. And I waited for the next bomb to drop. I didn't have to wait long.

Two years and two months after the Clara Faye Affair, a middle-aged man watched as his young, sad-eyed companion casually handed me the next explosive. The younger man had suspected his live-in girlfriend of being unfaithful, and had subsequently installed a recording device on their home phone. The first recorded call took place within minutes of the device being activated; the recording documented his girlfriend and a man making plans to meet at her apartment, the next day, during her lunch hour. Something about the male voice on the recording was familiar to the young man, but he couldn't put a name and face with the voice. The young man's girlfriend, a nineteen year-old redhead, and the male voice, referred to each other as "baby" and "babe", no names were mentioned. After listening to the tape several times, the young man placed a call to his dad and asked to borrow a video camera, explaining his unpleasant predicament. The dad was eager to help.

A plan was hatched. The younger man would return to the couple's apartment a few minutes before lunch the following day and set up the camera. There were two bedrooms in the apartment, and a decision was made to hide the camera in the master bedroom, because the other bedroom belonged to the couple's two-year-old daughter. He doubted any activity would take place in the toddler's crib.

The night before the rendezvous, the twenty-one year-old young man surveyed the room he shared with the nineteen year-old girl. He noted the bed's mattresses were level with the flat surface of a cluttered desk. The desk stood across the small room, a few feet from the bed. For the first time since moving in together, he was thankful for the girl's poor housekeeping skills, as the clutter and clothes littering the desk would provide a perfect hiding place for the video camera.

The next afternoon, father and son waited in a borrowed car, watching the apartment from across the parking lot. They witnessed the young woman pull into the lot and park her vehicle. She exited her car, alone, and entered her building. The young man breathed a deep sigh of relief, believing she had changed her mind about the afternoon encounter. The boy wanted to leave, return to work, but his dad said they should wait a minute or two longer. Before his dad completed the sentence, a truck, being driven by a man wearing a baseball cap, entered the complex and parked in the far west corner of the lot. The man left his truck and entered the breezeway of one of the buildings, although not the building where the young man resided with the girl. The younger man knew immediately it was a ploy intended to create deception, in the event others were watching. The younger man had no doubts about this, because as soon as the truck entered his line of vision, he had recognized it and immediately connected the voice on the tape to the man in the truck. It was his wife's supervisor, Mr. Dick Crisco.

The younger man's knee-jerk reaction was to run across the parking lot and barge into his apartment, confronting his common-law wife, and Dick, on the spot. But the older man, recognizing his son's pain, and understanding pain and anger could entwine and create a hellacious scene, placed a gentle but heavy hand on his son's arm and advised him to stay put.

"You've set up the video. Let's see how it plays out", he said to his son.

So, for what was an eternity to the younger man, the two waited and they watched, until finally Dick left the apartment, followed shortly thereafter by the girl. Later, the young man told me her red hair was "shining in the sun like new copper" when she left the apartment and walked to her car. And he wanted to cry. He had always loved her hair, but now the sight of it made him sick. Knowing Dick Crisco had just had his hands in her hair and on her body, was almost more than he could bear to think about.

Father and son entered the apartment and retrieved the video from the camera, they shoved it into the VCR and settled onto the sofa for the viewing. For several minutes the video revealed nothing but the couple's quiet, messy bed. Both men were surprised at the clarity of the film, there were no dark or shadowy places on the screen. The walls of the room were the generic white of cheap apartments, the windows were absent of curtains, covered only with ill-fitted blinds, allowing natural light to fill the space. If a person were to enter the field of the camera lens, there would be no mistaking their identity. This was something the young man had not anticipated. Indeed, he had actually been worried about poor lighting, considering the only electrical light in the room was a small table lamp beside the bed. He had been concerned the bright light coming in through the windows would create a hazy effect on the film. It had not.

The two men watched the tape in its entirety. The younger man did not return to work that day. He had wanted to go the metal recycling yard where his girlfriend and Dick worked and confront the illicit pair. His dad, fearful that humiliation, adrenalin and the raging testosterone of a twenty-one-year-old would affect the boy's judgment, stayed with him throughout the day and convinced him to try a different approach.

On that same sunny afternoon, while father and son, strangers to me, were watching their home movie, I sat in a chilled theater with my own children, watching Muppet Treasure Island. I had spent the last three days being treated with Intravenous Immunoglobulin and Methotrexate infusions, doctors advised me to rest and stay out of the sun. My children had been so sweet and understanding during my treatments, not once complaining about sitting around the house for three days. So on the first day free of nurses and needles, I decided a day away from the house, in a dark and cool movie theater, would be a treat for the kiddos. I wouldn't exert too much energy, nor would I be exposed to sunlight for any length of time. It would be a pleasant afternoon for the three of us. And it was affordable, it was Dollar Day at the Movies.

Before leaving the house, I opened my Day Planner so that I could double check my schedule, as well as that of my children. There had been so many doctor's appointments lately, I was afraid I may have overlooked something on my agenda. The kids were both on a local competition swim team, and I was fearful the medications had fogged up my recall of dates and appointments. There were no appointments written on the day's date, August 18, 1998, but there was an apology, a handwritten note to me from Dick:

"To my beautiful Danita. I'm sorry about blowing up last night. I love you more than anything and I'm so thankful to have you. There is no one else like you. XOXO Dick"

Cissy and Garrett and I munched on popcorn and Cokes, and laughed at the silly antics of Kermit and Fozzie Bear. We were having a great time. And then, without prelude, smack in the middle of Miss Piggy's grand Boom Shakalaka entrance on the back of an elephant, a familiar and ominous feeling quietly began to niggle at the corners of my senses. It wasn't yet a thought, just a feeling, and I tried to push it away. I hated the feeling for interrupting the afternoon, and I refused to allow it to get to me. I said a silent prayer, in the hope of holding the feeling at bay:

Father in Heaven, I don't like what I'm feeling. I don't like feeling this way about Dick. He promised he would stay true to our family and as far as I know, for two years he has been faithful. But something has caused a feeling of distrust and concern to rise up in me. I don't understand where the feeling is coming from. I've felt it before, in the days of Dick's affairs and I don't like it. So I'm asking you to take it away from me. If I'm conjuring up fantasies, as Dick has accused before, then please take them away from me and remove them for evermore, because You know I want a happy and stable family for my children, and these feelings aren't happy ones. Likewise, if there is something I am feeling but not seeing, and then I ask You to show me. I've made excuses for my husband's behavior in the past and I don't want to do that anymore. So if he is up to his old ways, please show me. But Lord, You know me and You know I need undisputable truth. Otherwise, I will continue to make excuses for him. So, if he is up to it again, please show me. And if he isn't, and I pray to You he isn't, then I need undisputable truth of that as well. Because I don't think this feeling is going to go away otherwise. Thank You for Your life, thank you for my family and forgive me for my sins. Amen.

"Will you order us a pizza for dinner, Mom? I think you look tired today and shouldn't cook", Cissy said.

We were in the car, on our way home from the movies. I *was* feeling tired from the medical treatment, and drained from my earlier worry. "You must have read my mind Sweet Girl! What kind of pizza would you guys like?"

"Yay! Pizza Pizza! Meat Lovers please, with black olives," Garrett said.

"Just black olives on one side, please. Extra cheese on my side", it was Cissy speaking.

As soon as we walked in the house, I ordered the pizza, changed clothes and began sorting through the day's mail. That's what I was doing when the phone rang.

"Hello."

"Danita?"

"Yes."

"Danita Crisco? Married to Dick Crisco?"

"Yes."

"I really hate to bother you like this. You don't know me, my name is Charles Stevens, my daughter-in-law, common-law daughter-in-law, Amanda works with your husband."

"Yes, I've met Amanda. Is she okay?"

The previous week Dick told me Amanda and her husband were having difficulties affording food and clothing for their little girl. He asked if I could sort through the clothes Cissy had outgrown and pass them on to Amanda's little girl. By way of Dick, I sent her two large bags of clothing. A few days after I sent the clothes to Amanda's little girl, Dick said Amanda wanted one of the puppies our dog had recently delivered. I was happy one of our puppies would have a little girl to love him, but I was confused by the request. "If they can't afford to feed their baby, why would they want a puppy? Another mouth to feed?" I asked.

Dick responded by telling me Amanda's husband had received a job offer at the local cable company and was now making much more money.

"Is she ok? Is the puppy causing too much trouble?"

"Uh, yeah, she's ok. My son isn't though. Look, I don't know how to say this but I've got something I think you need to take a look at. Now listen, what I'm about to say to you may cause you to cuss me out or you may want to hang up on me. But please, hear me out. I don't know how to say it except to say it. Amanda and Dick are sleeping together".

His words were iced water and boiling water pouring over me all at once. I was freezing and burning hot. I felt as though I was being submerged in a pool of hot lava then tossed into the Arctic Ocean, drowning. My heart raced and pounded heavily in my chest. My tongue turned thick and dry inside my mouth, but I heard myself ask, "Are you sure?" and I wondered why I bothered asking.

"Yes, Ma'am, without hesitation I can tell you they are screwing. But if you need proof, I have it on tape. I'll be happy to meet you in a public place and give you a copy of the video. I have some other proof that may help you believe me. I can tell you that piece of shit has got a tan line from hell. Evidently he's out in the sun a lot without a shirt on."

"Yes, he is outside very often. He likes to fish. Oh my lord, I'm finished this time."

"What do you mean when you say "this time"? You mean he's done this before?"

"Yes. Several times."

"Why in God's name have you stayed with him?"

"I don't know, stupidity I guess. He always promises to change and I always have faith in his promise. Plus, I have to protect my kids from being exposed to his trash. But this is it, the kids and I can't do this anymore."

Dick was due home soon, so Mr. Stevens and I made plans to meet the next afternoon in the parking lot of a local store. He and his son would deliver to me a copy of the video. To burn nervous energy, I began throwing some of Dick's clothes into a laundry basket. While I pulled his clothes out of drawers I thought about something Dick said the night before. "One of the women from work wants me to drive a boat for her this Saturday. It's her little girl's ninth birthday and she's rented a boat to take her daughter and some of her little friends out on the lake. She thought I could drive and she could keep an eye on the girls. She's never driven a boat before and I didn't want to say I wouldn't do it. I hope you don't care."

My mind had raced with anger at Dick's abrasive lack of consideration for our own children, I reminded him they had a swim meet that Saturday. Dick is a careless driver on land and on water, and I told him I thought taking a bunch of kids out on a boat would be asking for trouble. I suggested this woman must lack common sense, "Why would a woman who has never driven a boat rent one for a group of nine year-old girls"?

Dick exploded, "All you think about is yourself! You're so fucking selfish! This is a little girl who doesn't have a dad. Why can't you think of her instead of yourself?"

"I'm thinking of our kids and your liability! Because I think of my family first", I had said.

While I was in the closet gathering Dick's clothes, Cissy came to the door, "Dad is on the phone, Mom. He said he has to work late and wants to speak to you."

"Please tell him I can't come to the phone right now, Sweetie."

In a few minutes she was back, "Dad said to tell you he loves you and he'll see you around nine tonight."

I called Mr. Stevens and told him Dick would not be home before nine that evening and asked if he could meet me with the tape that night instead of the next day. We agreed to meet at Wal-Mart in half an hour. Later that evening, with my kids tucked into bed, I watched a horror film. Dick and Amanda's rendezvous was a "wham, bam, thank you ma'am," kind of moment, with Crisco ending the encounter by asking Amanda why she hadn't made lunch for him. It was heart-wrenching and disgusting and it was obvious the two had been together before: there was no hesitation between them, no awkwardness. They were very familiar with each other.

I did not cry when I watched my husband having sex with the nineteen year-old girl. The video sickened me and proved I was married to a disgusting, soul-less pervert. The video was the undisputable truth I had asked for earlier in the day.

I thanked God for answering my prayers so quickly, even though it wasn't the outcome I wanted. I said a few quick prayers under my breath, *"Help me to have strength both physically and mentally; help me to be strong for my children; and Lord, even though I don't want him in our lives, Dick is the father of my children, so please help him to become a better man."* Instantly, and that is not an exaggeration, I was overcome with more mental strength and clarity than I had felt in years. A feeling I cannot describe as anything other than raw strength and assurance formed in the crown of my head and cascaded through the rest of me. It wasn't physical strength of power I felt, it was more like a strong force flowing through all of me, body and mind.

When Dick came home that evening, I was sitting at the kitchen counter, absently perusing a Southern Living magazine.

"Hey Baby doll, did you have a good day?" He kissed me on the lips and hugged me.

"I had an eventful day."

"The movie was good?"

"Yes. Did you have a nice lunch? I noticed you forgot the spaghetti and meatball plate I fixed for you."

"I know and I've been kicking myself all day, my mouth was watering for your spaghetti and I'm about to eat it now because I'm starving. I had a horrible lunch. I had a hot dog from the sandwich truck that comes around. I'll never eat from that truck again, I've had gas all day and night."

"So it wasn't any good?"

"No, not at all. But then nothing is good when I compare it to your cooking."

"How about Amanda? Was she good?"

I made certain I had eye contact with Crisco when I asked him about Amanda. The slight hint of surprise in his expression would probably have been undetectable had I not been watching so closely, but Dick recovered quickly and as usual, landed on his feet.

"I don't know and don't care how Amanda was. Why would you ask a stupid question like that? She's a kid, a short little redneck kid and she's married, with a kid of her own. Don't tell me you're going to start this shit again. I thought you were finished accusing me of stuff. You promised me you would never accuse me of anything like that again. This is really hurting me. It hurts like hell when you think bad things about me", he mumbled unintelligibly as he turned to go to our bedroom.

"Where are you going, Dick?"

"To bed, I'm not listening to your stupid accusations. You're crazy Danita. You need help. Somebody, somewhere, sometime in your life messed you up and that's why you can't trust me! I love you more than anything and it rips me up to know you don't trust me. You'll never know how much I love you. I don't know why you don't know how much I love you."

The lies spilled out of his mouth as easily as if he were reading a nursery rhyme. Lies had always been easy for Dick, and in the past I would become very frustrated with him when I knew he was lying; frustrated because I could never trip him up in his lies, never get him to admit the truth. He could spin a web of deceit more intricate than a spider's web. He would snag me in the sticky web and no matter how hard I fought to remove the web of lies, he always won. I was never able to persuade him to tell the truth, our arguments usually went unresolved and ended with Dick on the sofa watching television while I steeped in frustrated anger. So I was surprised when I realized serenity was gliding through, surrounding me during this non-serene hour. Inherently, I had always known God was with me, but tonight, I actually felt His physical presence. I knew He was looking out for my children and me, I knew we were going to be ok. I was uncertain of the future, but without doubt, I felt a supernatural mental strength that could have only come from God. There was a strong, spiritual presence *standing beside* me that could have only been Him. I had never felt anything like it before.

I didn't react to Dick's twisted commentary. Instead, I calmly said, "Dick, you're not going to bed in this house. You're leaving."

He spun around quickly and pointed his index finger at me, "Like hell I'm leaving! You can leave! Why would I leave my own home?"

"You're leaving because I'm tired of your behavior and your lies. You had sex with Amanda today and I know you did. And you're leaving because I'm tired of the evilness you bring home with you. When you walk in the door Satan walks in with you and he closes the door behind you. I can't raise Cissy to be the kind of woman she needs to be or marry the kind of man who will love and respect her, as long as you act the way you do. And how can I teach Garrett to be the kind of man he should be when you act like a sick, sex addicted maniac? No, you're leaving and you're taking your devil with you. These kids deserve better than this. I deserve better. If you want other women, if you want to behave like a single man, fine. You can be a single man. You've got it. You can have the life you've always wanted and I'll have a good life with my children. That's all I want. I'm finally letting go, Dick. I don't care about making a life with you any longer. You have proven to me, multiple times, that you do not want this family. You have your freedom now, so please, just leave."

"You have lost your fucking mind! I did not have sex with that ugly little redheaded bitch! My God, she's a kid! And I would not do that to you and our kids again! Never! Who's telling this shit? I'll kick their damn teeth in! I'll stick my boot so far up their ass they'll have to pull it out of their mouth. Who's saying it, that damn aunt of yours or Tammy?"

"You told me Dick. You showed me."

"What the hell are you talking about?" He shook his head and placed his hand on his hipbone, "I should have listened to mom when she told me you were crazy because you *are* crazy g**dammit! A lunatic! You're a damn crazy ass liar, I haven't shown you anything! Other than work, I haven't been anywhere near that girl so there is nothing for you to see!"

If I had not seen the video of my naked husband in bed with Amanda, I would have believed his lies. His anger and indignation would have convinced anyone of his innocence and my insanity. He was that believable. But I had seen the film with my own eyes, heard his voice with my own ears; a voice I knew better than my own. There was no way around the truth.

"Dick, there is a video of you and Amanda. Her boyfriend and his dad recorded you and Amanda having sex this afternoon. You can't concoct a story and dig your way out this time. You don't have to admit it, I don't care if you don't admit it. You can continue to put together your artificial stories all you want. I know the truth, I've seen the video. You need to leave this house."

"I'll never admit to something I haven't done! You're fucking crazy! There's no tape and you know there isn't! You can go to hell and take your bullshit with you!". Dick glared at me from the crazed eyes of a man losing control, yet I didn't feel the familiar fear of his temper. As far as I was concerned, Dick's words were just moving air around the room.

"She didn't take her shirt off", I began. "She was wearing yellow, leopard print panties that you pulled off and tossed across the room; black nail polish on her toes, a tattoo on her ankle, the sheets on her bed are green and you asked her why she had not made lunch for you. Now leave, because you are no longer welcome here."

He knew he was busted, and he realized a smoothly woven story would not replace the truth this time. He picked up his laundry basket and walked to the door, placed his hand on the knob and turned to face me. He looked at me expectantly, because in previous arguments when he was ready to storm out the door, this is the point I would ask him to stay. I would ask him not to leave. I would tell him we should work things out for the sake of the kids. He got none of that from me tonight.

Dick hesitated at the door, "Well, I'm leaving and I'm not coming back."

"I don't want you to come back. You are no longer welcome here."

He opened the door and looked back once more, then he was gone. It was late, a weeknight and I knew my mom had to work the next morning. I called her anyway, I knew she wouldn't mind.

"Hello."

"Hey, Mama."

"What's wrong, Danita?"

"He's at it again."

"Oh no! What is he thinking? What's wrong with him? Who is it now? Is it that Clara Faye again?"

I relayed the day's events to her. She asked what Cissy and Garrett were doing and she offered to come to my house.

"No, I'm ok. He's gone and I'm finished with him for good. The kids are in bed already. As far as I know, our argument didn't wake Cissy or Garrett, neither have come out of their rooms, so I'm sure they're still sleeping."

"Oh my God, I can't believe this is happening again. He's sick, Danita. There is something wrong with him. Bad wrong. That's all I can come up with. Every time ya'll start to move forward financially and make some headway, he pulls this shit. It's like he doesn't want to be successful or make life easier for the kids. What are you going to do?"

"I don't know for certain what I'll do, but this much I do know; he will not do this to me again because I'm going to divorce him. And I know the kids and I will be ok. I feel stronger than I've felt in years", I said.

"Oh me, I forgot all about you just completing that treatment. And the doctor told you to keep the stress down and not overdo anything. To think he was doing this while you were at home hooked up to IV's. That is low down and sorry if you ask me. Are you sure you don't want me to come to Cartersville?"

"No, I'll be ok. I'm going to call Jean and then I'm going to bed and I will sleep. My stomach isn't turning and churning like in the past. I'm not nervous or worried. I don't feel broken and worthless this time. I feel strong."

"I hear the strength in your voice. But oh my God, those poor kids. Why does Dick have to put them through this over and over and over? He couldn't have asked for two better kids than those two. They are so pitiful, and they love him so much. Does he not ever stop to think of what his cheating does to them? You know, they're little now and they forgive easily. But one day, well one day I guess they'll continue to forgive him because of the kind of kids they are. They may forgive, but they won't ever forget because you don't forget this kind of abuse. One day they'll be grown and they won't allow him to pour his shit on them anymore."

We said goodnight.

"Call me if you need anything. One more thing, I'm glad those two babies have you. You're a good mom, Danita. Dick Crisco should thank his lucky stars to have married somebody like you. I don't care how high he looks or how low he looks, he won't ever find better kids or a better wife than what God has already given him. I love you."

We said goodnight again and I called Jean in Cheyenne. By this time it was 1:30 AM in Georgia, 11:30 PM in Wyoming, it was late and I knew Jean would be sleeping, but we have the kind of friendship where the hour on the clock doesn't matter.

She saw my number on the caller I.D. and answered with a groggy greeting, "What's wrong?"

"Dick."

"Oh no," she groaned. "Not again."

"Yep."

I relayed the ugly details to my friend; she listened without interruption until I stopped talking.

"Now what?"

"I'm finished. Done. Over and out."

"Well, I must say, you sound stronger and better than you have in times past. You know I'm here if you need anything."

"I know. Thank you, I guess I just need you to pray."

"You know, you and I love our kids and I think we are pretty dang good mothers and wives. We are happy when our families are happy, we're loyal to our family and we would never cheat on our husbands. How did two girls like us end up with selfish men who cared more about themselves than their children?"

"That's a mystery we'll never solve," I said.

Early the next morning the phone rang, the LCD screen displayed Dick's work number. I let the phone go unanswered.

I decided to clean the house, at first glance, it didn't look dirty but it felt dirty. I started cleaning in the master bathroom where, along with one of his nasty spit cups filled with the foul-smelling spittle of saliva and Copenhagen, I found two pair of Dick's dirty underwear, discarded on the floor. "He's never cared about the extra work he creates for me", I thought as I put the spit cup in a plastic bag. I walked out of the bathroom into the bedroom and began stripping the sheets from the bed. I saw a sock peeking out from underneath Dick's side of the bed. I bent down and found several dirty socks, several pair of dirty underwear, dirty tee shirts and three old spit cups filled with napkins and spit. *All shoved under the bed.* An idea came to me and I quickly reacted. I gathered up Dick's dirty socks and underwear, I walked through the house and found several more repulsive spit cups. I placed all the items together in plastic bags. I put the bags in the trunk of my car and then I woke the kids for breakfast, before taking them to the Dellinger Park pool for swim team practice. I told Cissy and Garrett I wouldn't stay for practice, but would return before it ended.

On a mission, I drove from the pool to the recycling yard where Dick worked. When I pulled through the gates I noticed Dick on the far side of the yard, working on a piece of machinery. Amanda's car was parked beside the office. I parked my car in front of the office and retrieved the bags of spit and dirty underwear from my trunk and entered the front doors of the main office. Amanda shared office space with two other women and two men. All of them knew me and all looked surprised when I walked to Amanda's work area and dumped the contents of the bags onto her desk.

"Gross!" said poor Amanda.

"If you want to screw my husband then you can wash his dirty underwear and pick up his disgusting spit cups too. And just so you know, sometimes he pisses on himself in his sleep", I said.

"Humph!" Poor Amanda again.

The others stood around the room in stunned silence. I turned and walked out the same way I walked in.

Dick was walking toward my car as I was driving out of the junkyard. He stood in the middle of the road, forcing me to stop. He walked to the car and got in on the passenger side. "Why won't you answer the phone? I've been calling you all day," he said.

"I don't have anything to say to you."

"But I love you. I can't lose you and the kids. I've messed up. I know I've messed up, but I'll make it up to you if you let me."

"No Dick. We're over. I can't play this sick game of yours any longer. Please get out of the car. I'll put the rest of your clothes in bags and leave them on the front porch. You can get them when you're ready."

"I'll kill myself if you don't let me come back home. I swear to you I'll kill myself."

"You're too selfish to kill yourself Dick. But if it's what you have to do, then do it. I refuse to let you play with the kid's emotions, my emotions, any longer. I've given you numerous chances and forgiven you multiple times. I've got nothing left, nothing that I want to waste on this fake marriage. Please get out of my car."

"No! I'm not getting out until you say you want me back."

"I'm not saying that because I don't want you back. If you don't get out then you'll go with me because I'm not staying here, and I won't bring you back to get your truck. You'll have to call Amanda to come get you." I accelerated toward the front gate of the property.

"Ok. Stop. I'll get out."

When the kids and I returned to the house that afternoon, the phone was ringing.

"Do you want me to get the phone, mommy? It's dad," Cissy said.

"You can answer if you want to Sweetie, but I can't talk. I've got things to do."

She didn't answer the phone, instead she came to me and placed her arms around my waist. "Dad's doing it again, isn't he mom?"

I tried to think of something to say, something that would take away the pain in her eyes. But what would that be? What could I say that would put a healing balm on her wounded heart?

"I heard him on the phone the other day. And I heard your argument last night. He's not going to change mom. He's done this multiple times. He's never going to stop doing this. We need to forget about him." Cissy let her gaze lock on mine, she was a little girl, but she had more wisdom regarding her dad's careless behavior than I had, and I was thirty-eight years old.

That evening, after dinner and baths and bowls of ice-cream, Cissy and Garrett climbed onto the tall Queen Anne bed I had shared with their dad since we were first married. Both kids were quiet for a few minutes, solemn while I scratched their backs. I knew their minds and hearts were full of unspoken worries. I waited for them to share their burdens with me. Cissy spoke first.

"I don't want dad to come back mom".

"I only want him to come back if he will promise to never, ever do this stuff again", Garrett said.

"He will do it again Brub. He always has. He'll say he won't do it again, but he will. You know he will. And he's always so angry. He's angry about everything we do", Cissy said.

"I guess you're right. Why does dad have to be that way Mom? Other dads don't do this stuff. Why does he want to spend time with other people's kids instead of Ciss and me?"

Their comments and questions crumpled my heart and stole my breath. Words were frozen on the back of my tongue, I didn't know how to respond to my hurting children. The anger I felt toward their dad, the source of their pain, made me want to peel his face off with my bare hands. I wanted him to hear the heartache of his children. I wanted him to know his little girl had lost faith in him. But I knew, even if they expressed themselves to him, he would have no empathy for their pain. Two years earlier he had walked away from Garrett and into the home of a woman and her children, while Garrett cried and begged him to please come home with us. He had turned his back on Garrett and kept walking while the woman and her kids stood at her front door and waited for Dick to come to them. *Surely to goodness Hell has a room designed especially for men and women who neglect and abuse their children. Whether the abuse is emotional or physical, hurt passed from a parent to his child penetrates the soul.*

The three of us sat on the bed and watched a sitcom or two. I asked if they wanted to sleep with me, have a slumber party. Cissy said she wanted to sleep in her own bed, Garrett said he wanted to sleep with me. Before sliding off the bed, Cissy kissed her brother and me goodnight, and as she left to go to her room I picked up the TV remote, searching for a news channel. I skipped past a young preacher on a regional cable channel, but something he said had intrigued me and enticed me to go back to his station. He was talking about how the choices we make can ruin or improve our lives. He spoke about how he had come out of an addiction to drugs after giving his life to Christ. His name was Lance and he mentioned his church was in Ball Ground, GA. Ball Ground wasn't too far from Cartersville...*perhaps the kids and I could go there on Sunday,* I remember thinking. At the close of his sermon, he said prayer lines were open and posted a phone number on the screen.

"Mom, can I please call that number and ask them to pray for Dad?"

I hadn't realized Garrett had been paying attention to the broadcast. "Of course, Buddy."

I can't describe the whirlwind of emotion I felt as my nine year-old boy picked up the phone and called a stranger, seeking help for his dad. Was it possible Dick did could not feel the love his children and I had for him? Worse, did he see and feel our love but simply not care? I didn't know.

I listened to Garrett's side of the conversation as he sat like an Indian Chief on the bed:

"Hello…Garrett…Garrett Able…. I'm nine. Yes…I need for you to pray for my dad. No, he's not sick…he's been bad…he's a bad dad and he yells at my mom and my sister and me because he has girlfriends even though he's married to my mom. He likes his girlfriends and their kids more than he likes us. I don't want him to have girlfriends anymore and I don't want my mom to cry anymore…I don't want him to get angry all the time for no reason. A bunch of stuff, but that's all for now I guess…… yes she's here….OK, let me tell my mom….Mom, she's going to pray with me and then she wants to pray with you….Ok Patti, I'm back… (long pause)…Amen. Here's the phone Mom."

"Hello."

"Ma'am, my name is Patti and that's an awesome little man you've got there."

"Yes, thank you, he is, he's a very good boy, a precious boy."

"Well, it's obvious he loves his family and wants his dad to change. And from the sound of it, his dad hasn't been all that great. But lady, I want to say that you or somebody has done a good job in raising Garrett. I don't think I've ever talked to a nine-year old who really understood that he could ask and receive help from our Lord. Even at nine, he realizes his dad's behavior is wrong. Let me ask you this, did you encourage him to call us?"

"No, it was Garrett's idea."

"Wow. Okay, well if it's alright with you, I would like to pray with you now," Patti said. And she did. She said a beautiful prayer for our family, asking God to change the heart of my husband and make him a whole man.

Patti invited us to call back anytime and asked if it would be ok if she followed up with us later in the week. She gave me scripture to look up. She told me to study and pray God's word. I thanked her and placed the phone on the table beside the bed.

"Well Mom, everything's going to be ok. I asked Jesus to save Dad and make dad like us more than he likes those other kids and their moms."

I pulled my son into an embrace and told him he was special and how much I love him. Then I went into the shower and permitted hot, steaming water to scorch my skin, and I cried. I cried for the heartbreak of my children and for the broken self-esteem their dad's behavior would surely cause them. I cried for the loss of our family and the loss of a dream. I cried because I had been so easily fooled and had then become so foolish. I cried until I was sick.

When I returned to bed, Garrett sleepily said, "Dad called while you were in the shower mom. He wants you to call him on his cell phone."

"Thank you little buddy. Get some sleep, ok?"

I didn't return Dick's call. He called several more times during the night and I left all of his calls unanswered. The next morning I checked our voicemail and heard him professing sorrow for his stupidity. He said he wanted to see the kids.

After their morning meal, I told Cissy and Garrett their dad wanted to see them. Both sat silently at the kitchen counter for several long seconds. Cissy spoke first.

"Ok. I'll see him."

"Me too," Garrett said.

Later that morning we drove to the recycling yard, Dick met us near the front entrance. He told me I looked beautiful and then he turned to face our children, both sitting in the back seat.

"Hey guys. I miss you. I love you," he said.

They responded with sad stares and silence, distrust written in their expressions.

"I'm sorry about all of this. I love you two and your mom more than anything in the world. It will kill me if I lose you," he said.

Tears formed in Garrett's eyes.

Anger burned white hot on Cissy's face, "If you love us then why do you do the things you do? You hurt us dad!" Angry tears puddled in her eyes and poured down her face.

"I swear to you, I will never do anything like this again. I promise you on my life I won't be stupid anymore. I just want to be home with the three people I love the most."

"I want to believe you dad. But I don't." Cissy said.

"What about you Buddy? Do you believe me?"

Garrett's face was scrunched in agony, his eyes were closed tightly in an effort to hold back the tears. But the tears fell anyway. In response to his dad's question, he shook his head and softly said, "No".

The three of us left the recycling yard and went through the motions of everyday life the best we could: we went to a swim meet, we shopped for milk and bread, we rented a movie and grilled hamburgers. On Saturday evening I told the kids we would be visiting a new church the next morning, leaving our house early because the church wasn't in Cartersville.

Dick continued to barrage me with calls and I continued to let them go unanswered. I knew if I spoke to him he would have a better chance of wearing me down and pulling me back into his sticky web of indecency. I was finished with his dirty life. For the first time in years I was beginning to feel clean, and it felt good. Strangely, until then, I had not realized I was soiled.

Around 2:30 on Sunday morning, August 23, 1998, I was startled from restful slumber, immediately frightened. It was difficult to hear above the loud, pounding heartbeat in my ears, but I could tell someone was in the house. I heard the sound of soft footsteps creeping over the hardwood floor. Adrenaline propelled me to my feet and to the far side of the bed.

"Whoever you are, you're about to get your head blown off!" I yelled (I didn't know where the guns were or how to load them, even if I could have found them).

"Baby! It's me", the serpent, I mean Dick, hissed. "I need to talk to you. Please, just hear me out. Please listen to me and then I'll leave if you still want me to." Dick's silhouette appeared in the doorway to our bedroom, filling the space.

The adrenaline left me as quickly as it had rushed in, and I felt weak and wobbly because of it. "Just leave. I don't want to hear your lies and I don't want to argue," I said.

Dick perched on the side of the bed, "Please, baby doll, just listen to me and then I'll go. Please, sit here beside me for a minute and hear me out."

I did not want to listen to him, but with his insistence I reluctantly caved.

"Ok. Talk."

"Something's changing in me Danita. I've seen what my life will be without you and the kids. Last night I was playing cards with Doug and some of his friends. We were in Doug's camper because Doug's wife has kicked him out. Everybody was sitting around drinking and talking bad about their wives and kids and I looked around and realized that where we were and what we were doing was a lot worse than being with our families. I was miserable and I think they were all miserable too. But we were all trying to act like we were having the best time of our lives. And I realized I could still be doing this in ten, fifteen or twenty years from now and my family will have moved on, gone on without me. I don't want that. I want to be here with you and the kids. We belong together."

Dick paused, I didn't respond. He continued, "I tried to sleep up in the top of the camper. I couldn't stop thinking of you and the kids here at the house. I kept wondering what you were doing. I could see you in the kitchen, making dinner and I cried. I could see Garrett with his water boots and shorts on, wading in the river. I could see Cissy flipping on the trampoline and cuddling her puppy. And I wanted to be here with you. I finally went to sleep but then I woke up with a burning sensation down my legs and back. Fire ants were all over me and I felt like it was a warning of some kind. Now, I know you won't believe me, but I think God is trying to tell me something."

"Ok, now you're going to be like an inmate and find Jesus?"

"No! It's not like that. I'm telling the truth. Something is changing in me. I want to be a better man for you and a better dad for Cissy and Garrett. Please give me a chance."

"Dick, you've had so many chances to get it right. And you've blown each and every one of them. You haven't cared enough to get it right in the past, why should I believe you now? Do you realize the hell you've put me through and how many times I've forgiven you? You have taken me for granted since the day we married, Dick. I cannot do this anymore! I won't do this anymore! Get out. Get away from me!"

"Please, just give me a chance to prove to you that I'm sincere. I never want to hurt you again. I never want to hurt the kids again. And I know I've been wrong in letting my mom talk about you and treat you the way she does. I'm sorry for never defending you when she put you down. I'm sorry I didn't defend you when she lied about you or hurt you when we were at their house and I'll call her and tell her. I'm sorry, baby. Can you ever forgive me?"

"I'll forgive you, Dick. But I don't want you in my life anymore."

"How can you forgive me and not want us together?"

"Forgiveness doesn't mean a person is stupid, Dick. Forgiving doesn't require the forgiver to have a relationship with the offender. And forgiveness doesn't mean a person is weak minded. Actually, I think forgiveness shows strength. I'll forgive you because it's what I have to do, but I don't want to stay married to you. You've done too much damage to our family."

Dick fell backwards across the bed and cried.

"Please don't do this, not now. Not when I finally realize what I've been throwing away all these years."

"Dick, you need to go. I have to get up early in the morning."

"Why don't you and the kids go with me to the Benefield's cabin at the lake tomorrow? They said we could go and use their pontoon boat. Let's just have a family day, ok?"

"The kids and I have plans already. We're going to church tomorrow, a church in Ball Ground."

"Can I go with you?"

"No," I said.

Immediately, deep in my spirit, something said: *Don't stand in his way.*

I was accustomed to Dick changing family plans at the last minute, especially if church was involved. I figured if I agreed he could go to church with us, he would pretend to be happy about it and then tomorrow morning he would try to entice me to skip church and go to the lake. But because of the voice in my spirit, I knew I had to agree for Dick to attend church with us. I agreed with a stipulation attached.

"Ok. You can come with us, but please don't try to change our plans, don't try to entice the kids with the boat and the lake. The kids and I are going to church. You can do what you want to do."

"I promise you, I won't try to change your mind. Can I come back here in the morning and take a shower? Doug doesn't have a shower in his camper and I don't have clean clothes there either."

"Ok. I'll see you in the morning."

"Can I stay here and sleep on a sofa? It's already almost five o'clock."

"I guess so."

The next morning I was aggravated with myself for giving in to him. Going to church with Dick felt like a lie and I didn't want to pretend anymore. *"Just get through the day,"* I remember thinking.

After showering, I roused Cissy and Garrett and returned to the master bedroom to finish dressing. Dick was standing at the foot of the bed, already showered, buttoning his shirt. I wanted to tell him he couldn't go with us, but the voice in my spirit spoke again, "Expect a miracle today."

There wasn't much chatter between the four of us as we drove the forty-five minutes to church. I was still aggravated with myself for even giving Dick the time of day, much less agreeing to spend a Sunday morning with him. I didn't trust myself to speak to him without arguing, so I said very little while my mind was reeling. Both kids were exceptionally quiet. Dick tried to engage each of us in conversation and was met with silence, we weren't feeling it.

After a few wrong turns, we finally found the church. It was hiding high on a hill down a narrow country road. In surprising contrast to the sleepy little town of Ball Ground, the church campus was bustling. Men with church credentials pinned to their chests were stationed about, directing traffic. A man in a golf cart was ferrying people from the lot to the front entrance of the church. The parking lot was overflowing with a cornucopia of people. Elderly men and women dressed in their Sunday best, families in casual attire, teens in jeans, bikers in leather, all were walking from their vehicles to the doors of the church and they all walked with urgency and purpose. Silently I wondered, somewhat apprehensive, "What kind of church is this?"

Once inside the church, the atmosphere was both electrifying and comforting. I can't describe it any other way. The church foyer was packed with people who greeted us as if we had met before. Smiles and warm eyes caressed our faces, strong hands shook ours and gentle arms embraced our shoulders. It felt like we were being welcomed home after a long absence.

A man with a name badge identifying himself as Ronnie, ushered us through a set of double doors and into the sanctuary. The cavernous room was filled with a confetti of people, and they all seemed happy to be there. I could sense an air of expectancy in the room and for a split second, I was afraid, and I wanted to leave. I had heard stories about snake churches...

Remarkably, Ronnie found four seats side by side on the next to last row of seats. He ushered us into the row, I went first, Garrett next to me, then Cissy, followed by Dick. As Dick took his seat, Ronnie placed a hand on Dick's back and said, "God's gonna bless you today Brother."

Dick leaned over and whispered, "Do you want to sit next to me?" I stayed where I was, refusing to look at him. I didn't want to be in the same room with him and I sure as heck didn't want to sit next to him.

A woman sitting behind me leaned into my ear and said, "You're where you need to be Sister. It's going to be ok, just you wait and see." I didn't turn around, but I couldn't deny the warmth her words left in my soul.

When the music began, the congregation moved to its feet as one body, and the most powerful and beautiful voice I had ever heard began to sing an unfamiliar song," Almighty God I raise Him up...all things are possible." I was spiritually and emotionally moved by the song, the music, the spirit in the room and the spirit within the person singing. "She sounds real. This isn't a fake, put on a Sunday face Christian," I remember thinking. I had been around many "pretenders" in many churches over the years, and I could usually quickly discern the phonies; this wasn't a stage show. This lady sounded like the real deal. "No one can fake that depth of spirit," I thought to myself. I strained to get a glimpse of the person singing, and was shocked when to realize the amazing, powerful voice flowed out of a pretty young lady no more than five feet tall and probably no more than twenty-four years old. I was even more shocked when I glanced at Dick and saw tears streaming down his face.

I was curious about Dick's tears, but remained unmoved by them. I had been fooled by his sympathy act and false apologies too many times, and I wanted to put him behind me. In the past few days I had tasted a life free of Dick's lies and it tasted good. I was ready for the kids to have a life free from lies and heartache. I wanted that kind of life for myself as well.

Soon Lance, the same pastor I had watched on television, welcomed everyone to the church and then he jumped right into his sermon. About ten minutes into his lesson, Lance paused and spoke words that made me stop and take notice.

"There's a man here and you're about to lose everything of importance to you. Because of your adulterous habits, you are about to lose your family. I'm here to tell you, if you don't stop what you've been doing... something you've done many, many times, you are going to lose everything. Up till now, your family hasn't been all that important to you. But oh, you just wait. When that little boy no longer looks at you like you're a hero and that little girl no longer sees you as a knight in shining armor. Or when your wife finds someone who treats her like a queen. Oh, you need to hear me now, because it will happen. And you're going to be left like the blind man on the side of the road. You'll be alone, calling for help and no one will hear you or care enough to stop and help you."

He was talking about us, but I had no idea how he knew. Other than greetings, we had spoken to no one before the service started. We had not completed a questionnaire. No one we knew attended this church and no one we knew was aware of our plans to visit the church.

Out of the peripheral vision of my left eye, I saw Dick stand. I watched as he walked down the aisle of the church with his arms raised above his head, as if surrendering. When Dick reached the altar, Ronnie and two other men gathered around him. I could tell they were asking him questions and he was answering. The men each raised one arm and placed his other arm around Dick and began to pray. Before long, the men were on their knees.

"What's wrong with Dad?" Cissy asked.

"He's praying," I answered.

Garrett observed quietly.

One of the ladies behind me leaned forward and said, "Come on baby, let's go pray for you while the men pray with your husband."

When we left church that day, Dick claimed to have experienced a life transformation. I was skeptical at first, but I had to admit he seemed sincere. I thought I could sense a difference in him, but I wasn't willing to trust that his words were true just yet. He definitely made outward changes: he stopped dipping tobacco and he quit swearing. Before long, I was one hundred percent convinced of my husband's salvation and transformation. From that Sunday into the next ten years, Dick would seldom miss a church service. He studied the Bible and absorbed the lessons therein. He taught classes and led Bible study groups in our home. I believed him when he said he could never turn back to his old ways.

"God will kill me if I ever go back to that life," he said.

Was he sincere? I think so. For at least six years I believe he lived the life he presented. But his demons were returning suitors and, though he kept them a secret, he could not resist his desire to please them. About the time our daughter was a senior in high school, signs of his old habits began to reappear: I noticed he was once again angry most of the time, I caught him in lies again. Things didn't add up with the household money. He began keeping two cell phones again, one he had tried to keep hidden from me. He lost his job and blamed someone else. Without telling me, he changed bank accounts and didn't add me to the new one. He refused to give me the passwords for online banking and our cell phone bill. And so on. I had no proof of anything, but everything indicated the old Dick was back in action.

One day, the cell phone bill arrived and he wasn't home to retrieve it. I opened it and saw that he had made numerous calls to three separate numbers. I called all three numbers and each belonged to a female. He had called one number eighty-seven times in less than a week. That particular number belonged to an eighteen year old girl. I had decided I would not say anything to our kids until I knew for certain what the truth was. I called Dick and confronted him about the calls, and as expected, he denied everything. As it happened, Cissy called me shortly after I had spoken to her dad. "What's wrong?" she asked.

"Nothing."

"Something's up. What's wrong?"

"No, nothing is up."

"Dad just called me and told me you are accusing him of stuff again. Now you need to stop it Mom! You know he's not doing anything. He wouldn't do anything again and you know it. Stop it. Don't try to create trouble."

I wanted to choose my words carefully. *Why in the name of Sam had Dick felt compelled to call our daughter?* "Cissy, you don't need to bother yourself with this. Let it go and let us handle it."

"Well ya'll have pulled me into this!"

"No. I haven't. I didn't call you. Your dad called you. If you remember, when we spoke earlier today I didn't mention any of this to you. I wasn't going to say anything until I knew for sure. I would not accuse your dad for no reason about something this serious. I wouldn't bring up the past if it wasn't being pushed in my face. He's been calling women and the proof is on the phone bill. One of them is a girl near your age."

"Who is she?"

I gave Cissy the name and she recognized it. Cissy called the girl and asked her, "Why do you and my dad call each other all the time? All during the night you talk to him. Why?"

"You'll have to take that up with your dad," the girl replied.

That was the extent of the proof I was able to gather. Once Dick knew I was on to him, he became less careless with his lies and more secretive with his behavior. From that time until two years later when Garrett caught him for the final time, I was just going through the motions of surviving. I knew he was lying but could prove nothing.

The Idea, 2009

Dick moved to Wyoming a few weeks after I told him I wanted a divorce. He wasted no time stirring up trouble for another family. Not long after Dick's arrival in Cheyenne, but before he was to return to Georgia for our divorce, we received troubling news from Cheyenne. The informant claimed Dick's current girlfriend was a married gynecologist with a practice in Cheyenne, he said she owned an obstetrics and gynecology clinic as well as a medical spa. This seemed farfetched to us... *a doctor and Dick?* After some investigative digging, I soon discovered everything the man had said was true.

We were not yet divorced, and Dick was living the highlife on this doctor's penny, vacationing with her, taking her daughters snowmobiling. While the kids and I were struggling to make ends meet, Dick was living without concern for anyone. Debt collectors were calling the house phone daily, searching for Dick because they couldn't reach him on his cell phone. Dick had promised to keep the family cell phone plan in place for an extended period, but instead, cancelled the plan without warning us in advance. He had promised to help pay the utilities until the divorce hearing, but reneged on that promise as well. I wasn't surprised. He refused to pay the debts he left behind. The pain and frustration of our lives permeated my every thought. Watching Cissy and Garrett suffer was the most excruciating pain of all. I needed to say some things to Dick, get some things off my chest, but I didn't want to talk to him. I knew talking would go nowhere, I knew he would twist everything back to me, so I decided to write him a letter. He probably wouldn't read it, but at least I would have the satisfaction of writing and venting my aggravation.

So I wrote the letter. But before I sent it to him, I decided I should have my close friend Jean, who happens to reside in Cheyenne, read it via email. Of my friends, Jean knew the history of Dick Crisco best. Jean had known Dick and me for many years, she had talked me through many rough nights, she understood my fear and pain and she never sugar-coated her advice. I could count on her to be brutally honest with me. Years before, when I first learned of Dick's infidelity, I had called him Wormdirt during a conversation with Jean. It was a nice substitute for the name I would have preferred to call him. In the years since, if I referred to my husband as Wormdirt, Jean knew it meant Dick was up to something.

Date: Wednesday, December 2, 2009, 4:55PM
Subject: Letter to Dick
1 file attch: lettertodickdoc.

Hey Jean,

I've attached a letter I wrote to
Wormdirt. Please read and tell me what
you think…… Should I send it? I want
to badly! It felt great putting these
thoughts in black and white!

Hope your day has been great!

D

Date: Wednesday, December 2, 2009, 6:37PM
RE: Letter to Dick

My, that's quite the letter.
While I understand the pain from which
your words arose, I don't think you
should send it to him. You know better
than anyone what he's capable of. I feel
he may try to use the letter against you.
I've never heard you use that language
before. Keep writing if it makes you feel
better, but don't send it to Wormdirt.

Take care,
J

Date: Thursday, December 3, 2009, 7:03AM
RE: Letter to Dick

Dear Jean (aka Voice of Reason),

I guess you're right. (You're always
sooooo practical…but that's why I sent
the letter to you for proofing). He's such
a hollow little worm, my words would
mean nothing to him anyway. But DANG!
They make me feel better. I'll take your
advice and keep writing. It's cheaper
than therapy.

XO
D

Date: Thursday, December 3, 2009, 8:01PM
RE: Letter to Dick

Wise choice, my friend.

Love ya,
J.

Letter to the Whoremonger

November 13, 2009

Dear Dick,

Well, they said you would never do it…but you were determined to prove them wrong, weren't you? They underestimated you. The fact that you could screw every whore in the state of Georgia at least once (some several times) has amazed many of the people that doubted you. And the fact that you accomplished such a lofty goal while married makes it even more remarkable. That many of the whores, most in fact, were also married just adds glitter to your status as the ultimate Man Whore.

And now that you're done with the whores, sluts, skunks and dogs in heat of Georgia, you've moved on to Wyoming.…no doubt trying to accomplish another life altering goal…screw every whore, married or single in that wonderful state. But you're getting so old. Do you have another twenty-four years of Pecker Power left in you? Explain something, please, you told me your pecker no longer worked. Really? How is it you've managed to put it to use so often? How do you do it? Perhaps your mail order, generic hootie enhancement medicines finally worked. I remember our son discovered a large bottle of little blue pills in your truck…I found more in a bathroom closet. You were taking several different brands…all at once. You were getting desperate there for a while. Was it the lovely lady you met online at the cheating wife website that had you so desperately anxious? Remember? Yes, I saw her photo. Classic Beauty. I thought her missing tooth and the tattoo of the Rebel Flag were awesome! Unfortunately, even though the tat was huge, and covered both cheeks, it didn't camouflage the cellulite dimples cratered on her flabby backside. Her cellulite made it look as if the flag was rippling in the wind.

I guess if the generic pecker medications didn't work, it's possible one of your Pancake Hut whores shared her Ecstasy with you. Come to think of it, you were losing weight and acting creepier than usual during those last few months that you graced me with your presence. Is that what you're doing to make old hootie work *for a few hours? I'm just curious, you were wiped out, exhausted when you came home from work every day. You would recline for hours like a zombie on the sofa, watching countless reruns of a stupid home video show. And you laughed, over and over; at the same videos…it was surreal. So maybe, just maybe, you were spent from your work day activity. Not the actual work of cooking eggs and bacon, but from the sexual activity you engaged in when you left the restaurant to make 'bank deposits'. I thought because you were home on time most nights and every weekend, you were faithful to me. Tired, but faithful. Plus, remember, you had assured me ol' Hootie no longer worked that well. Shriveled up. Dead. That's what you said. How could I have fallen for your lies? Again? In the past, most of your affairs had been conducted during work hours (however, there was the convenient store clerk you brought into our bed after I left for work). But you are such an excellent, believable liar; you had convinced me you were a reformed man, a Born Again Christian, no longer capable of telling a lie or looking at another woman. I'm tempted to scream LOSER at this point in my letter… but I don't know if I would be screaming the name at you or myself.*

Our divorce will be final next week. You know, on the day we married twenty-three years and eight months ago, I believed we would be married forever. I loved you. On the day we met, I was sunbathing outside my apartment. You were across the parking lot, in front of your condo, removing the top from your Jeep. I thought you were the most beautiful man I had ever set my eyes upon. I was dating several others when we met, nothing serious. They were what I considered the stuffy business types. Boring. You were different. A very manly man, in my eyes at least. My trusting eyes. We hit it off immediately. You asked if I would like to have dinner and go dancing with you that same evening. I had a date already. You asked me out again for the next night. I had another date, previously planned. Finally you said, "How about two weeks from this Saturday?" I told you I would be free that particular night, and would love to dance with you. In the meantime, we found an empty afternoon and you asked if I wanted to ride out to Stone Mountain and hike. I was thrilled. I had to return by six that evening for a date with another guy. By the end of our day hiking up Stone Mountain, canoeing and petting the horses, I was smitten. I did not want to return for my date. But I did. And you sat on the steps outside your condominium and watched me drive away with him in his BMW. I desperately wanted to be sitting beside you on the steps rather than sitting in the front seat of my date's car. I ended the date early. I walked over to your place, knocked on your door and asked if you wanted to go for an ice-cream. We bought the treat and ate on the steps outside your condo. Later, you walked me to my apartment and gave me a big bear hug as we said good-night.

The next evening, we drove out to Stone Mountain again, we picnicked and watched the Georgia sun set. We drove away from the granite mountain with the top off your Jeep and you sang along to country love songs. I really didn't like country music, but I loved hearing you sing. In that moment, I fell in love with your gentleness. I never went out with another guy again. Not ever.

Life changed quickly once we were married. Our wedding was beautiful, the reception very nice. During greetings, an old boyfriend walked up to congratulate us, and he told you how fortunate you were to have me as your wife. You didn't thank him. You coldly said, "Yeah, I know." I was embarrassed for you, myself and for him. He didn't deserve the attitude you gave him. During the "reception after the reception" you got drunk. When we made it back to our hotel room, you plopped down clumsily on the sofa. When I came out of the bathroom you were nude and sprawled across the end of the bed, passed out from too much alcohol and too little food. Throughout our entire marriage you accused me of ruining our wedding night. Funny though, that honeymoon night, when I woke up at four in the morning and saw that you were still passed out cold, I thought the same thing about you.

Very soon I realized not all fairytales have a happy ending, but we were married. I was committed to you. Marriage was a lifetime commitment for me. Everyone had told me it would take about a year to adjust to marriage, so that's what I kept telling myself. When you began to criticize everything I did or said, I justified your behavior by telling myself you were just having a more difficult time adjusting to marriage than I was. A week into our marriage I saw the corner of a magazine hanging over the top of the bathroom cabinet. "That's odd", I thought. I stood on tiptoe and pulled the magazine down. It was a pornographic magazine. My stomach flipped and my heart beat rapidly. I never knew you to purchase such material. You had never shown or mentioned an interest in. "Ok, lots of guys read these magazines", I justified. When I asked, you told me it didn't belong to you. You said my brother left it there while he was staying with you before we married. You grab the magazine from my hands and tossed it in the trash. "I don't need this stuff, I have you. I love you," you said. I accepted your explanation.

One morning, a week later, while putting away your clothes, I found the same magazine, the one you had discarded in the trash with broken eggs and empty Campbell soup cans. This time you say, "Ok, whatever, it's mine, it's just that girl on the front reminds me of you. I wanted to keep it to be reminded of you when you're not here."

I told you the woman on the magazine's cover looked nothing like me. "She looks like a young version of your mother," I said. You said nothing.

I asked if you were masturbating to the photos and you exploded, rage coming from your lips and eyes. "Yes I am! And it's a hell of a lot more fun than fucking you!"

I was devastated but I had to go to work, I cried all the way to Atlanta. Throughout the day I thought about what you said to me and I got sick to my stomach. I was humiliated and crushed by your words, but I told no one. "Who is this person?" I wondered. You were not acting like the beautiful man I had known while we dated. Where was the considerate, gentle soul I fell in love with? Jekyll and Hyde came to mind. I was already confused by strange changes in your behavior, behavior that started as soon as we were married. You stayed up late every night, never came to bed at the same time with me. On our days off, you would suddenly get up and go outside, get in your jeep and leave; without saying a word to me. It was in the days before cell phones, I wouldn't hear from you for hours and I worried about you because I loved you. I worried, "has he been in an accident?" Infidelity never entered my mind in those days. I kept telling myself we were still adjusting to married life and when we figured out how to live together, things would get better. When you admitted you preferred masturbating rather than a relationship with me, you bruised my spirit. I became self-conscious of my body, filled with self-doubt. From the day of your confession until the day you left, I heard your sneer every time you touched me, "...it's a hell of a lot more fun than fucking you!"

Later that afternoon, on the day of our magazine argument, you called while I was at work and apologized. You said you never meant to hurt me. You said you had only said what you said to hurt me, because I had hurt you by asking the masturbation question. You wanted to know how I could think such a thing about you. You loved me more than anything, you said. You said you would never intentionally hurt me, especially not like I had hurt you when I asked about masturbation. I forgave you and I apologized to you, I apologize for hurting you with my rude question. Years later I would think of this first exchange of mean words and apologies as the first steps, the learning steps of a horribly choreographed dance between us; a dance of pain and misplaced blame. We would argue, you would dip me in blame and I would spin an apology around you. It was a dance of heartache, deceit and degradation.

A couple of weeks after the magazine incident, our first phone bill arrived. I opened the bill and was shocked when I realized it totaled close to a thousand dollars. Page after page of the invoice showed calls to a 900 service. I knew what those 900 numbers were. My first job out of college was in customer service for the phone company, where daily I had dealt with upset customers who denied these calls on their bills. The customers always argued that the charges were a mistake and demanded the calls be removed. At the phone company we knew someone inside the home had made the calls, perhaps not the customer, but someone in the home had made the calls. Until now, I had never had any calls like that on my bill. But when I saw our charges, and I saw the calls were made during the day while we were both working (a few of them had been made late at night after we were sleeping), I knew there was a mistake. A big mistake. I called the phone company and explained the situation.

They asked me the usual questions:

Q. *"Who is home during the time of the calls?"*

A. *"No one."*

Q. *"Has a neighbor borrowed your phone."*

A. *"No. Our neighbors are old and they have their own phones."*

Q. *"Are there any teenagers in the home? These calls are to sex lines and are usually made by teenaged boys."*

A. *"No teens, no children, no neighbors. We are newlyweds. There is a mistake. Please credit my phone bill for this amount."*

Reluctantly, the phone company representative agreed to credit our bill. When you arrived home, I showed you the bill and relayed to you my conversation with the phone company. You were dumbfounded and said you knew for sure the phone company was "doing this kind of thing to make money!" We agreed we would pay very close attention to the phone bill and other utilities, to make certain there were no mistakes. I filed the problem with the phone bill in the back of my mind and went about my daily business of working and trying to figure out how to be a wife. And how to pay our bills. You and I were both working, but you were having trouble collecting all the money owed to you from your construction accounts. We both had car payments along with our rent, food and utilities. After these bills were paid, there never seemed to be any money left. Collecting payment from your accounts was getting more and more difficult, you said.

One Saturday morning, a week or two after the phone bill incident, you left early to collect from your contractors. While you were gone I decided to sweep the front porch. We lived on East Main Street, where the homeowners and renters were expected to keep a presentable yard and exterior. Our landlady, Mrs. Scott, whom you accused of being a "nosey old hag", had been born in the house we rented and now she lived across the street. Remember how she loved to tell us her dad built the house with his own hands in 1919? Mrs. Scott kept a close watch on her birthplace and that Saturday morning she saw me on the porch and walked over to say hello. A few minutes into our chat, she asked if you were "out of work". I told her you were working everyday but having a difficult time collecting from your accounts. She said, "Well, I was just curious. He leaves before you do every morning. But then he returns a few minutes after you leave. He stays home all day and leaves again a few minutes before you arrive. So, I guess I thought he was no longer working. I just wanted to check in with you, I don't want you to get in trouble with your bills."

Immediately I thought of the 900 numbers on the phone bill, the calls placed during the work day. I remember feeling my stomach churn and my face turn red and hot. Throbbing pain filled my temples and a cold, dark heat, a feeling that would eventually become very familiar to me, crawled thru my muscles and settled in the pit of my stomach. I remember being unable to focus my vision, seeing, *but seeing nothing at all. I really don't remember what I said to Mrs. Scott; most likely I stumbled on my words and made an excuse for you. For some reason I felt I had to protect you. I guess I was trying to salvage my dignity as well. When you returned home, late that afternoon, I told you what she had said, and you accused her of being a nosey old woman with nothing better to do than make up lies. You said you had a good mind to walk across the street and give her a piece of your mind. Then you said you wouldn't give her the satisfaction of letting her see you upset and we would just look for another place to live.*

I didn't know what to think anymore. Incidences from previous days started making sense and falling into place. A few times I came home from work and found the heat on. I always left for work about fifteen minutes after you and I always shut the heat off before I left each morning before leaving the house, it was an act I had integrated into my morning routine. When I mentioned the oddity to you, you said, "That old lady probably came over and turned the heat on to keep the pipes from freezing." Other days, I would find lights on. There was no question I had shut off the lights prior to leaving the house. Again, you blamed the landlady. An awful, knowing, gnawing feeling began chopping away at my conscience and my heart. Something was wrong, and I mentioned my feelings to you. You said the only thing that was wrong was me. You told me I had a problem with conjuring things up in my head and trying to make them real. You told me to stop whining and nagging. I actually wanted to believe the problem was with me and not you. Then, the second phone bill arrived, and it was also loaded with calls to 900 numbers, but the bill was lower this time, just under five hundred dollars. You asked me to call the phone company again and ask for a credit. I refused. I knew these calls were coming from our home, but you still denied them. And because you think you can convince anyone to believe you, you called the phone company yourself, and this time they refused to remove the calls, they refused to credit the bill. We were responsible for the calls to the 900 Service. We didn't have enough money to cover the charges, so you called your mom. I don't know what excuse you gave her, but in a few days, she sent a check to pay our phone bill. Your mom paid for your calls to sex lines. The previous month, I had told her about the phone calls to the 900 services. After you asked her for the money, she called me and inquired about the phone bill. I told her the calls came from our home, but she didn't believe me, she believed you. She echoed your comment, "Do yourself a favor and stop nagging him. If he did make the calls, be glad he's doing this instead of running around on you." I was appalled, and taken aback by her attitude.

I asked her, "Don't you realize this means he has a problem? He's staying home to make these calls rather than going to work?"

Your mom groaned, "Oh my god, you're his only problem."

One day, not long after she paid our phone bill, your mom called me and asked me if you had trouble having sex. The odd question baffled me. Where did that come from and why, I wanted to know, "I was just wondering," she said. For a long time, I pondered your mom's bizarre question. Years later, when I finally realized you had sexual addictions, I wondered if perhaps you had been sexually molested as a child. I asked you about the possibility of molestation. Your mother has always claimed she had been molested by an uncle, and you know as well as anyone, if she meets someone who doesn't act just as she feels they should, she says they've either been molested or they are a molester. So, along the lines of her theory, maybe it had happened to you. You said you didn't think so. "But then again", you said, "she left me, but never my sisters, with her crazy mother and uncle."

Eventually, when I ask your mom to help me get you into counseling for your sexual addictions, she screamed at me and repeated I was your only problem. You agreed with her.

Do you remember, a few weeks after our wedding, your mom began to call me at work and discuss your old high school girlfriend? Your mom told me you would always love Mary and would never love me as much as you loved Mary. I asked your mom to stop talking about Mary and she accused me of being insecure. I wanted to hang up when she began talking about your old girlfriend, but I wanted to develop a good relationship with my mother-in-law. She continued to call and tell me all sorts of things about your relationship with Mary; details previously unknown to me. She would talk to me about Mary until I became upset, and then she would tell me not to say anything to you. For a long time, I didn't. But one day I couldn't take it anymore, and I told you. You immediately called your mom and she promptly denied ever saying anything about any of your old girlfriends. Do you remember she told you she thought I was trying to cause trouble between the two of you? She said I was trying to come between mother and son. You came to me angrily, "Mom says you're lying about all of this. Why would you lie about my mom?" It was then I recited to you some of the things your mom had told me, things you had never revealed, things I wouldn't have known unless someone told me. You knew then I was telling you the truth, yet you never confronted your mom about the issue of her lies. You never stood by me on that subject or any other for that matter. I realize now your mom was throwing seeds of discontent in our already fragile marriage. As you said, she was the one who was in love with Mary and would never be happy with anyone else you chose to marry. Unfortunately, at the time, I still held high regard for your mom, and I allowed her skewed mental state to contribute to my dwindling self-esteem.

*And while I'm on the subject of your mom, I just want to say she's a **crazy woman**. Since you left Georgia, she has called our daughter and upset her numerous times. It's odd that she would exclude our kids from the trips she takes with the rest of the grandchildren, yet she doesn't mind drawing them into her insanity. She has no consideration for upsetting and demeaning Cissy and Garrett. Remember when your mom accused Garrett of saying Jake* *was stupid? Garrett didn't say that Jake was stupid, what he said was, "Jake, that's stupid," referring to a show they were watching. But your mom twisted it to be something else. She is still fabricating stories and twisting details. Just like you.*

Another thing: While the kids were growing up, you never cared if they visited your parents or not. If it had been up to you, they would have stayed home. I encouraged their visits. I've learned your family constantly degraded me on those visits. Your lack of concern about whether our kids visited your parents, is one thing I wish I would have agreed with you on.

I'm getting sidetracked here. Back to the second phone bill, our second month of marriage. I realized you had made these calls to the 900 Service, you tried to convince me otherwise, but I knew. For a few days I contemplated our short, rocky marriage. I concluded that I should leave you. You had betrayed me with your lies, the phone calls and magazines. Foolishly, I still didn't believe you would ever have a physical relationship with another woman (I was wrong.) The overwhelming heartache from realizing you were drawn to something as sick as phone sex and that you were willing to pay, or have your mom pay for it, was almost too much to bear. So, I told you I was leaving. You began mocking me, accusing me of "running to mama". I wanted you to understand I was leaving the pain and private humiliation you were heaping upon me, I wasn't running to anything. But you didn't get it. You started screaming, "You're going to leave me!? You think you're going to leave me? I changed my whole fucking life for you! I changed everything for you!"

What? What did you change for me? I had been thinking your drastic change occurred after we were married. I didn't understand what you were telling me. You had changed for me? What had you changed from that had been so wonderful? What was so great in your previous life that you now hated me because of the change? More than twenty years later you finally revealed what you were and why you had deceived me while we were dating:

- *You had been addicted to cigarettes (I had never seen you smoke).*
- *You had been addicted to alcohol (I had seen you drink very little).*
- *You had experimented with and taken several different types of drugs.*
- *You had always been addicted to women.*

*This part of your life was foreign to me. You finally told me your reasons for keeping these parts of your life a secret from me. You said you knew I was different from all the other girls you had dated, and you knew I would never have dated you if I had known the truth about. You said you thought you could change: "**I thought I could change.**" Do you remember saying that? You thought you could change? I never asked you to change for me, why would I? While we dated I* *thought you were perfect. I would never have asked you to change, because I realize that kind of change is impossible. Change starts from the inside and works its way out. Change doesn't occur just because another wants someone to change, change comes from within. More to the point, I thought you were perfection. I had no reason to want you to change. I was clueless about your inner struggles. But you blamed me when you could no longer masquerade. Do you realize how unfair that was to me and to yourself? I married a stranger.*

I remember walking across the street to tell the landlords that I would begin packing my car in a few minutes, leaving you. I was going home. They ask me to think about my decision. I told them I had thought about it. I went back to our little house and started loading my things into my Honda. In a few minutes, Mr. and Mrs. Scott came over and ask me to stop packing; they wanted to talk to me. They told me I should reconsider my decision to leave. They said I hadn't given my marriage a chance. Mr. Scott told me, "It's much harder for men to adjust to marriage than it is for women." He said I needed to give you more time and space. Mrs. Scott said it would be wrong for me to leave you and I should probably try harder to understand you. Eventually they told me I had blown things out of proportion.

The biggest problem with the Scott's assessment of our marital situation is I had not revealed all the details to them. I was too embarrassed. You were already blaming me for your problems and I was beginning to believe you, I thought the Scotts would believe you too. The Scotts had only half the story when they offered advice.

Humiliation, shame and pride, all wrapped up in a secret package, is very destructive to a young woman's spirit.

The Scotts helped me take my things back inside the house. Everything was back in place when you returned later that evening. We made up, apologized and vowed to work harder on our marriage.

We had a rocky start and our marriage was difficult. Made more difficult by your mother's constant meddling. After conversations with and visits from her, you would tell me that no one liked me. "No one, not even members of your own family like you," you said. I never questioned you. I just sank further into myself. Before long I thought I was unworthy of being loved. Like the hunter that you aspire to be, you saw the fear in my eyes and you preyed on it. I had a fear of being seen as a failure, and you used it against me. You knew I was too embarrassed to tell family and friends what was going on in our house. And so it went; you continued your verbal assaults on me, I continued to pretend that things were great.

Eventually we left the rental on Main Street and moved to an apartment in Gwinnett County. The move put us closer to our jobs and we liked living in a complex with other young married couples. Do you remember how, for a while, things were pretty good between us? Sometimes they were even great. There were a few fights over things that seemed important to me and insignificant to you or vice versa, but we got through most of them. Certain things caused heated arguments, such as your tardiness when we had plans. Your forgetfulness regarding paying our bills on time always bothered me. Your habit of leaving the apartment door open, not just unlocked but ajar, when you left every morning, while I was still sleeping. You hated my shoe collection, even though most were purchased long before we married. Remember tossing my shoes around when you were angry with me? When I mentioned these things to a friend she told me she had similar issues with her husband. "No marriage is perfect," she said. So, I decided it was another area in which I was overreacting, another character flaw for me to improve on.

About a year after we married, we began construction of our first home on the ten acres of land we had purchased during our engagement. When our house was about half finished, we discovered I was pregnant. We were both overjoyed, or so I thought. You were attentive, loving and caring during my pregnancy. It seemed parenthood was a positive turning point in our marriage. I knew you were going to be a fantastic dad because you had been wonderful with my young nephew. I had sugarplum dreams when I thought of future Christmas mornings gathered around a large Frasier Fir, a fire roaring in the fireplace, steaming mugs of hot cocoa and happy little children running around the house.

After our baby girl was born, I fell in love with you all over again. I loved watching you hold her. I loved the way you were so gentle with her, as if she were a fragile porcelain doll. Three days after she was born, and one day after we came home from the hospital, your parents and your seventeen-year-old sister came to visit. They stayed with us in our small two-bedroom, one bath apartment for over a week. Presumably, they were there to help with our new baby. It was a difficult week. Rapidly, the relationship you and I had tried to repair during my pregnancy began to unravel during their visit. Your felt she needed to invite your other sister and her husband and your uncle and his wife, to our apartment for dinner each night. I was physically exhausted from a long labor and delivery, frustrated with trying to nurse our baby in front of your family. Cissy developed colic and wasn't sleeping, neither was I. I told you how tired I was, I asked you to please ask your mom to hold off on entertaining. You told her what I had requested, and she told you I was being selfish and whiny. Later I learned from your sister and your aunt they had each told her they didn't need to come over every night. They had visibly witnessed the fatigue I was dealing with and mentioned as much to your mom. But BJ had lied and told them both I was fine, that I wanted company. This went on for a week. I cried tears of joy the day your family left. I was hurt because you didn't stand up for me, didn't respect my request for rest and privacy. I had just given birth to a beautiful nine-pound baby. I was fatigued, and postpartum hormones were fluctuating, yet you *allowed your mom to ignore my pleas for rest. Your mom told you I made her feel unwelcome; you told me to stop being selfish.*

I was tired, Dick. I just needed a few days of repose. I wanted to relax with you and our little girl. I wanted you to defend me and tell your mom to take the party elsewhere. But you didn't. After the birth of our daughter your mom found more opportunities to belittle me. She made up blatant lies and you believed her. You claimed to despise this woman, yet you let her treat me like rubbish. You know, for years I witnessed your mom treating you poorly and I felt sad for you. I never understood how a mom could show so much love for one daughter, show a lot less love for her middle child and not much of anything for her firstborn, her son. I was always amazed that you allowed her to degrade you, our marriage and eventually her grandchildren, our children, with her insults and hurtful words. I finally realized you wanted her love and approval and I believe you thought you could earn it by being non-confrontational with her. Not too long after Cissy was born, you began to accuse me of trying to control you. You showed no respect for me as a wife or as a mother and again, you compared me to your mom.

"You're just like my damn mother!"

*When in anger you compared us, I wanted to believe your remarks were fueled by frustrations, not something you truly felt. Years into our marriage, I finally realized you actually believed what you said. Why else would you treat me as if I **was** your mother? You wrongly believed I didn't love you; you accused me of following you around town, as she had done when you were a teen; you believed if I wanted to spend time with you I must have an ulterior motive. You never believed that I loved you enough to simply want to be with you. Was it really so difficult to believe you were loved? Were you emotionally crippled because your mom had never loved you enough to want to spend time with you? Was it because she had never found joy in you... her child, her boy? Looking back, I can clearly see our relationship was doomed before we ever met.*

Do you remember the time I showed up unannounced on your job site to have lunch with you? You made ugly accusations: "You want to be stuck up my ass just like my mom! I can't do a damn thing without you wanting to be stuck up my ass!" I know you remember saying it. That ugly, hurtful phrase became very familiar during our marriage. Our arguments were always peppered with angry comparisons of your mom and me. One thing I never understood is this: when I defended you against your mom, you became upset with me. What was that about? Recently, after you left, I found an entry in a journal you had kept for a week or two. You described the way your mom sent you to Oklahoma almost every summer to visit your paternal grandmother. While in Oklahoma, you spent time with an uncle you loved and adored but, you say in the journal, for "much of the time as a little boy, I was alone". And you say you liked it that way. But did you really? As an adult you don't like being alone. You need constant reassurance that someone is thinking of you and wants to be with you. I think you feel this way because you never felt loved or accepted by the people who were supposed to love you the most. One time, your sister Vee told me your mom couldn't handle you when you were a little boy, so she sent you away every summer. Later, Vee said when you became a young man you were "getting into trouble", so your mom and dad sent you to Atlanta to live with your uncle. As a boy, were you always aware your mother didn't want you around? I cried for the little boy you were, the one who felt unloved and unwanted.

Three weeks after our baby girl was born, we moved into our new house. I was so proud of it because you had built it with your own hands. My brother, your sister's husband, your uncle and a few others had helped, but most of the work was done by you. For a while it seemed things were improving for us emotionally and financially. Every evening you greeted me and our baby with hugs and kisses. Before long though, things became dark again. You seemed to resent having a family and you started coming home a little later each night. Delinquent notices from the bank began showing up in the mail. The fuse on your temper became short and quick again. I knew something was wrong but when I questioned you, you said it was nothing. I could not break through your wall and the old frustrations of 'knowing something was wrong but not knowing what' haunted me.

One afternoon I popped a movie into the VCR and rather than seeing the home movie we had recorded, there were images of nude women on the film. You had filmed page after page of naked women and placed them on video for safe keeping. Again, that cold, dark heat pulsated through me. Why had you done this? What were you thinking? When you came home I questioned you about it and you said you were "just goofing around with the camera". I was supposed to accept that as an ok answer.

"When did you purchase the magazines? We don't have money for our bills but you're purchasing men's magazines?"

"I found it on a job site," you said.

"But why would you video the photos? And film over home movies of our child?! That's sick! Why would you do that?" I remember asking.

"Why do you want to gripe and bitch about everything!? You're just like my damn mom; you've got to nag me about everything I do. And why were you going through my damn stuff? That's all she ever did, snoop and bitch!"

Blaming me was your standard way of responding to confrontation. You always managed to direct the blame to me or someone else. You never took responsibility for your actions. Before long, I accepted the blame you placed on me. At times I stood with you and placed blame on someone else. With each argument, with each insult, I lost a little of myself. I didn't even realize what was happening. Twenty-four years later, my parents told me they watched me 'go downhill' with each passing year of our marriage, and they felt helpless to do anything about it. You knew what you were doing, didn't you? After our arguments, you would apologize, bring home a beautiful card and sometimes stop by Wal-Mart and pick up flowers. And always, always, you vowed to never hurt me again. You always had a good explanation for your anger and I was always willing to accept your apology. Because I remembered, the sweet, kind man I fell in love with. Each time you offered a glimpse of that man, I convinced myself the bad times were over. The true Dick was coming back to me.

Things between us improved after I found the video, you became very attentive to our family and home. Your work increased and became steady again. You offered to help around the house and yard more frequently than before. We began attending a little church in town and began socializing with other young families from the church. Before long, we were happy to discover I was pregnant with our second child. At this time, I had not yet allowed myself to think of you as an unstable man. When questions about your odd behavior rose to the surface of awareness, I swatted them away as I would an annoying fly. It would be years before I allowed the truth to settle in my mind. The excuse I made for you was simply that you were still having a difficult time adjusting. By the end of the first trimester of my second pregnancy, the troubles in our marriage were hard to ignore.

I'll never forget the day you came home and told me we were going to lose our house. It was a beautiful day…my belly swollen with new life…our little girl and I outside watering our rose garden. We heard you roaring down the country road before we saw you. "DaDa"! Cissy said, already recognizing the sound of your approach. Seconds later, your grey Ford Ranger appeared on the horizon of the graveled driveway, coming to a sudden stop a few feet from Cissy and me, kicking up dust. You jumped out of the small cab of the vehicle and bellowed at me, "There's no use in planting another fucking thing! This damn house is going back to the bank!" You went on to say you had just left the bank and they told you they were going to foreclose unless payments were brought up to date. Up to date? I had no idea how far behind we were on the mortgage, you had told me you were taking payments to the bank on the days you were paid. This was another fist of deception to my gut. I had been strolling along, thinking life was improving, while behind the scenes everything was falling apart.

After much worry and negotiation, to save our home, my parents agreed to co-sign a second mortgage with us. You agreed to pay every payment on time. You had first asked your dad, but he said he couldn't co-sign with you. Yet after the loan was signed, he shook hands with my dad, and vowed to make half the payment if you failed to pay.

I never saw the late notices from the bank. When they came in mail, you tossed them in the trash or left them in your truck, forgotten. Two months after securing the loan, the bank called my parents to inform them of your failure to make payments and disregard of late notices. My dad called yours and asked him to make half the payment as he had agreed. Your dad swore at my dad and told him it wasn't his responsibility. **The apple doesn't fall far from the tree.**

Several weeks later, I woke one morning to find my car missing, repossessed. You told me you had mailed the payment the prior week. You just didn't understand why they would repossess the car. You said you were going to find out who did this and sue them! Of course, we never got the car back and you never sued anyone. You had never made the payment. What had you done with the money? To this day, I don't know.

If it seems like this letter is a recap of our lives, I guess then, that's what it is. Dick, I have years of tears and heartache bottled up. Memories I had pushed to the back of my mind have resurfaced and I feel the need to put them on paper. I have to tell you, it is difficult to relive these things I'm writing, yet it feels good to lay it down. You always told me to write a book; maybe I'll finally do it. Perhaps that's what I'm doing this very minute.

When I was eight months pregnant with Garrett, I drove your Ford Ranger to the Department of Motor Vehicles to renew my license. Cissy was with me, 21 months old at the time. When it was my turn at the desk, I was informed by the clerk, a family friend, that my license had been suspended for lack of vehicle insurance. She told me if I got behind the wheel of the truck, it would be the obligation of the officers on duty to pull me over and issue a ticket. I didn't know what to do. Thankfully, she noticed my fear and the sweat pouring down my pregnant face (there was no air conditioning in the truck) and had sympathy for my situation. She said if I promised to go directly to the insurance office, she would tell the officers to leave me alone. I did as I was told and when I returned later that day with the documentation proving I had purchased insurance, she renewed my license. That evening, when you came home, I told you about my experience. You didn't have much to say. You shrugged your shoulders and said, "I guess you should have paid the insurance." With what? When did you give me the money to pay the insurance? I thought you were taking care of our bills.

Two weeks later things got considerably worse. Late one night, a couple of weeks into my ninth month, there was a knock on the door. It was a deputy from the sheriff's office, you were not home from work and I had not heard from you all day. When I saw the officer at our door, my first thought was that something terrible had happened to you. I remembered the night I was seven years old and a police officer came to our door to tell us my Grandpa Crawford had been injured in a horrible accident. I was afraid the deputy was at my door with the same type of news. I needn't have worried. The officer was there to arrest me. Seems I had written a check for fifteen dollars to a grocery store and the check was returned insufficient funds. You had a habit of throwing mail in the trash, especially mail you didn't want me to see, so I can only assume the bank's notices had made it to the trash. When I wrote the check to the store, I was unaware of the negative status in our bank account. Unknown to me, you had cashed out the account. Would it have been too much trouble to tell me, Dick? Ah...I would have asked too many questions, is that it? I had never seen a notice from the bank or the grocery store regarding the fifteen-dollar returned check. Our mail came to a post office box. You retrieved our mail from the post office on the way home from work. Sometimes the mail made it inside the house, sometimes it didn't, it just depended on the content of the piece of mail, didn't it? This important piece of mail obviously never made it inside the house, because a week after the officer came to our home, I found certified letters from the Big Star Grocery shoved underneath the seat of your truck. Letters you had signed for at the post office. Mail you had sworn you had never received.

That night, the night the officer came to our door, I tried to explain to him I knew nothing about the returned check. He said he was sorry, but he would have to take me in to the Cobb County jail.

"Oh my God, no! This is a mistake. What about my little girl?"

For the first time, the officer noticed Cissy toddling around and asked if anyone else was home with me. I told him you were not home, and I had no way of getting in touch with you. He softened and said he would not take me in so long as I promised to go to the jail and pay my bill first thing the next morning.

The fine was three hundred and fifty dollars...for a fifteen-dollar check. A complete waste of money due to your lack of responsibility. How difficult would it have been for you to tell me you had spent the money in our checking account? How much effort would it have taken for you to pick up a single envelope and bring it inside the house? You didn't want me to know you had spent the money, so you handled the problem the way you handled everything else...you ignored it.

When you finally came home that night, and I told you about the officer's visit, your reaction was typical Crisco: "How are you going to pay for this? I don't have the damn money!" you said. "I guess you can figure out a way to pay it or you can go to jail."

For the past ten months, I had been secretly saving money for Christmas; reluctantly, I emptied my savings jar and you drove me and our little girl to the detention center where I used the Christmas savings to keep myself out of jail. On the way home you said, "Aren't you proud? We got out of this mess without having to ask anyone for help?"

I was disturbed that you took this so lightly, I felt sick and dirty from the whole experience. I did not feel proud. And there it was the end of August, December only four months away. I knew I didn't have time to save enough money for Christmas gifts.

"No, I'm not proud. It never should have happened. If you had brought the mail inside, if you had let me know there was no money in our account, this never would have happened. What's there to be proud of?"

Of the Christmas money I had saved, one hundred dollars was left. When we returned to the house, I hid the remaining money in a decorative Japanese Ginger Jar, high on a book shelf in the den. I hoped I would be able to add a few dollars to it before Santa arrived.

Dick, I know you remember the rainy Monday morning, a couple of weeks after my 'brush with the law', when I woke to the wracking pains of labor. It was a week past my delivery date, yet you thought I was teasing when I said it was time for the baby. Finally convinced, you and our little girl drove me to the Piedmont Hospital in Atlanta. Once I was situated in my room, you drove our daughter to a relative's house, so they could watch her for the night. Rather than return immediately to the hospital, you drove in the opposite direction, to our house. From there, you phoned my hospital room. Astonishingly, you said you had no money for gas and didn't know how you would get back to the Atlanta. Reluctantly, I told you where the rest of the Christmas savings was hidden. I asked you to please not take more than twenty dollars from the jar. When you returned to the hospital, mere minutes before our son entered the world, you told me you had found no money in the jar. You said you had to borrow gas money from someone you worked with. I knew you were lying, Dick. We were the only adults in the house. Who else would have taken the money? The money was in the jar and you spent it.

You acted indignant when I questioned your truthfulness. Confronting you was a waste of breath and it was just easier to drop it. I wanted to walk away from you then, September 1989. But what would I do? By now I was filled with self-doubt, I thought I would never make it on my own with two babies under two years old. And I told myself you were just having another difficult time. Even I was tired of my same old song and dance excuse, but it was the best I had at the time and I didn't want to raise my children without their dad.

By then, I had already learned to hide my feelings behind an invisible mask. Most everyone thought we had the perfect little family. My pride, my embarrassment would not let me expose you for the fraud I was beginning to realize you are. And back then, I really believed you would be so overcome with love for our children that you would want to become the best man you could be for them. I hoped you would crave the respect of our children as much as I did. I believed I could fail at anything in life and survive…except where my children were concerned. Failing them was unthinkable. Giving up on their dad was admitting failure. I couldn't give up.

After our son was born, you became even more withdrawn, more distant. You worked longer hours and brought home less money. When you weren't working you went fishing, hunting or you lay on the sofa and watched television. I told myself you were overwhelmed with our growing family, the mortgage, business troubles, etc. When we gathered with family and friends you transformed into the most amazing and loving husband and dad; you became the living version of my dream. During church picnics or family dinners, when you seemed to be in love with our family, I was able to convince myself this was the real you. Sometimes you could keep up the pretense until we arrived home, and then, away from your audience, you returned to your hateful, irritable, true nature. Most of the time, your act ended as soon as our family was alone in the car with you, returning to the house we all shared. It's easy now to see the resentment you held against us, but during those early days of our family, I didn't recognize it for what it.

For years you lashed out at me because of your displeasure at being a husband and dad, a position you considered beneath you. I'm still angry with myself for allowing your bitterness to control me. When you were in a good mood your small nuggets of love and attention seemed genuine, I held onto those nuggets for dear life, convincing myself your periodic transformations from selfish jerk to loving husband would one day be permanent. I believed your episodes of poor judgment and easy deception were simply your way of responding to stress and that one day, you would learn to cope with the problems of life. I became very skilled at making excuses for your problems. I believed the excuses myself.

Soon after our baby boy was born, your mom and dad began to visit on a regular basis. This was unusual for them. You had never had a close relationship with your parents and your mom and sisters despised me. Often you told me your mom and her mother hated little boys. You claimed your grandmother had advised your mom, on the day of your birth, "It's a boy, you may as well kill him now". Knowing this about your mom made her visits after the birth of a grandson a bit puzzling. Yet, you seemed happy to have them around. I like to believe you had hoped you, your dad and our son would have a special relationship. I wanted that for you and our son. Perhaps you thought your parents would finally show you the love and attention they had neglected giving you during your childhood. You had longed for the love they showered on your baby sister. I knew this, and I had ached for you many times because of it. So, I was happy for them to visit, especially if it meant they were finally becoming the parents you desired. Plus, you were usually in a good mood when you knew they were on their way to Georgia. Their frequent visits meant your moods were better more often. I liked that. Things seemed to be looking up again.

I tried to be happy to have them around. For the most part, I enjoyed your dad's company. But your mom's habit of making ugly, biting remarks, and calling it teasing, was difficult to take. During my first visit with your family, your mom said, "Well, at least if you have children, maybe they'll have normal foreheads. Yours is flat, Little Dick's protrudes, so we can at least hope your kids will have normal ones." At the time, I didn't know how to respond to your mom. I was very uncomfortable around her and I thought her habit of staring at people was strange and rude. Growing up, I was taught it's wrong to criticize a person's physical features or their financial status, so your mom's criticism of me and of you, put me in a terrible situation and made me uneasy. I didn't want to be rude to her, so I kept quiet. The entire time I knew her, your mom continued to make derogatory comments about people, always critical of a person's physical appearance; it is one of her most annoying habits. I came to think of it as 'picking a person apart' and never understood her need to find fault with others. Eventually I realized she had low self-esteem and her way of feeling better about herself was to put others down. Acquiring that knowledge didn't make me feel any better when she insulted me or the people I love. It angered me when she criticized you or me in front of our children. It was a behavior I didn't want either of our children to possess. In the beginning, I had hoped things would get better with your mom once she got to know me, but it soon became clear she didn't want to like me or to accept me into her family. Rather than improve with time, her rude remarks became more bitter and cruel. To keep peace, I continued to "keep my mouth shut"(your phrase). Most of the time, I didn't bring the incidents up with you. I knew your mom would deny making the remarks, I had seen her do so in several situations, and I knew you would not believe me anyway. But when our children were born, and her remarks turned to them, I could no longer keep quiet.

One time I caught your mom coldly scrutinizing Cissy. When BJ realized I had seen her, she said, "It's too bad that red spot is on her cheek. It'll ruin her looks."

As a baby, you'll remember, Cissy had a small, faint red spot on the lower half of her face. The spot would become a deeper red when she was hot. We never noticed it unless we were looking for it. Your mom really pissed me off when she 'picked Cissy apart', I had to say something. "Your granddaughter is so beautiful, nothing could ruin her looks," I said. I wanted to say more, I wanted to slap your mom for insulting our baby, but to save an argument, I refrained.

Later, after Garrett was born, BJ, "And to think you didn't want him." I was furious with her and I refused to hold back, "What the hell are you talking about?"

*"You were upset when you found out you were pregnant", she said. Your mom's comment was appalling. She is an evil woman and to quote a line from the Grinch song, her "heart is an empty hole." I said to her, "BJ, I've always wanted him. Who wouldn't want him? When I learned I was pregnant, I became very concerned about how we would pay for his birth because my husband, your son, wasn't working and we had no insurance. Practically every phone call we received came from a collection agency and we were struggling to purchase baby food for Cissy. Those were all very stressful things, but it doesn't mean Garrett wasn't wanted. I've always wanted him. You better listen to what I'm about to say and you better remember it! If you **ever** say anything like that to my son, or my daughter for that matter, I will tell them what a liar their grandmother is! What kind of sinister monster are you? Who would say something like that about their grandchild? You undoubtedly! The same woman who told her own son he didn't*

have the sense God gave a goose. You are malicious!" **I wish I could find the words to describe the masked evilness that dwells within that woman.**

When I found your mom going through my purse, so deep in thought reading my checkbook ledger that she didn't hear me approach, I had a better understanding of why you accused me of snooping. It's what she did, so you assumed I snooped too.

When Garrett was six months old, I began getting sick. Every time your mom and dad came to visit, I would get ill within an hour or so of their departure. Most of the time, when they came to visit, they arrived late Friday evenings and left on Monday morning after breakfast. Sickness wasn't common for me, I was seldom sick as a child and even when I was pregnant I didn't experience the morning sickness so common with many pregnancies. I remember thinking it was an odd coincidence that I would get sick within an hour of their departure, every time they visited. The pain in my stomach was always excruciating and my head would hurt so terribly I felt it might explode. At the time, it never occurred to me that you or your mother could be responsible for the change in my health.

After the first episode of extreme diarrhea, when it was evident the Imodium I took wasn't alleviating the symptoms, my mom suggested I obtain paregoric from the pharmacy. In those days, paregoric could be purchased over the counter, if the consumer signed for it with the pharmacist. You came home from work, that first time I was ill, and found me crumpled on the sofa. I asked you to go to the pharmacy and you said you were too tired. I asked you to drive me. "You have to sign for it anyway. Just drive yourself," you said. You offered to stay with the children while I drove the twelve miles into downtown Canton. I made the drive, even though I was so weak I had trouble standing without supporting myself.

Now I realize your lack of concern for my health reflected your hatred for me. The way you spat out, "just drive yourself" wasn't simply aggravation, as I thought back then. It was pure contempt.

By the time I got to Mid-City Pharmacy in Canton, I was weak, my legs could barely carry me. The pharmacist noticed my condition and asked me to take a seat while he prepared the paregoric and appropriate paperwork. He told the counter attendant to call someone to drive me home. "My husband is home with our children, he won't be able to come into town. There is no one else. I'll be fine in a bit."

"Honey, I know he would prefer to drive here and pick you up, if he knew how sick you are," the clerk said.

I wanted to tell her you already knew, that you had refused to drive me into town, but I stayed silent. It was my secret. I was too embarrassed to admit I was married to a man who didn't care. In those days, I wouldn't say anything that would cast a bad light on you. Unkind words and derogatory comments about *you never escaped my lips, because they wouldn't go well with the pretty fairytale I was trying to create.*

The pharmacist handed me the medicine and advised me against taking it while driving. "This is a strong medication. It's derived from Opium. Don't take more than is required, and don't take it until you're home. Don't drive after you've ingested the paregoric."

By the time I made it home, I was practically crawling. I went into the kitchen, took the medication and followed the sounds of the TV into the den. I sat beside you on the sofa and leaned into you. You asked, "Aren't you going to make dinner?"

"This is probably a terrible virus, I don't think I should handle our food. And I'm too weak to stand up, Dick, could you make sandwiches or something for yourself and Cissy?"

Do you remember how upset you became? "Why didn't you get our dinner up when you were in town, then? Would that have been too much trouble for you?" You screamed at me and called me a selfish bitch. "All you ever think about is your own goat smelly ass!" The insults you hurled at me were endless, but I was too sick to care, too sick to fight.

I asked if you would give our son a bottle, I told you I didn't think I should nurse him, in case I was contagious, and I asked you once more to feed our little girl. In a huff, you went into the kitchen and slammed cabinet doors and drawers. You took care of the children and fed them, but the entire time you kept saying, "I'm starving. There's nothing to eat in this damn house."

That evening, after the paregoric took effect, I heated some leftovers for you. The smell of the chicken casserole was nauseating to me, and sent me running to the bathroom. When I returned to the kitchen you were peppering your casserole with Cajun seasoning, you spoke without looking at me, "I'll do this myself. Go sit down." Your tone was not gentle or soothing; it was bitter and angry and filled with resentment.

The periodic episodes of vomiting and stomach problems were becoming a cause of concern for my parents and two of my aunts. One day, my Aunt Mary Dean said she had been thinking about the health problems I was having. "Have you noticed you only get sick after Dick's parents visit? His mama is crazy, I'm afraid she's poisoning you. Your symptoms are just like the symptoms that lady in Canton had. The one whose husband tried to kill her with arsenic."

I laughed, "No, no, no. BJ's nuts and she hates me, but I don't think she would do anything like that."

Mary Dean was not satisfied with my answer, "Well, I want you to promise me you'll be careful around her. Don't let her near your food or drink. Don't you think it's strange that she never visited Dick until ya'll were married? I mean, it's strange to me that you only get sick when she visits. That woman scares *me. I don't really know her, but I know a crazy person when I see one and she's crazy."*

I promised her I would be careful around your mom. But I wasn't, I didn't think there was anything to be careful of. I remember thinking Dean watched too many crime shows on television.

Then one day my Aunt Mae called, "Now I don't want you to get upset with me, but there's something on my mind and I won't feel right until I tell you what I've been thinking. Danita, if something happened to you and I hadn't warned you of what I've been feeling, I would never forgive myself. Do you think Dick could be doing something to make you sick? I mean, this just makes no sense the way you keep getting sick all the time. You've always been as healthy as a horse! I know you said you think it's a recurring virus, but the kids aren't getting sick and Dick sure as hell never gets sick."

I assured her you would never to anything to harm me. I was your wife, the mother of your children. "Only a monster would hurt his children's mother", I remember saying to her.

"Well, there are a lot of damn monsters in the world, but the problem is they look like angels."

I brushed her concerns aside, confident both my aunts had heard too many horror stories and watched too much crime TV. I didn't tell you about their concerns.

In an effort to regain my health and stamina, I decided I would exercise more, stay away from junk food and get outside more often. I began a morning routine of bundling the kids up, loading them in the double stroller and walking. In my weakened physical condition, it took great effort to push the stroller up the steep hills surrounding our home. I tried to make it an adventure for the kids. Both were mere babies, but I would make up stories for them and pretend we were on the wagon trail or mountain climbers or Hansel and Gretel. One morning, as I pushed the stroller up the steepest incline, I happened to look down at my hands as they gripped the stroller handle. The knuckle on the index finger of my right hand was red and swollen. It was slightly tender, but it wasn't what I considered painful. I assumed I had been bitten by an insect and thought nothing else of it. A few days later I woke with my hand in severe pain and noticed my left index finger was now also red and swollen. When you woke, I showed you my hands.

"You've probably been bitten by something. Don't worry about it", you said.

I thought you were probably correct, and I began medicating myself with left-over antibiotics and aspirin. The following weekend your parents came to visit. By the time they arrived, the color of my right hand had turned a deep purple-red. The skin on the back of my hand began to have a smooth, hardened look and feel to it. My left hand showed signs of becoming just like my right hand. I showed my hands to your mom and told her of the excruciating pain.

"You are such a hypochondriac. You've always got to have something wrong with you, don't you? You've either bumped your hands or something bit you," she said.

"That's what I've tried to tell her, but she won't listen!" you said.

Your parents returned to Louisiana on Sunday afternoon, and by Sunday evening I was sick again. The stomach cramps were fierce, and I spent most of the night on the bathroom floor. You never came to check on me. The next morning, I told you I thought I needed to go to the emergency room. Do you remember what you said, Dick? You said, "You're just like my damn mom and sisters, always acting like something's wrong with you. Get over yourself!"

You left for work without asking if I would be okay or if I needed anything. Later in the day, Mary Dean called to check on me, she knew your parents had visited over the weekend and she was concerned. My family was convinced there was something disturbing behind my deteriorating health, but I wasn't worried. I didn't think there was reason for them to be concerned, either. I admitted to Mary Dean I was sick again, and she asked if I had taken paregoric. I told her I had none left and had no money to purchase more. Within a couple of hours, she was at our door with medication for me and food for the family. She had driven from her home in Jasper to plead with me to see a doctor. She also said I should get in touch with the arsenic survivor in Canton. I did neither. Arsenic poisoning, poisoning of any kind by another person, sounded too crazy to say out loud. It was an unfathomable concept.

A couple of weeks after your parent's visit, the kids and I drove to White, GA to visit my Aunt Mae. As soon as I walked in, she asked, "Why are you limping?"

I told her I wasn't aware I was limping.

"Well you are! What's that crazy ass BJ or her sorry ass son done to you?" I laughed and told her I was probably limping because I was usually carrying a baby on each hip, a heavy diaper bag on one shoulder and a purse on the other. She warned me to be leery of your mother. "That woman makes my skin crawl. She's evil, but she's good at covering it up. You be careful around her. Be careful around the whole damn bunch, Dick included. I don't trust him any farther than I can throw him."

I shook my head as I laughed the warnings off, convinced I came from a family of overly suspicious people.

I never visited a doctor for my stomach ailments. Remember how you would tell me doctors were good for nothing but getting rich "off poor people" and would only make me sicker? You said I was getting viruses because I didn't take care of myself. I knew I wasn't getting enough exercise and hadn't been eating properly. Your evaluation of my health crisis seemed probable.

I remember being so thankful that you and the kids never came down with the virus. I remember saying to you, "If anyone has to get the bug, I'm happy it's me. I would hate for the kids to be this sick. There's no way you would be able to work with if you come down with this stuff, it's the worst pain I've ever felt; including childbirth. And the overall sick feeling is horrid."

I remember my mom saying a virus this severe would probably kill babies or the elderly. "Just be thankful those two babies haven't come down with it", she said.

Several weeks after the first bout with the virus, my hair started falling out. I would find large amounts of hair in the shower. Clumps of hair were left in my hairbrush, long wavy strands of dark hair clung to my pillows each morning. This worried me. We didn't have medical insurance and I was hesitant to spend money consulting our family physician, so I mentioned the hair loss to my gynecologist during a postnatal visit to his office. He said hair loss, weeks or even months, after the birth of a baby was normal with some women. He assured me it was hormone related. "Once your hormones settle down and get in balance, you'll see the hair loss stop." I respected my doctor and his was a logical explanation, so I tried to not worry about my thinning hair. But it didn't stop. My hair continued to shed, I lost more weight and my stomach problems continued, though happening less frequently than before. I thought I was on the mend. Occasionally I still became sick when your parents visited but I contributed this to stress of dealing with your mom.

My hands were a different story. Do you remember how they were? The pain increased and was so severe, I couldn't hold a toothbrush without great effort and discomfort. My fingers were grotesquely swollen and remained a purplish red color from the knuckle to the base of my finger. Sometimes, the pain was excruciating, rendering sleep impossible. When my hands became so engorged and painful that I had to change our sons diaper by pulling the taped closure away from the plastic diaper with my teeth, I finally admitted I had a problem that wasn't getting any better. I told you I felt I had to see a doctor about my hands. Mentioning the possibility of a doctor's visit sent you in a tailspin.

"Why do you want to run to the damn doctor every time you think you have something wrong? I'm tired of this shit! There's nothing wrong with you! All you want to do is waste every fucking dime I make!"

I was upset by your reaction. Anyone could look at my hands and see that something was wrong. I held them out and asked you to look at them, even though you had watched me struggling to use them during the last weeks. I reminded you the only physician I had visited was my gynecologist. It wasn't my nature to see a doctor for minor illnesses and you knew this. Still, you kept up your tirade, "Go on and waste my money. That's all you know how to do!"

I had worn borrowed maternity clothes during my two pregnancies, the tennis shoes on my feet had holes in the toes and I hadn't had my hair cut professionally in over a year. Even the Christmas and birthday gifts you gave me were returned to the store at your request. No one could accuse me of being careless with money. But for the entire length of our marriage, you accused me of wasteful spending. I guess you thought the tobacco you kept in your mouth throughout the day was money well spent. Did you consider Copenhagen and Skoal tobacco a necessity for our family? Were your frequent purchases of hunting and fishing equipment essential for the well-being and development of our children? During those days, I didn't know you were spending money on other men's wives, but you were, and that was one of the reasons we couldn't afford the basics of life.

Your voice was inflamed with detest when you screamed, "We can't afford for you to see a damn doctor just because you got a little pain in your hand! Hell, I hurt all the time, and nobody worries about me"! I did not want more trouble with you, so I put off calling the doctor's office for several more days. Early one morning, I woke with tears rolling down my face. The pain had been so terrible, I had wept during sleep. Quietly, I sat up and swung my legs off the side of the bed and raised my arms above my head, hoping to alleviate the pain and swelling. The slightest touch caused searing pain, and as I raised my arms, my right hand brushed against the covers, causing me to wince loudly. In the early morning darkness, you asked, "What's the matter with you? What are you whining about now?"

Without answering you, I slid from the bed and went into the bathroom to shower; sometimes the hottest water I could tolerate would ease the discomfort a bit. Both my hands were swollen and misshapen, only my thumbs would bend without searing pain. I could no longer grasp or grip, with either hand. I couldn't snap my fingers or hold a pencil without breathtaking pain. I couldn't twist the shower knob with my hands, instead I used my forearms in a shoving and rolling motion to adjust the faucet controls, the process took great effort. That morning, knowing you were awake, I asked you to adjust the water for me.

"Do it yourself. I've got to work all day while you do nothing but sit on your ass. I fuckin' work! Why don't you see if you can't get a job today?" In retrospect I can hear the animosity in your voice, but at the time, I didn't recognize hatred and contempt. Later that morning, after you left for work and I had the children settled, I decided to make an appointment with Dr. Fry. His receptionist said he would be able to see me the next day. I didn't tell you about the appointment because I didn't have the stamina to fight you; the constant pain in my hands drained me of energy. The following afternoon I loaded both kids in their car seats, placed the double stroller in the trunk of the car, and drove into town for the scheduled doctor's visit. I remember I didn't want to wait with the children in a lobby filled with sick people, so I asked the receptionist if she would mind if I waited outside. "Oh, sure, go ahead. It's a beautiful day! I would wait outside too, if I could. I'll open the door when we're ready for you.

When Doctor Fry saw my hands, his knee-jerk diagnosis was arthritis. I told him I knew of no one in my family with arthritis. My grandparents had lived into their late seventies and eighties with only minor arthritic problems. Even so, he said he was almost certain arthritis was the problem. He ordered lab tests to confirm. I didn't think the frequent stomach ailments and hair loss were related to the pain in my hands, so I didn't mention these other symptoms to the doctor. It had been two weeks since I had last experienced diarrhea and vomiting, and in my mind, this confirmed my self-diagnosis of a lingering virus, which now appeared to be gone.

A few days after the lab work, Dr. Fry called, "Well, the good news is you don't have arthritis. The bad news is, I suspect you may have a rare autoimmune disease. I'm referring you to Dr. Gabriel at St. Joe's in Atlanta. He's tops in the field and he'll get to the bottom of this. I'll have my receptionist make the appointment. She'll call you when it's set."

That afternoon, Dr. Fry's office called with the date and time of my appointment with the specialist. I knew I would have to tell you about the referral to an Atlanta physician and my stomach churned at the prospect of another angry altercation between us. As I expected, you yelled, screamed and threw a man-sized temper tantrum and said there was no reason to spend money on another doctor. You demanded I cancel the appointment. For once, I did not obey your demands.

My aunt and her mother-in-law had agreed to babysit while I saw the physician at St. Joseph's. My appointment was at nine o'clock on Tuesday morning; I arrived early and completed an extensive questionnaire, regarding my medical history. I listed everything I could remember, including my recent bouts with diarrhea, vomiting and hair loss. A nurse ushered me to an examination room and asked a few more questions. Eventually, the doctor entered and introduced himself; he looked at my hands and asked more questions. He told me he felt it was probably an autoimmune issue but wanted to do some more lab work. For the time being though, he said, he wanted to put me on a medication called Prednisone, sixty-five milligrams per day. I had never heard of this medicine, but he said it would take the swelling out of my hands. He said when the swelling was gone, the pain would go away too.

"You'll be surprised how much better you'll feel when we rid you of pain", he said.

This sounded like great news to me, because by this time I thought my only relief would be amputation and I would have willingly agreed to it, that's how bad the pain was. Several days later, Dr. Gabriel called with the results from the lab. He said they were inconclusive and more tests were needed. I guess it was then I should have asked him to check for poisons in my system, but it never entered my mind. I didn't think poison was a possibility. I thought poison was a crazy idea my aunts had conjured up.

You were angry when I told you the doctor wanted to do more tests. You accused him of greed and dishonesty. Your lack of concern for my health puzzled me. During the last few weeks it had become apparent I was ill. My weight had dropped to 102 pounds, I had not weighed so little since college. My hair, usually full and wavy, hung in thin, limp strands. I was determined to get an answer regarding my declining health, so I agreed to more tests, all of which were inconclusive. My aunts, and occasionally my parents, still tried to persuade me to be tested for poisons, and I continued to disregard their requests. Looking back, I realize I was foolish not to listen to them. Would you be in prison now if I had listened to the people who love me? I'll never know the answer to that question, but I think about it often.

As my physical condition deteriorated, so did our finances. We could not afford the cost of the doctor or the lab fees, so I discontinued my visits. The medication had alleviated the swelling in my hands, the pain was now tolerable. The prednisone also ended the weight loss, but the other ailments continued. When I told you I would no longer see the doctor, you were visibly relieved. You wrapped your arms around me and told me everything would be alright. I wanted to believe you.

Do you remember how small our house payment was? $575.00 per month for a five-bedroom home, on ten acres. And we couldn't make the payment. You were away from home long hours working your construction jobs, but there was never enough money. Not even for groceries and utilities. One very cold Friday in December, just a few days after our little girl turned three…a couple of months after our little boy turned one, I heard Bonzo barking. I went to the window and watched a large truck back down our driveway and pull beside the house, next to the propane tank. The driver and an assistant stepped out of the truck and began the removal of our propane tank, our home's source of heat and cooking.

I called the propane provider and asked if they would hold off until I could get a payment to them. I explained I had two babies who wouldn't do well without heat. "Well, I'm sorry about that", she said, "I guess you and your husband need to pay your bills on time."

I sat on the floor and cried as they hauled the tank away. My sweet little girl wrapped her dimpled baby arms around my neck, patted my shoulder and said, "It be ok, Mommy". Dear God, my heart broke for her that day. When you came home that night you noticed the missing tank. You walked in the front door and asked, "Why did you let them take the tank?"

I replayed the events that transpired that afternoon; I repeated the conversation with the lady from the propane company.

"You could have stopped them if you had really tried!" you said.

"They need money from us Dick! Utility companies expect to be paid for their services. Did you collect your pay from anyone today?"

"No. I couldn't find anyone to pay me. That's why I'm so late getting home. I drove all over Roswell looking for Dave." It was the same story you gave me every Friday and the story was getting old.

Later that night my parents brought a five gallon can of kerosene and a kerosene heater to our house. We set the heater in the den and built a fire in the fireplace. I placed quilts and blankets on the floor for the children to sit and sleep on. I heated their bath water in the microwave. For the next week, we had cold sandwiches and salads for dinner, cereal for breakfast. Then, the very next Friday, Amicalola EMC shut off our power. No lights and no heat, no hot water. I remember feeling beaten and defeated. When you came home later that day, the kids and I were huddled in front of the fireplace. Except for the glowing light and heat from the fireplace and kerosene heater, the house was cold and dark. Casually, as if suggesting we drive across town to visit a friend, you said, "Well, I guess we'll move to Louisiana. Dad says he can get me a job with a large craft and hobby store in Baton Rouge, a management position. We can live with Mom and Dad for a while."

I can't begin to describe the anger and frustration I felt toward you that day. How could you even think about moving us to the place you had claimed to escape from only a few years before? How could you ask us to live with your mother? A woman you hate? A woman who hated me?

"What about our house and land?" I asked.

"The damn bank can have the sonofabitch. I'm tired of trying to keep this damn place up!" That was your answer.

In reality, you had done very little to keep our house up. Instead of working every day, you were spending hours with the trashy women you came across. But I was unaware of the way you spent your time. You're such an accomplished liar, I believed you when you told me you were working all day. I thought you were telling the truth when you said the 'no good people' in construction were "screwing you" by withholding the money they owed you. You said to keep your employees, you had to pay them even when no work had been done. That made no sense to me, and we argued when I said as much.

"You don't know anything about how a business works", you said.

You were relying on our parents, yours and mine, to pay our bills while you screwed around with women. Your mama is still paying your bills, while you party in Cheyenne. You are almost fifty years old, a big Baby Huey that cries and pouts to the mama he hates. Twenty years ago, I was naïve, I believed almost everything you said. I was convinced the disruptions in your personality were temporary. I believed your aberrant behavior was a reaction to the problems arising in our lives, rather than the reason for the problems. So later that night, when you came to me and gently said, "Dad says I definitely have a job waiting for me in Baton Rouge", I didn't question what you said. I accepted it, even while I grieved for the loss of my home and dreaded the move away from family, to a place where I knew I was hated. I regarded this job as an offering of hope. My family saw it as a death sentence.

Like a dog kicked into submission, I went into autopilot. I began packing up the house, crying with every box I sealed, every closet I emptied. Throughout the packing process you admonished me for my sadness. You said, "I'm tired of killing myself for this damn house! Stop your damn whining!" You said you had a great job waiting for you in Baton Rouge and you didn't understand why I wasn't happy about that. Never did you empathize with me or try to understand my sadness. Within a few days your dad drove to Georgia from Louisiana, we loaded a moving van, and without so much as an apology from you, we moved to hell.

The "great job" was a phantom. There was no employer waiting for you in Baton Rouge. To this day I don't know if you lied to me, or if your parents lied to you, to ensure our move to Louisiana. Eventually you found work in construction with an old high school friend of yours. There was still no insurance and the pay was very low. Emotionally, we were worse off than we were in Georgia. Even you seemed sad.

We spent a year in Louisiana. For twelve months I had to deal with your mother and your sisters treating me as if your irresponsibility was my fault. I couldn't drag you out of bed and off to work any better than they could, but they acted as if your laziness was something I controlled. For twelve months, I was subjected to their hatred of me and their jealousy of our children. I had to listen to them while they talked about me as if I were not in the next room. Your mother started on your old girlfriend again, and for twelve solid months she told me how much you loved Mary and that you would never love me as much as your loved her. For twelve months I listened to your twenty-one-year-old, selfish sister call my children brats, and me a bitch. When I defended our children and myself, your sister and your mother fought me. The mother you despise and the sister you called a "spoiled bitch" pushed me down and knocked me backwards over the kitchen bar. Your sister hit me repeatedly as your mother wrapped her hands around my neck and choked me. I was weak from illness and medications, I was in no shape to physically defend myself, and they took advantage of my condition. When you came home I told you what had occurred that day. When you asked your mom and sister about the fight, they said I was lying. **Both** said it never happened. I told you our three-year-old daughter had seen the entire attack. You asked Cissy, and she told you what happened as best she could. But you didn't believe her. I suggested you could call the police for proof, because your sister had called 911 and demanded, "Come get my sister-in-law and her brats out of my house". You sided with your mom and sister. You cast your children and me aside. That's when I began to loathe you.

I'm curious…do you treat your girlfriends and their children the way you treated our kids and me?

My health deteriorated in Louisiana. Day by day, I became weaker. Your mother acted as if I was faking the illness and said as much to her neighbors. I remember one day after breakfast, I was so sick I couldn't stand up. I felt as if I had been drugged. I was weak, my vision was blurry, and my tongue was so heavy I could barely speak. I sat on the sofa and waited for the feeling to pass, but it worsened as the morning rolled on. Our little children were aware something was wrong with me. I remember their little hands rubbing my arms and legs and face, while I slipped in and out of awareness on the sofa. You were working, your dad was out of town, but your mom was home. I was vaguely aware of her walking around the house, tinkering in the kitchen and vacuuming the carpet of the den, the room I was in. She never asked how I was feeling. When I asked her to call 911, she asked me how I thought I would pay for an emergency room visit.

"Because I'm sure as hell not paying for it!" she said. She never called an ambulance. By the time you came home from work, your mom was gone. She left without speaking. She didn't ask if her grandchildren had eaten, she knew they had not. They had not eaten a bite, because I had been unable to lift myself from the sofa all day.

When you walked in the door, our little girl ran to you, crying, "Mommy's sick, Dada".

You walked to the sofa and asked what was wrong. Your voice came to me muffled, as if in a tunnel. I couldn't answer, couldn't speak. You lifted me in your arms and carried me outside to your parent's backyard and placed me on a reclined lawn chair. Both our babies followed.

"I think Mommy needs some fresh air", you said.

"Put your hands on mommy's legs," you told the children.

And then you prayed for me. It was the first time I had ever heard you praying to God.

I was sick for three more days, gradually improving each day. I never went to the emergency room, nor did I see a physician.

I seldom said anything about the pain in my hands, the mental fog I experienced, or the headaches that never went away. I had learned my lesson about revealing how I felt. On the occasions I mentioned not feeling well, you or your mother would tell me to stop whining and complaining. Eventually, I stopped saying anything to you at all regarding my symptoms, but I embarked on a personal mission to find an affordable doctor. I contacted a physician in Georgia and he referred me to the Muscular Dystrophy Association in Baton Rouge. He explained the clinic would be free. At the time, I had been diagnosed, (misdiagnosed, but it would be years before I knew this), with an illness in the Muscular Dystrophy group. It would be a few months before there was an open appointment with the MDA, in the meantime, my hands were 'crippling' again. By the time I had the first visit to the Muscular Dystrophy Clinic, my hands were in the same swollen, discolored and painful condition as before. During the second MDA appointment, the physician told me the lab tests indicated I did not have any of the Muscular Dystrophy Diseases. Before I left he said to me, "Perhaps you should consider being tested for heavy metals. You have some unusual symptoms and it's possible you've come in contact with a poison of some kind."

That was my final visit to the MDA Clinic, we were moving to Wyoming in a couple of weeks, so you could attend Cheyenne Aero Tech. I had high hopes the move would be a new beginning for us. But the MDA doctor's comment was eerily reminiscent of my aunt's comments, and I couldn't stop thinking about what he had suggested. So one afternoon, before we left Baton Rouge, your mother, you and I were sitting in her den and I decided to tell the two of you what the doctor had suggested. I still didn't fully believe anyone in my life would want to harm me, especially you, but something within urged me to tell you and your mother what the doctor insinuated. I wanted to watch your reactions. When I said, "the doctor thinks I may have been poisoned in some way," neither of you showed an interest. There were no questions from either of you inquiring of the type of poison he thought it could be. There was no curiosity about how I might have encounterd poison. Nothing. I'll never forget the way your mama looked at me. The look she gave me made the hair on my head feel prickly. Still today, I can see the cold, stone-faced expression she presented. A few days later, we left Baton Rouge... I had never been so happy to see a place disappear in my rearview mirror as I was to watch your parent's house fade from view. I thought I was finally leaving hell.

With you driving the large moving van, and me following in our car, the drive to Wyoming took three days. By the time we crossed over the border separating Colorado and Wyoming, much of the swelling in my hands was gone. The pain had subsided greatly, and I had only had diarrhea twice, early in the trip.

I loved the two years we spent in Cheyenne. For the first time in our marriage, it felt like we were on the same team, finally working together for a common goal. We lived in an old, tiny apartment, a former military housing development for F.E Warren Air Force Base. We had very little money, but that didn't matter to me. The children were happy, you seemed happy and my health was great for the first time in almost two years. Our plan was to move back to Georgia after you finished the Aerotech program. A couple of months before you completed the A&P program, I was changing the sheets on our bed and found a pair of lady's underwear crumpled in the covers. They did not belong to me. I asked you about them and you immediately blamed our babysitter. "I bet that girl had someone here while she was babysitting," you said. I wanted to believe you, but I didn't. I guess I've relied heavily on denial as a survival mechanism, because once again, I pushed the thought away and told myself I was being suspicious for no reason. After all, you were home when you were supposed to be. As far as I knew you were at work every day and in class every night. I chided myself, "When would he have time to have an affair?"

We were in Wyoming almost two years before your parents came to visit. In fact, we seldom heard from them. Your birthday was a week before we were to leave Cheyenne, your parents decided to come visit before we left the state. To celebrate your birthday, we planned a short trip to Jackson Hole with them and our children. The morning of the day we were to drive to Jackson, you told us you had to do some maintenance work around the apartment complex. You said you would be finished by ten o'clock that morning. Your parents and I packed the car so that we would be ready to go as soon as you came home. Ten o'clock came and went, then eleven. I phoned the office at the complex and asked Jane, the manager if you were around, "No, he didn't have to work today. Dick said his parents were here and you all were going out of town. Danita, do you know Allison? Check with her." I knew what Jane was implying but I couldn't ask any more questions, your parents would be furious with me for questioning you. I made an excuse to leave and I drove around the apartment complex looking for you. You were nowhere to be found. I returned to our apartment to wait with your parents, around noon you showed up with a birthday card in your hands. When I asked where you had been you were indignant, "You know where I've been! Working my ass off like I always do!"

You were incensed when I told you I had spoken with Jane and she said you weren't working, "That crazy bitch doesn't know what's going on! If you don't believe me, I'll show you the work I did today!" I dropped the fight. Why waste my breath on your lies and self-righteous attitude? You stormed off to the shower yelling, "I've got a good mind to stay here! I don't need this shit!" As I retrieved the birthday card you had tossed into the trash, your mom said to me, "Why do you always have to upset him? Why do you always do this to him?" I showed her the card, "Happy Birthday to a Wonderful Man! I love you, Allison."

"That's just someone that cares about him as a friend! My God, leave him alone!" Your mother was in denial too. She still is.

The underwear and the card from Allison were just the beginning of my new patch of trouble. I guess it was the beginning of my very slow walk towards acknowledgement of your instability. The beginning of my troubles began the day we met. Your problems began when you were still just a little boy. But you kept those things secret from me for years. You didn't admit your early exposure to sex and pornography, or the emotional issues they caused you, until years after we were married. And even then, you didn't want help for your problems. Your sexual addictions had been left to grow and fester like untreated boils. When they ruptured and spilled their infections into our marriage, I tried to treat the gaping wound by wiping off the pus and covering it with a bandage. In a few days, the boil always seemed to be healed. It (you) would look good on the outside, so I thought all was well again. But underneath the surface, your infection continued to grow and spread, eventually filling your soul and your spirit. Your visible behavioral problems, the 'boil', was only a small indicator of the severity of your disease.

Why did I ever believe there was anything good in you? What made me think you were just going through hard times? How could I have believed your behavior was your way of coping with stress? Why did I make excuses for you to others as well as myself? Why did I believe you could be anything more than a lying, disgusting, womanizing adulterer? I can't answer my own questions. I don't know why or how I continued to find saving qualities in you. I guess part of the reason was I wanted you to be something you were never capable of being to begin with: an honest and responsible husband and dad. You took advantage of the faith and hope I had in you. You trampled on me and then on our children. Like a wild, roaming tiger your eyes were set on your prey, in your case, the prey was married women. And like a wild conscienceless predator, you ran over, chased down and tried to destroy anything standing in the way of you and the women. Sometimes your behavior mimicked a tiger in a zoo pen, frantically pacing back and forth, stopping frequently to roar hatred toward the zoo keepers. You were the caged tiger; we, your family, were the keepers of your pen. Sometimes the tiger escaped, and he mutilated the human lives he crossed. But he always sauntered back to his cage. Why? At first, he seemed happy to return to his home. Before long, the wild-eyed glares and the roar of hatred, resentment and contempt always returned. Why did you come back? You only prolonged our misery.

It may appear to you and others that I walked through life with a blindfold tied around my eyes. And for a while that's exactly how it was. But eventually, it wasn't like that at all. In the beginning I had great hopes for you and our family. If I was blinded by anything, it was faith that you could do anything you set your mind on. Even when I suspected infidelity or deceit, I still held onto hope of a better life with you. Yes, I continued to make excuses for your behavior, but I wasn't blind. I was determined to give my family every opportunity to survive. My understanding of the monster within you was limited to what you permitted me to witness. I was ignorant of your heartlessness and your inability to empathize. Evidence of your lack of emotion and your inability to experience guilt and remorse was kept tucked safely behind the mask of a normal man. When I finally recognized you for the despicable little man you are, we had two beautiful children and I had a different reason for trying to keep the marriage together. I knew of your attraction to married women long before I knew of your addiction to pornography. Until recently, when you began seeing the married gynecologist in Cheyenne, your women of choice were always what you referred to as Trailer Park Trash.

The friends you chose were as bad as the women: alcoholics, drug addicts and other adulterers. Not the kind of people I wanted around my children. I chose to stay with you to protect my children from you, the women and your friends. I knew if we divorced I would probably have to share custody with you. Who would protect my children from the influences of you and your women? I thought I was protecting our children. But, I wasn't. You still found ways to expose them to your disgusting sickness. I didn't know what you were doing, and I could never have imagined the low level to which you were willing to stoop or the carnage you would expose to our kids. I hate myself for staying with you. You never deserved our children and they never deserved to have a sick bastard for a dad. These days our son calls you the Sperm Donor rather than dad. His title for you is much more fitting than the endearing name of dad.

Probably one of the hardest things for me to anchor my mind on, is not that you cheated, but that I stayed. What happened to me? Now that I'm removed from the blanket of heartache, lies and insults you wrapped me in daily, I feel strong and worthy. I no longer think of myself as someone you were doing a favor for. That's how you made me feel, you know. My thoughts were muddled with lies: **No one else would ever want me. You had settled for me when you could have had someone more deserving of Little Dick Crisco. I was worthless.**

But the very hardest thing of all, is realizing my blind determination to make my marriage work, may not have benefited my children at all. I should have left your sorry butt the first time I had proof of an affair. Or even before, when I realized lies slip off your tongue as easily as melted butter. How did I assure myself I was helping the children by choosing to stay? Why could I not see the pain in their little faces? How did I persuade myself having you around was better for them than your absence? I was a fool. How did I convince myself that each affair, each episode with adult web sites and phone sex lines, would be the last? How could I do that to my children and myself? For almost twenty-four years, I unwittingly enabled you to live your dirty, seedy, secret life. I'll never understand what happened to me, or how I allowed it to happen. I will regret my choices until my last living day.

Now you're in Wyoming, with yet another man's wife. Playing dad to another man's children. Sleeping in another man's bed, with another man's wife. Eating his food, driving his car. She's paying for your dates, purchasing your clothing and food. You've finally found the Sugar Mama you've been searching for. I doubt she realizes how dearly she'll pay for your attention and affection. Oh, you'll drain her bank account at the first opportunity, but I'm speaking of a more expensive form of payment. I'm referring to her loss of self-esteem, the loss of respect from her daughters and the cost of the anguish and humiliation she will cause them, her husband and her own parents. All because she believes you are a Knight in Shining Armor. Soon, but most likely not soon enough to save her family, she will see the rusted, peeling places in your dull armor. She'll realize her knight is nothing more than a carefully crafted illusion created to gain her trust and admiration. *I feel sorry for this woman, seemingly an intelligent woman, because you've fooled her. Haven't you? But mostly I feel terrible for her husband, her two little girls, and her parents. Her family is experiencing, at her hands, the same emotional pain you inflicted on our children and me. Strange, don't you think, her hands, the hands trained to deliver babies safely into the world are creating emotional scars for her own babies? You don't really care about that though, do you? You're only concern is for your pecker and your wallet. Everything else you toss aside, simply shoving the cares, worries and concerns most fathers deal with into a drawer, just like you do the bills you never pay.*

Do you remember several years ago, when we found your mother's dad through a genealogy web site? You were excited when we discovered his name and the names of your mother's half siblings and you called her to tell her of the discovery. You felt she would want to be in contact with them. She had always told you she didn't want a relationship with him, but you felt enough time had passed and she should contact him. The history she relayed of her dad had always been a bit foggy and confusing, the information she revealed about him was always jumbled and I was never able to tie it all together. I was apprehensive about your call to her, but you felt certain she would want to contact him. You were wrong, remember? She told you she wanted nothing to do with him.

"She told me I could call him if I wanted to, but to leave her out of it," you said. You chose not to call, but we wondered what had caused your mom to have so much hatred for her dad. Now I wonder this: Are you the same kind of man your mother hates? Are you and your grandfather the same type of man? Is that the legacy your mother passed to you?

My prayer is the legacy dies with you.
Danita

P.S. I'm purging myself of the anger and frustrations that has lived in me for twenty-four years. Writing has helped. I'm enclosing a list I made for your mom; a list of things I wanted to get off my chest.

<u>*B.J. Things I Think You Should Hear:*</u>
B.J, you've said I blame you for the choices Dick has made. That is not true. I do however, think you blame yourself. Dick is responsible for the choices he's made as an adult. I think the way you treated him as a child contributed to his mental problems, which causes him to make poor choices. For example:

1. You emasculated him from the time he was a very small child. When he was still a little boy, you told him over and over that your own mother, his grandmother, hated him for being a boy. You told him his grandma said you should just kill him since he was a boy. (Tell me BJ, why would you hurt your child by telling him something so cruel? He understood she hated him for something he had no control over: his gender.

2. *You made him urinate like a girl. You would not allow him to stand at the toilet; instead you forced him to sit like a girl. Why would you do that? What do you think that did to him emotionally? Especially when he learned other boys, his cousins, stood to urinate? I remember when I was toilet training Garrett, you said to me, "I never let Little Dick stand. I made him sit." I told you Garrett would stand.*

3. *Dick told me you made him stay clean, even if he went outside to play. He was unable to get dirty like other boys. You forced him to stay clean, like a girl. Don't you wonder if you made him feel as if you wanted him to be a girl?*

4. *You told him he didn't have the sense God gave a goose. You told him he would never amount to anything. Well, BJ, he took you at your word. He believed you.*

5. *You've told all of us, on many occasions, that you "tried to make Little Dick be the perfect man." The problem with that is your idea of a perfect man was a man who never had sex. You told us that too. You emasculated him in the hope of preventing him from having sex. As a result, since his early teens, he has spent his life trying to prove to himself he is a man like other men. Unfortunately, he thinks the way to prove his masculinity is by having sex with as many people as possible. The behavior started in his teens and goes on today. Many times, you've laughed and told the story of catching Dick sneaking in and out of his bedroom window. I never laughed when you told the story, because unfortunately, Dick never stopped sneaking around. He gets some sick kick out of it. And for his kids and me, it was never funny.*

*One more thing BJ, did you ever stop to think about Cissy and Garrett when you chose to take your other grandchildren on trips, yet leave Cissy and Garrett behind? Do you remember telling Cissy that Micha said there would not be enough room in the condo for her to come to the beach? You wanted me to tell her, and I refused. Because I knew you would twist the story and deny it. You've told everyone that you invited Cissy to Europe with you and your other granddaughter, and that Cissy declined. Cissy knows the truth; you invited her **after** she learned of the trip. She learned of the trip because she called her cousin and invited her to go on a graduation trip with us. "I can't go. Grandma is taking me to Europe," replied your other granddaughter. Nothing was said about Cissy going. So when you twist your story, you should remember this: Cissy knows the truth and so does the other granddaughter. Do you ever feel remorseful for showing a difference in your grandchildren? Do you ever feel bad because you support their dad in his adultery and push them to the side?*

Moving On

Through a series of events, several conversations passed between the husband of Dick's latest girlfriend and me. I was not surprised to learn of the drama Dick had created since arriving in Cheyenne, but I certainly hated hearing about the heartbreak of another family. I realized this woman had no understanding of the true nature of Dick Crisco. Her husband had shared Garrett's Facebook note with her and she had refused to believe it, even accusing her husband of writing the letter.

After a few days of deliberate thought, I decided I would share the history of my marriage with the doctor. She could do as she pleased with the information I would give her, but at least she would go forward with open eyes.

A Letter to the Doctor

December 3, 2009

Ener,

There are some things you should know about Dick Crisco. I wish someone had warned me about him when we started dating twenty-six years ago. Unfortunately, I had to learn the hard way during our twenty-three years and eight months of marriage. It's possible that nothing I say will matter to you, but I feel this letter is necessary, as you have two daughters to consider.

Dick left our home on September 28, 2009. He arrived in Cheyenne on October 1, 2009. He went home from a bar with you on October 3, 2009. (He says you met online before he left Georgia.)

Our divorce became final November 18, 2009. Our settlement required him to begin paying alimony one month before the divorce was final. He is required to pay me for the rest of my life. As of today, he has paid nothing. Yet, it seems he has money to throw around in Cheyenne. He is currently in contempt and he will be arrested if he doesn't bring the alimony current. He refinanced our daughter's car before coming to Cheyenne. He never had intentions of paying the loan. He doesn't care if her car is repossessed nor does he care about the predicament he's placed her in. My daughter loves her dad and has tried to forgive him for the hell he made her live in. But, as someone said to her last week, "That Fucker has never cared about you or your family."

Little Dick needs to send $2300.00 to prevent Cissy's vehicle from being repossessed. He agreed in the settlement to make our house payment. As is his usual way of dealing with his responsibilities, he's paid nothing. Currently he owes $7000 for the house. His parents, my parents and I are paying for Dick's responsibilities. Not to mention the numerous other debts he left unpaid.

On the surface Dick is a very likable person. He appears honest, reliable, outgoing, and dependable. He is none of these things. Dick is constantly on the make. It's easier for him to tell a lie than to speak the truth. A lie forms in his *mouth before his brain can process the thought. He is a sleazy red-neck who just happens to be capable of fooling women, men and children.*

You have two young daughters. I am very concerned for them. Dick has a volatile and explosive temper. He will be able to hide it for a while, but it will surface sooner or later. He can't control it. Many times, I have been the victim of abuse at his hands. He has slapped me, knocked me down, dragged me around the house by my ankles, and punched me in the face with his fist. Once, while I was holding my son, age four, he rammed his fist through a screen door, hit me in the face and almost knocked me backwards off the steps. Garrett remembers this vividly. Like many abused women, I never filed charges against him. The police were called to our home on several occasions. (Bartow County Georgia).

One day, if you're around long enough, you and your daughters will experience his anger and his physical and verbal abuse. It's my belief you haven't yet seen this side of Dick. The way he speaks to me, when he and you call me, leads me to this conclusion. The man on the phone sounds nothing like the Dick my children, his parents, his co-workers and I know. While you're listening, he speaks respectfully and kind. Usually, the comments he makes to me are for your benefit, they actually have nothing to do with the conversation he and I are having. The next time you and he decide to call me, have him put his phone on speaker so you can hear both sides of the conversation.

Several years ago, I was being treated with Methotrexate, IVIG and steroids while my considerate husband was out screwing the secretary of the recycling plant he was employed with. I didn't find out until the woman's husband presented me with a video he made of Little Dick and his wife while they had sex during lunch (at their home).

All of Dick's affairs have been conducted during the work day, by the way. He was always home in the evenings and on the weekends, making it very difficult to uncover his lies. Dick has caused too much pain and humiliation over the years. His multiple infidelities of this past summer were my breaking point. Since I no longer had to worry about raising our two children and protecting them from the trashy women Dick loves, I was more than ready to jump off this train wreck. Unfortunately, Dick has left me with a mountain of debt. He sold his truck and took my only form of transportation when he left for Wyoming. I started a shuttle business in 2007 when I was forced to leave Delta Air Lines due to health issues. He knew my car was my only source of income, but he didn't/doesn't care. I'm sure his plan is to eventually have you paying his bills. One of those debts will be the previously mentioned alimony he agreed upon in our divorce settlement. Again, he is required to pay me weekly for the rest of my life. Dick is terrible with money management and is always on the look-out for a 'get rich quick scheme'. Apparently, after going to your home and having sex with you, he decided his money troubles were over. His words, to a mutual friend, "I fell into a damn gold mine". Think that comment speaks loudly and clearly of his intentions.

He may have already played on your sympathies. Perhaps he's given you a heart wrenching story and you've loaned him some money (don't expect to be repaid) or you've allowed him to borrow your vehicle or stay in your home. Nothing about him surprises me. Not too long ago I defended him like a mother bear. I was so foolish.

No one knows the real Dick. I know Dick better than anyone, but even I don't really know him. He has a dark, evil, ugly mental life which he keeps locked within. He acts his fantasy life out at times, but you will never know about it. He can screw a woman at work, then spend time in sex chat rooms or internet sites and come home and act as if he's a saint. He will have women in your bed while you are working. He has sex with you in your husband's bed now; do you think he will be more considerate and respectful of you? Dick will think nothing of bringing a woman into your home and having sex with her in your bedroom; while you're working he will play.

Dick has many of the characteristics of a sociopath. He is a sexual pervert. He is addicted to pornography, specifically, internet porn. To protect our children from their dad's lewd behavior, I had to place parental controls on our computers. He had been covertly visiting porn sites for years; in the end he was blatant with his sickness. Check the web browser on his Blackberry, you will find several questionable web sites. Of course if you confront him, he'll say he doesn't know how it happens. Those sites "just pop up" on his phone and computer. He subscribes to several dating web sites as well. With some sites, he uses an alias. With others he uses his actual name or a variation of it. He has several different e-mail addresses thru which he communicates with the women he meets online. He is addicted to phone sex chat lines. Check his phone bill. In the address book of his phone, he has been known to use male aliases for his women. For instance, he listed a woman named Kendal as Alex. Sherri might be David and so forth. You think he won't do this to you? So did I. Dick is addicted to sex and to women. He disrespects women. He loves their sex. His level of addiction is severe. He went to counseling one time and he became angry and said the counselor didn't know what he was talking about and refused to return for more sessions. Dick cannot control himself. For years he sat on the pew of a church and said "Amen" and "that's right, brother," on Sundays and Wednesdays, but was screwing several different women all the while.

His own mother said to one of her grandchildren, "I know my son is a sick man." Another family member who knows Dick very well says Dick should never have married. "Not when he was twenty-two, not now and not when he's eighty. He will never be able to be with one woman."

Dick cannot maintain long-term relationships. Our marriage lasted twenty-four years because I wouldn't give up on it or him. Once though, in 1998, I had finally had enough. My son and I had been chased all over town by one of his lunatic women. She called me and said Dick had told her I was crazy and she should carry a gun to protect herself from me. He told her he would provide her with a gun (Dick owns an arsenal of weapons). I do not like guns, I don't handle guns, I am afraid of guns. But this woman believed him. He of course was denying their relationship to me. After being assaulted in Wal-Mart by this woman, and after she described the sheets on my bed and the towels in my bathroom, he could no longer deny their affair. I was determined to divorce him, but he begged and pleaded with me to stay. Once again, I fell for lies. He seemed so sincere. I should have gone with my gut instinct and left him then. I would have saved my children and myself years of heartache and humiliation.

His friendships last an average of a year. His adulterous affairs last from two months to several months.

Dick can pour on the charm. Dick is a practiced liar. He's very talented and creative with his lies. He is so good that even this past September when I had hard evidence of his continued infidelity, he almost had me convinced that I was mistaken. Even when our son caught him this past July 31, he tried to talk his way out of it with me. (Not with our son however. Our boy had been exposed to too much of his dad's evilness and was finished). This time, I knew I was getting out of this hell he created, but still, by the time he finished his elaborate story, I was almost convinced. You can know in the core of yourself that he is lying, but he can make you believe he's telling the truth and everyone else is lying. With Dick the blame is always placed elsewhere. As with most sociopaths, he has no remorse for the pain he causes others. He is incapable of feeling guilt.

Dick is careless and irresponsible. He has never paid bills on time. He has had family members co-sign loans and then he walks away from the debt, leaving the co-signer to cover the loan.

The first time he talked about his mother he told me he had to move "five states away from her to keep the crazy bitch from controlling my life." No respect for his mom. It should have been a red flag.

When he left Georgia and moved to Cheyenne two months ago, it was not only because he had met you online, but also because he was running away from the mess he created here. He knew his gig was up; he left because we refused to keep his secrets any longer. When our son told him in July, "I will not cover for you ever again. I loathe the man you are. I will always love you as my dad but I will never respect you as a man," he meant it. Garrett had tears streaming down his face when he said these things to Dick. Dick sat there like a piece of stone. He was unmoved, untouched by his son's outpouring of pain.

But when he's feeling sorry for himself, or he wants another's sympathy, Crisco can make tears pour like water. Incredibly, it seems you've fallen for his masquerade.

Our son posted a note on Facebook about life with his dad (this note has swept across Facebook; people we don't know have written comments about the pain they felt upon reading Garrett's heartbreaking words). Crisco read it and made no comment. Not even, 'I'm sorry I did this to him'. He was cold to his son's heartbreak.

On August 1, 2009 I told Dick I was finished with him forever. I was serious this time, I knew there was no turning back, but he thought he could talk and fabricate his way thru. It had always worked before, but not this time. Still, he would not leave the house. He didn't leave until the Pancake Hut situation and then he fled like the coward he is, leaving the kids and me behind to deal with the embarrassment.

He has probably told you he went to L.S.U., he fed me this concocted story when we first met and told me he had also played football for the LSU Tigers. The only time Dick has been on that campus was to attend parties. I didn't discover he had never attended LSU until two years after we married. The only college Dick attended was Cheyenne Aero Tech, and that was at my persistence. He received his A&P license in 1993. He worked for a contract company who provided fuel for Delta Air Lines. Dick was a fueler; he filled the aircraft with fuel. Dick has never worked as an aircraft mechanic. (He was fired from the fueling job because he left work while on the clock to have sex with one of the secretaries…in a company van). Before he attended Cheyenne Aero Tech, we lost our home to bankruptcy because Dick was screwing women rather than working, I had hoped getting him away from construction would help. It didn't. He screwed a teenage girl in our bed at Pinewood Village Apartments in Cheyenne…while I was working. The same manager of the apartments today, was there in 1993. Ask her about Dick and the girl, a young girl who worked in the leasing office. A few years after we returned to Georgia, while I was working with Delta Air Lines he screwed a convenience store clerk in our bed…with our two young children across the hall. I worked full time for many years, but Dick likes to tell his women "all my wife has ever done is sit on her lazy ass while I've killed myself paying for our damn house." He called our home "this damn house" in front of our kids. Only a selfish, cruel man would say these things in front of his children.

The first fifteen years of our marriage Dick moved us around quite a bit. He would quit paying our rent and we would have to move, again and again. I managed to keep our children in the same school system all those years by driving them to school from our out of district homes. When we moved into my current home in the summer of 2001, I was determined to stay. My boy, eleven years old at the time, said to me when we moved in, "please don't let dad move us again". I fought like heck to stay here. Dick does not like the responsibility of a mortgage or anything else related to a family.

Dick has never held a job for more than five years. Prior to moving to Cheyenne and obtaining his current spot selling cars, his most recent position had been as a manager/cook with Pancake Hut. He worked with Pancake Hut for one year. He was fired in September, 2009, (two months ago) for sexual harassment. Four different women filed claims against him. The confrontation with the corporate lawyer was his big finale' and he made a snap decision to run. He came home from his termination meeting and packed the white utility trailer he has with him *in Wyoming. He was infuriated with the attorney from Pancake Hut because he couldn't charm her into believing his story. She had proof of sexual harassment, but that didn't stop Dick from trying to convince her otherwise.*

Personally, I think he also failed a drug test. (He didn't allow me to see his termination papers, he told me only about the sexual harassment charges). I also believe this is the reason he didn't get the job with Great Lakes Air Lines in Cheyenne. They offered him a job contingent on his drug screening and background check. He claims they retracted the offer based on an arrest that occurred before we were married. He was arrested more than 25 years ago for stealing a coat from Rich's Department Store in Atlanta, Fulton County, Ga. I don't believe that's the reason for the job retraction. Pancake Hut and several other companies he's worked for have processed background checks and it was never a problem.

In July 2009, when our son discovered the latest affair, and refused to keep his dad's life a secret from me or anyone else any longer, Dick began openly going to a biker bar, smoking Camels (I had never seen him smoke before) and coming home drunk. I'm sure there were several drugs he could have picked up at this bar. Drug use is speculation. However, his behavior supported the possibility.

He will attempt to make you believe everyone has treated him unfairly; he wants his women to feel sorry for him. He uses your compassion to get what he wants. He once said men would take advantage of a sympathetic woman because men "can sniff out compassion and sympathy like a blue tick hound. They use it to their advantage." He is currently using this ploy against you.

About eighteen months ago he began calling my first cousin. She and I are eight months apart in age and we grew up like sisters. She says in the beginning she thought nothing of it, he had always called and teased my cousin and her older sister. But then he began to tell her things about our intimacy. Most of which was not true. He told her he just needed someone to show him how to help me get through menopause...he loved me so much and he hated to see me suffer. Sounds like he was being kind and compassionate about my circumstance... except she knew I had gone through menopause about five years prior. She told Dick he was making her uncomfortable with the things he was saying, and that she would tell me if he didn't stop calling her. He continued to call and tried to play on her sympathies. She called me and told me what he had been doing and saying. When I confronted him about it, Dick said she was not telling the truth. My cousin has never lied to me. Dick seldom told me the truth. He accused her of calling him. As usual, he was placing his blame on someone else. For years I believed him when he did this little sympathy act, now I know I was a fool. I'll be happy to give you my cousins phone number if you would like to speak with her.

Dick is very needy. He cannot be without a woman. You need to know this: No matter how much destruction and havoc he causes in the lives of others, Dick always comes out smelling like a rose. He always comes out on top. It takes a while to see through the elaborate wall of lies. Sometimes it takes years.

He likes to tell people that I got him into debt. You will see from the liens and judgments against him, I had nothing to do with it. Dick is an impulse shopper. He spends needlessly. He filed bankruptcy about three years ago, for the second time. I was not on the bankruptcy. Once again, we almost lost our home.

He also told his lawyer he left me a 2006 Grand Jeep Cherokee to drive. That lie was to save face because we used to attend church with the attorney. We've never had a 2006 Jeep. A few years ago, I purchased, with money from my 401K, a 1992 Jeep Cherokee... no longer roadworthy.

That's the only vehicle Dick left here in Georgia. And that Jeep belongs to my son. Why did he lie about that? Because he wanted to appear generous and sympathetic to the attorney. Before Dick left town, he tried to convince me to put the title of the Jeep in his name. He would have gone to a title pawn to gain money from the Jeep. He's done this with cars in the past. A word of caution: never be fooled into signing property over to him. You will lose the property.

I no longer have contact numbers for the women from a few years ago, but I can give you their names if you want to look them up. See if the story he's told you, isn't similar to the ones he told them. I can get you in touch with some of the waitresses if you wish. There have been numerous women, many more than the ones mentioned here.

I really can't tell you how many homes Dick has wrecked over the years. I don't know how many women he's actually had affairs with during our marriage. But I can tell you this...you are not the first, and you won't be the last.

Dick goes hard and heavy with anything for a while. A few years ago, we attended a church in Ball Ground, Georgia, (World Harvest Church). Dick claimed he had a life altering experience and became a Christian. He claimed he would never go back to his old ways.

"God will kill me before he allows me to hurt you and the kids again."

He began attending church every time the doors were opened. Prior to being "saved", Dick had once screamed at me, "I've changed my life for you. I changed everything for you!" I had no idea what he was talking about. After he was "born again", I asked him what he had meant when he said he had changed everything for me. He confessed he had drank excessively, taken several different drugs and had several different women prior to meeting me. I asked why he never told me the truth. He said he knew I would never have settled for that behavior and he thought he could change permanently. I told him he had been unfair to me and to himself by choosing to keep his life secret from me. I loved him and married him based on the man he was when we dated. That man disappeared on my Honeymoon night. He stumbled, slobbering drunk to our room and passed out on the bed. But throughout our marriage he has blamed me for our wedding night being a disaster. He never accepts responsibility. He always places blame on others.

While attending World Harvest Church, Dick made a public testimony of his history of affairs. In front of a congregation of more than 1000 people he asked the kids and me to forgive him. The church even broadcast a portion of it on a national Christian Station. His parents watched the broadcast in their home in Cabot, Arkansas. Friends in Alaska and Wyoming watched it as well. I guess you could say Dick had his fifteen minutes of fame for infidelity.

You may wonder why I stayed with him for almost twenty-four years. In the beginning I believed every word out of his mouth. Why wouldn't I? He was not caught in an affair until after the children were born. After the first affair, I agreed to stay with him and work things out. I forgave quickly. Two years later, it happened again. This time I was ready for a divorce, but allowed him, once more, to convince me he had changed. By the third time, just a few months later, I realized he would never change. I also realized when he wasn't with me he was with unsavory people. Drug addicts, alcoholics, bar hoppers, etc. I made a conscious decision to stay with him for the sake of our children. In retrospect, I second guess my choice. I'll never know if I made the right decision. I knew I could protect my children from his 'friends as long as we were married. If we divorced I would have to share custody with him and I didn't want my children exposed to his women and his trash on Holidays, during summers and on weekends. I stayed and tried to make the best of a sad situation. Sometimes things were good, even great at times. During those times I had high hopes of Dick moving past his demons. But that was never to be. Last spring, early summer, Dick stopped running from the Devil. He stood still and allowed all his demons to catch up with him. And by some stroke of misfortune, you have found yourself trapped in his false life.

If a man loved his daughter would he call her a bitch? Dick does, to her back. Would he go to a bar rather than to a restaurant with his family to celebrate his son's 20th birthday? Dick did. He claimed he was sick, but I have the bank receipts to prove he was in a biker bar. He knew it would be the last time he would see our children for a very long time. He didn't care. The bar and the women were more important to Dick.

Ener, your behavior baffles me. Do you love your children? Do you cherish them? You have allowed your daughters to spend time alone with a sociopath. A sociopath you've only known a few weeks. Why would you allow your young daughters to go off with a man you barely know? Where is your responsibility to your daughters? I'm sure in your position you've seen the aftermath of sexual abuse towards children. Dick preys on women and all of them have children. Dick was most likely sexually abused as a child. His mother claims she was abused by her uncle and Dick says she left him with the uncle who molested her. Either you're selfish with no concern for your daughters or you're very irresponsible. Either way, *you're taking a chance with your children. I don't know if Dick has ever harmed a child sexually, but why take a chance? I found a homemade video made years ago, when our daughter was a baby. He had recorded photos from Hustler Magazine on the video. Then he placed a pornographic film in the VCR and filmed our TV screen, recording the ugly movie onto a VHS tape. While the movie was playing on our TV, our nine month old baby crawled across the floor in front of the TV. I was sick to my stomach.*

I know you are still married. That makes you no different than the convenience store women, the mill women and Pancake whores he's preferred in the past.

My children have never known the man I fell in love with. They have never witnessed the way Dick treated me during our dating and engagement relationship. Dick was so kind and considerate. Humble. There was a vulnerable quality to him that I adored. He showered me with praise, gifts, and romantic dinners he cooked himself. He took me boating, taught me to fish. He was the consummate gentleman. He showered my nephew with love. I adored and cherished the way he played games with my nephew, the way Dick showed so much patience when he taught him things. This was proof, I thought, of the wonderful husband and father Dick would become. I was wrong.

I will never say I regret marrying Dick because I have two wonderful children with him. I would not have these same two children with anyone else. I will tell you I am sorry for marrying a man who had such disregard for the feelings of his children. My children would probably tell you Dick had little to do with their becoming the wonderful young woman and man they are today. However, they would probably tell you he is responsible for the emotional pain and trauma they may deal with at times. Unfortunately, I am responsible for some of that pain as well. I dealt with chronic emotional stress and upheaval because of his adultery and verbal abuse. My children suffered, they witnessed me suffering, they witnessed his volcanic outbursts of anger and many times they were the target of his anger. In retrospect, I was an absolute idiot for staying with him. As the saying goes, "I couldn't see the forest for the trees". Now it seems ridiculous that I believed I was protecting them. Yes, I kept them from his women and disgusting friends, but I couldn't prevent what they saw and heard in our home. How could I have known he would be so careless and disrespectful toward our son that he would take him to meet his women? How could I have known he would talk scum about women in front of my son? It never occurred to me he would hurt our children that way. I thought he was only hurting me.

He will be kind and sweet to your daughters for a while. But one day, one or both will do something to anger him. At that time, they will see the temper I've described to you.

Just as Dick was new to Atlanta when we met, he is now new to Cheyenne. Like you, I knew nothing of his history. At least you can investigate, listen with open ears and study the man before you make a lifelong commitment to him. There was no one to provide history for me, no one to really warn me about Little Dick. However, after we were engaged he and I went to Louisiana, so he could introduce me to his family. While there, I met his sister Vee for the first time. Late one night after a crawfish boil, she tried to warn me. She told me Dick would never settle down. He would never be happy with one woman. She also said, "My brother lies. He lies about everything. I've taken beatings because of his lies." When I mentioned this to Dick, he told me his sister was as crazy as their mom and grandmother. I believed him. Why wouldn't I believe the man I was in love with?

Dick may tell you I'm saying these things because I want him back in my life. That won't be the truth. Two weeks ago he sent me a text and asked me if I thought we should stay together. I told him no. He has proven he will never change. The night before our divorce, he was at a Cheyenne sports bar and called to see if I wanted to stay together. Nothing could make me return to that life.

As his mistress you will be treated very well. If you become his wife you will be treated as a worthless nobody. You will become disposable property. He has no respect for women. He will love your income, but not you.

Dick will try to convince you the things written in this letter are false. I realize for the most part, you will not be able to verify the information I've given you. Make an attempt to learn the truth.

He will probably say I'm a crazy ex-wife, that's the reason he left me, I'm a crazy bitch, etc. His latest reaction, since coming to Cheyenne, is to sadly say, "I don't know why you would think these things about me. I don't know why you would say such a thing". **My answer is always the same**, *"For whose benefit are you making these denials? I know you; this is the life I lived. Dick, are you forgetting who you're speaking with? You know these things are true."*

One day I sent him a text and asked him to please send our daughter's car payment, I asked him to send money for the electric bill and the house payment. Our divorce was not final at the time. When he called me later that evening, I could hear conversations and restaurant activity in the background. This is what he said to me, "Why would you need money for the house payment? I paid the house and all utilities up and in advance before I left." **That was not true.**

This past summer, our son read text messages from Dick to a woman named Jill. I noticed on the phone bill there were several calls to the woman but none from her. There were several text messages from him to her as well. I called Jill and learned from her that Dick had been stalking her for months via his cell phone. She and my husband had never seen one another via photo or in person, yet he had begged her to meet him. He found her phone number in a forwarded text sex joke and started contacting her. She said to me, "Your husband is a stalker. I was married to a man just like him. I date a police officer and I know to stay away from Dick. I am afraid of men like your husband."

Danita

A few days later, I received an e-mail from Ener:

Danita,

I received your letter today. Wow. I appreciate the concern and I will do some research. I, too, have a fairly sociopathic husband. I am sure he has convinced you and Garrett that if I was not seeing Dick that he and I would be back together and all would be happy. that is not true. We are going to get divorced. He, too, has been taking advantage of my income and has not worked in 2 1/2 years.

I am sorry for all the things that Dick has done to you and your family. Even if you are exaggerating it is quite awful.

Please let me clarify some things. He has not spent any money on me or the girls. He did buy dinner once or twice and has paid for a few beers. I have paid for a few meals and for any activities we have done with my kids. That is as far as the money thing goes. he has said he does not have any money and is looking for a different job due to not selling as many cars as he needs to.

My big concern with your letter and this email is how derogatory it is to me. I do not understand the big problem with me seeing Dick. I get that you think he is already cheating on me and that he is a big fat liar, but why does that make me a "whore" and a slut. Yes, technically you were still married when we met and I am still married. But we were both separated and have filed for divorce. Especially if you were the one wanting the divorce why is it such a big deal that he is seeing me? I appreciate the advice and will look into some things, but please don't make me into the bad guy. I am just having a fun relationship with a guy who has so far been kind to me and fun to be around. I am not planning on marriage or anything like that.

I cannot help Dick with his money issues since I have to deal with my own. If he gets arrested then so be it. He is a big boy and will figure this out on his own one way or another.

Thanks again for the info and advice.

Ener

Date: Mon, 7 Dec 2009 15:14:34 -0800

I read Ener's email and sat back in a bit of disbelief. She had missed the point of my letter by a long shot and focused instead on what she believed were insults of her character. Granted, I had not written the letter to make her feel good about what she was doing and I had used words such as whore…simply because she fit the dictionary's definition:

Whore – a person considered sexually promiscuous; a person considered as having compromised principles.

I felt it important to inform Ener of Dick's troubled history. Perhaps I gave too much information. Maybe not enough, I don't know. But I know this much, she ignored my warning and has subsequently witnessed first-hand Dick's volatile temper and lies. Yet she continues a relationship with him. From the outside looking in I could easily ask, "What is wrong with that woman?" But having been on the inside of Dick's sickness for a long time, I know very well how easy it is to fall into his web of lies. *Something about him makes you **want** to believe him.* So in the end, I don't question what's wrong with her; because I *know*.

March 21, 2012,

We're approaching three years since Crisco moved to Cheyenne. It's been more than two years since I wrote the letters to him and Ener. For various reasons, during this time, I've put down my writing. At times it was just too difficult to remember and face my foolish determination to make a life with Dick; other times I just didn't have the time to write. But during these months, the irony of the situation has never been far from my mind. Throughout our marriage, Dick hated to work and now he lives with a woman who can and does support him. I remember the way he complained if I asked him to plant a flower in our yard, yet he spends hours shoveling snow off Ener's driveway.

During the last two years, there have been several court hearings between Crisco and myself, the last one just a few weeks ago. Crisco doesn't like paying alimony and he has engaged lawyers and the court system to fight me. I'm certain I haven't seen the end of the alimony fight.

These days, Dick lives rent free in Ener's 10,000 square foot home while Garrett and Cissy struggle to pay apartment rents and tuition. I have lived with friends, camped on my ex sister-in-law's sofa, slept in my car and lived several months with the King family (former friends of Dick). But it's okay. We have survived and we don't have to listen to a bully berate us; insult us; criticize us; mock us; scream at us; cheat on us and lie to us. We're good and getting better every day.

And I've forgiven Crisco. Forgiveness didn't come easily. For a long while I was consumed with hatred and anger. Ugliness and bitterness seeped out of my pores and spilled into my conversations. Hatred burned like a fire within me and threatened to consume my happiness. Thick vines of bitterness began to wrap around me like Georgia Kudzu, choking me. I knew what I had to do. I didn't want to do it. Forgiveness, *the need to forgive*, wrestled with me at night and kept me awake. So I forgave. Even before I actually felt it, I made a conscious decision to forgive. I began by asking God to forgive me of the dark hatred living in me. Then I told God I forgave Crisco. I realized that wasn't 100% true, so I said, "Well God, that's not totally accurate. I'm trying to forgive him. Please help me." God and I went back and forth for a few days, then late one night, I phoned Crisco and told him I was choosing to forgive him.

"Well, that's nice of you," Crisco replied (something along those lines anyway).

My action of forgiveness didn't appear to be life changing at first. I didn't hear bells chiming or angels singing and I felt only slightly better about myself. What I really wanted was to return to full blown hatred mode because of the way Dick received and responded to my offer of grace. I mentioned this to a friend and she opened my eyes, "It doesn't matter how he received it. You did what you know is right. What Dick does with the forgiveness is on him, not you. You've done your part." Ok, cool. I can see how this is true. It was then, with my eyes wide open, that God revealed something to me in a silent whisper, "You've been saying you gave Dick forgiveness, and you did. But the Gift of Forgiveness is through Me. When you spoke words of forgiveness to Dick, you looked to him for a response. *Look to Me.* My response is important, not Dick's. I'll deal with Dick. Give him to Me; he is no longer yours to worry about." And that was that.

I still have moments of disbelief when I think about the longevity of my denial, my naïveté. There are still days where I want to kick myself for being stupid. But the hatred I felt for Dick is gone. The love I had for him is gone. Apathy has replaced every emotion I once felt for Dick.

I still wish he had known how to feel true love for his children; I still long for him to know how to unfold a blanket of fatherly love over our children. I no longer hope for it to happen, but I wish it had been possible. Something sidetracked Dick years before I met him, his life was touched and perverted by a silent monster; he was never interested in destroying the beast. So, based on advice from above, I'm leaving Dick and his demons in God's Hands.

Letters to a Princess and a Warrior

April 21, 2010

Dear Garrett,

Today I was going through some old family photographs and I came across one of you when you were just a little guy; you are protectively holding a fish. I've seen this photo many times before and for reasons I never understood, it always stirred up deep emotion and tugged at my heart.

You look so beautiful in the photo; your eyes are clear and blue. But there is such sorrow in your expression. The sadness puddled in your blue eyes always seemed out of place to me because you loved fishing and you had obviously just returned from the lake, your shirt is still wet down the front.

Finding bugs and worms underneath rotting logs, searching for lizards and baby snakes around my flowers, frog hunting by flashlight and fishing were your favorite pastimes at that age. Even more than fishing and hunting for these creatures, you loved having them in your hands. The wildlife you captured were priceless treasures to you and you always handled them gently and carefully, even the ugliest of frogs. You gave them names. And when you would bring them to me your blue eyes would sparkle with admiration for the creature; your snaggle-toothed grin spread wide with joy. This photo shows none of your zest. It reveals something else. That day, all those years ago, my camera's lens caught sadness in your eyes and even today it makes my heart skip a beat. Nothing brings me closer to loss of breath than knowing you and your sister are unhappy. In this photo, you are clearly melancholy.

Your expression was completely out of character considering the activity portrayed in the scene. So for the hundredth time, today I found myself studying the photograph: you hair is cut in a buzz; you're wearing a blue T-shirt from the Cheyenne YMCA; your beloved red and yellow Little Tykes motorcycle is to your left; you're holding a fish, standing in the garage of our house near Pine Log, Georgia. You are not smiling. Your lips are pressed tightly together. You are looking directly at the camera, but your eyes, always so full of light and laughter, are serious. What's causing the sadness haunting your eyes? Haunting me all these years later? I'm the photographer behind the camera; I was almost always the one to document our lives. And you're looking at me in a way that now makes me feel you are trying to say something to me. What Buddy? What did you want me to know? Why didn't I see it at the time? I flip the photo over and look on the back. Nothing is written there. Then I pick up the next photo in the stack and it all becomes clear. Realization hits me like a lead balloon.

In the second photo you're still holding the fish and you're still looking directly at the camera. But now there is a look of contempt in those beautiful blues. Your dad is standing next to you with, as he would say, a "shit eating grin" on his face. And I know. This is **the** fishing trip.

I'm so sorry for my lack of understanding. I can never apologize enough for not protecting you from the sickness of this man. I could try to blame my ignorance of the situation on working full time on a midnight shift, the fog of chemotherapy or being married to a masterful liar. But in the end, I know I should have known. No matter what, I should have felt your unspoken pain. Can you ever forgive me? Never in my darkest nightmares could I have imagined your dad would take you to meet those women. Or that he would expose you to his filth in the ways he did. Or that he would make you swear to never tell me. What kind of sick sonofabitch does that to his child? When he took you fishing I really believed he was choosing to spend quality dad and son time with you. I imagined the sweet memories you were creating together. I thought he loved you and Cissy as much as I did, and I knew I would never willingly expose you to anything that would physically or emotionally harm you, so it was outside my realm of possibilities that he would ever be so neglectful of you. I thought he loved you that much too. Now I realize the bastard is too sick to love anyone or anything but himself.

My heart still breaks knowing he hurt you. I live with guilt, knowing I didn't protect you from his madness. How could I have been so blind and for so long? So stupid? I hate him for hurting you and Cissy.

Once, not long after these photos were taken, I considered divorcing him. You overheard me talking to your dad about a divorce and when he left the house you came to me and said, "Mommy, please promise me you won't marry us another dad." Your plea ripped my heart into a zillion little pieces because I thought you couldn't imagine a world without your dad. As they say, hind sight is twenty-twenty and I've come to believe you asked me not to "marry you another dad" because you were afraid. At the time, you knew things about your dad that I didn't know, and I believe you felt if your own dad, your real dad, could hurt you in the ways he had, what would a step-dad be capable of doing? If that was what you were trying to say to me, please forgive me. I'm so sorry for my misinterpretation of your plea.

Last summer, fate set unseen, unfair wheels in motion and once again placed you in position to discover and reveal your dad's ugly double life. My heart shattered as I watched your heart break. With tears streaming down your beautiful face you said, "Mom, I don't know why I always have to be the one to break your heart. I don't want to break your heart again."

I told you then and I'm telling you now: You are not the one to break my heart.

I remember saying, "You're the messenger not the heartbreaker".

Between wet, guttural sobs you said, "I really believed he had changed, Mom. I hoped he had. I guess I've always known he wouldn't. I just wish he had been sincere and I wish I wasn't the one to have to tell you."

I remember telling you I didn't understand why God seemed to choose you to be the messenger of the news. Or why you had to be the one to see the sinister side of your dad so often, while he kept the truth tucked away from the rest of us. A few months have passed since that night and I think I have an idea of why God chose you to bear the burden of the message. First of all, it's plain as day now, your dad was never the true man of our house. He didn't want to be accountable for himself or for our family and he shirked his responsibilities at every turn. From the time you were very small, you picked up on this defect in your dad and you took it upon yourself to be the protector of your sister and me. You worried about whether or not we would have to move again. You worried when I had to take medication. You worried if I wasn't at the front of the pick-up line after school. You worried if your sister wasn't home on time. *And Heaven help anyone who said a negative word about your sister.* You worried about our animals and the strays you saw on the side of the road. When you became a teen my friends said you had a Hero

Complex because you always wanted to rescue your friends, especially the girls, from painful situations. By that time in your life, I knew your desire to protect was much more than a Hero Complex. So, I think, one of the reasons you always *had* to be the one to discover and reveal the monster is because you were the only man in our household. Your dad would have never owned up to his transgressions unless he was caught red handed. Even then, caught in the act, he tried to lie his way out and blame others.

The other reason I think you had to be the messenger of the ugliness, and this realization is difficult for me, is that for me to leave that nightmare behind, *I had to feel your heart break.* It was the most painful thing I've ever witnessed. You, my strong nineteen year-old son, stood broken with anguish and heartache before me and it almost killed me. I had seen your hurt before, but never like this. I had seen your tears before, but not pouring like waterfalls from your eyes. And when you said, "I love you Mom but I can't watch him do this to you anymore", I knew I was done. I felt the door close on that life. I literally heard the click of the key in the lock. For years you had tried to protect your sister and me from the things we did not know. Cissy had seen a lot, but not as much as you and you had wanted to keep it that way. But this night, those years of pent up secrets and emotions spilled forth and I vowed to get out forever. You asked me if I was sure and I said, "Without a doubt". You see, until that night, I believed I had protected you and Cissy from the worst of your dad's affairs, from the worst of his temper. I thought I had taken the brunt of his criticism and emotional abuse and buffered you from the wickedness. I thought I had protected the two of you from the worst of him. I'm sorry I was so wrong. I didn't protect you at all.

"Wow. You're free, Mom. We're all free! We're a family of three now. I guess that's really what we've always been," you said.

"I should have left him long ago. Really, I wish I would have left him the day after you were conceived. The only good thing to come of this union was you and Cissy. I could have prevented a lot of heartache if I had left him before you were born."

Once more I told you I was sorry. I said to you, "One of the reasons I stayed for so long, once I realized he would never change, was to protect you and Cissy from exposure to the horrid people he liked to hang out with. And the nasty women he's always migrated to. I knew if I divorced him he would have been given visitation on the weekends and summers and I wouldn't have been there to protect you. And then he started going to church and everything seemed good. I really thought he had changed. How could I have been so fooled? I didn't protect you at all," I repeated.

Like the mature young man you are, you said to me, "Mom, don't beat yourself up. You did what you thought best and we'll never know how it would have been if you had divorced him when we were small. More than likely, even if dad had been given part time custody he would have left town and we would have never seen or heard from him again. We know he would never have paid child support. But on the other hand, he may have stayed in town just to make life miserable for everyone. The past is gone. Now you, Cissy and I can start over."

You told me you would not return to the house while he was there. I understood but my heart broke again for you; this was the house you had once asked me to promise we would never leave. You promised you would visit while he was working. We were having this conversation in the church parking lot, the summer night was heavy with honeysuckle and humidity, you looked toward the sky and began to sing, "It's a marvelous night for a moon dance, with the sky up above in your eyes…. Just think Mom, you can start dating again." I scoffed at that idea and you said, "Well at least you can go out and have intelligent conversation again. You've never been able to do that with Dick!" I laughed, because you were right.

Garrett, you're an amazing young man. I'm so proud of you. You will be a wonderful husband and dad one of these days. As you've said, you "know what kind of man not to be".

Stick to your convictions, my son. I'm so thankful life with Crisco didn't steal your light. Your passion for life explodes in the lives of others and their lives are better because of it. I have no doubt, when you have a family of your own, you'll love them with that same life giving passion.

I'm proud of you.
I love you
Mom

July 23, 2010

Dear Cissy,

I barely remember life without you and your brother. It seems your spirit has been with me my whole life. I remember the trusting way your blue eyes studied my face the night you were born. The way you seemed to concentrate on the sound of my voice. The way you *felt so familiar* to me. It seemed I was familiar to you too; you snuggled contentedly in the curve of my arm as if you had already been there many times before.

When you and I were alone for the first time on your birth day, I caressed your face with kisses and promised to do my best to make the world a beautiful place for you. I promised I would never let you down. I promised to never break my promises to you. I failed on all three promises. On that cold winter night in 1987 I could never have imagined or envisioned the pain you would suffer just because you were born into our family. By no fault of your own, you had the misfortune of being fathered by a man with no desire to be a husband or a dad. The problem is his, not yours. I realize that doesn't make the pain less painful. Please hear me clearly: You and Garrett were never the cause or reason for his anger and temper or his poor choices. His ego and his other problems were the driving forces behind his frightening outbursts. Don't ever believe, not for one second, that his problems were anyone's fault but his own. Crisco is the kind of man who puts himself above others, even his children. He believes his life and his desires are more important than anyone else's. I'm so sorry you had to grow up in that kind of atmosphere. I'm painfully aware my choices caused us to live in that insanity for far too many years. I will never forgive myself for the choices I made.

On the day you were born I believed your dad was a good man at his core, a man who longed for a sweet and solid family life the same way I longed for it. My ignorance and lack of critical judgment caused you more pain than I ever realized. I'm so sorry and I hope you can forgive me someday.

Recently I was sorting through a box of old photographs and I found one from the Halloween you were five. You're dressed like a fairy princess, the twinkling rhinestone tiara crowning your beautiful head doesn't compare to the sparkle in your missing toothed smile or the brightness of your blue eyes. *It's your eyes that break me.* Your beautiful blue eyes shine with the innocence of hope and love, promise, anticipation and expectation. In your beautiful eyes I see what you were feeling. *You felt like a Princess.* I wish I could go back in time and wave your magic wand and save that princess feeling for you…so that you would keep it forever and ever. *Because you are a Princess.*

As a little girl you were full of the sweetness of life. You found joy in everything: swings, books, puppies, kittens, sand and buckets. And you brought joy to every life you touched. For a time you believed everyone was good. Too early, the ugly side of life began to invade your safe little world. Little by little you saw and heard things that I did not. You picked up on lies spoken that I never heard. You met a monster that I didn't know existed. Can you ever forgive my ignorance?

I wanted to marry a man who would love his children more than life. A man who would never dishonor his family. A man who would hold his children in such high esteem, his son would feel like a mighty warrior and his daughter would feel like a beautiful princess. And in turn our children would have the utmost devotion and respect for their dad. I wanted to marry the kind of man who would offer his children such powerful encouragement they would feel incapable of anything less than conquering the world. I thought I had married that kind of man. I failed greatly in my choice of husband and dad. Either from lack of caring or lack of capability, Crisco chose not to be that kind of dad.

It's no excuse, but I was fooled. While we dated, I based my judgment of his 'dad type' character by the way he treated your cousin, Justin. And the way he treated the children of our friends. I greatly misjudged that one, didn't I? If only I had seen past his masks.

In retrospect, there were many red flags and warning signs. By the time you and your brother were pre-teens it was obvious you held no reverence toward your dad. I often wondered about it and assumed it was because of his numerous affairs, and I guess the affairs were part of the big picture. But there were uglier reasons, hiding and festering like open wounds in the secret places of your beautiful heart.

By the time you were ten you held more wisdom that I will ever possess. One night after Crisco had brought more hell into our house, you came to my bedroom and said this: "Just leave him mom. He's never going to change." How is it that a sweet little girl could see what her mom could not? I guess I refused to admit the bitter reality of our lives. I wanted things to be so much better for you and Garrett. I thought keeping our family together was best for all of us. I'm sorry for not listening to you. I'm sorry for not asking deeper questions, for assuming you were just angry with your dad. I lacked understanding. My heart weeps when I think about the heartache you've felt because of my lack of understanding.

Crisco allowed me to see the masks and shadows of who he actually is. While I was working and you and Garrett were alone with him, he let the mask fall away and he stepped out of the shadows. You got to see the evilness in him much more often than I did. And when I did see it, I made excuses for it. You *never* made excuses for him. You had seen the sickness of your dad and you knew the vile nature he kept tucked behind his easy smile. Recently you and Garrett have told me of the times you walked in on him while he was watching porn. I hate that sonofabitch for his selfish insanity. I hate him for exposing you to his darkness. If I could cut his pecker off and feed it to him I would. It angers me to think of the things he exposed you to. It infuriates me to know he brought his women into our home while you and your brother were there. I'm angry about it all, and most of the anger is directed at myself. How could I not have known? I should have been aware of his selfishness and his sickness. I don't know how I missed it so badly. Never, ever would I have thought he would blatantly disregard the feelings and the innocence of his children. He had never allowed me to see the full perverted side of his personality. I had come to expect him to treat me badly, but I never thought he would extend his resentment and disgust to you and Garrett.

In time your outgoing and happy personality began to grow quiet and withdrawn. I thought it was because of your age and changing hormones. I didn't realize you were beginning to have self-doubt because of the controlling and degrading way your dad treated our family. Like me before you, you began to lose yourself because of the insulting nature of Dick Crisco. But you're back and you've regained strength. Recently Garrett said to me, "Every time Cissy stands up to Crisco she'll get stronger. Every time she refuses to allow him to put her down, she'll get stronger." And I see that it's true. Your gorgeous smile and eyes light up more frequently these days. And your beautiful laughter fills a room as it did when you were a little girl.

Last January, in your wisdom, you said to me, "dad is incapable of loving anyone". I hope you always remember that his inability to love does indeed extend to everyone, not just to you and your brother. You and Garrett are two of the easiest people in the world to love.

My Sweet Girl, you're an amazing young woman. I'm so proud of you. If someday you choose to marry and have children, you'll be a wonderful wife and mother. You have life experience to help you in making good life choices. You know what kind of man to stay away from. You know the signs…and if you ever see those signs, run like hell and get away. It doesn't matter if you've been married ten minutes or ten years. GET OUT.

You'll be a much better mom that I have been. You've felt the pain of my mistakes, you'll know what not to do. Or what you should do. I have no doubt you'll see a situation for what it is and deal with it head on. Be true to yourself. Don't ever get pulled into a life that degrades you.

As you know, I believe everything happens for a reason. For years I've believed the only reason I was allowed to marry Crisco was so that you and Garrett would be born. I can't imagine a world without the two of you in it. I believe God has awesome plans for your life. Cissy, you have so much to offer the world…both the world at large and your own little piece of it.

The grace and dignity you've brought to my life is absolutely flawless.
I'm proud of you.
I love you.
Mom

Epilogue:

Well Crisco, This Is Another Fine Mess You've Gotten Us Into...

Able vs Able. Is it ever going to end? Yesterday I once again found myself in a courtroom, facing Crisco. Once again he was trying to wiggle out of his responsibilities. Once again his mama or his girlfriend paid an attorney $250.00 an hour to fight me. Once again they 'threw good money after bad".

A space of fifty feet and a lifetime separated Crisco and me...and as I looked at his haggard face, I realized his life choices were finally catching up with him. While he sat in the witness chair, spewing lies and false accusations, I wondered what I had ever seen in him. How had he fooled me? I wondered how such a snake had fathered my two beautifully amazing children

Watching him toss arrogant smiles to his attorney while my attorney questioned him....Hearing him say, "my girlfriend, she's a doctor, she is able to pay for her own home and her own bills"(something he can't do), I was overcome with empathy for her...she has no idea what he's doing to her life.... And I was so very thankful he is no longer an active part of mine.

It was staggering to watch my attorney, J Lovett, riddle Crisco with one sharp question after another. And quite amusing to watch Crisco stumble and trip over his own lies....falling ever deeper into the pit he was digging. Oh, Crisco was quick with his deceptiveness and practically anyone would have believed him in a different setting…but he was no match for Mr. Lovett.

And then there was the judge. He had Crisco's number from the beginning and held nothing back.

From the judge:

Mr. Able, I don't know what lured you to Cheyenne, Wyoming, but I strongly suspect it had nothing to do with employment….

Mr. Able, You're a kept man. You've got a Sugar Mama paying your way…

Mr. Able, I suggest you get a job….

Yes indeed, a lifetime to pay alimony is a long time. That's why I suggested Mr. Able find a job, and this time he should try to figure out a way to keep it…

Mr. Able and his bow-tied attorney hightailed it likkity-split out of the courthouse so fast no one noticed. By the time Lawyer Bowtie asked permission to be excused, the gallery of lawyers, courtroom observers, Mr. Lovett and myself were distracted by our laughter, making it difficult to stay focused on anything 'Laurel and Hardy' were doing. But I imagine Crisco and company hit Highway 20 toward his lawyer's Canton office… licking their wounds with each turn of the wheels.

The End

Contact the Author:
Information and speaking engagements.

Danita Clark
DanitaClark2018@live.com
www.facebook.com/DanitaClarkAuthor

Author's Blog:
www.RedClayPonderings.com

Made in the USA
Middletown, DE
02 April 2018